PRINCESS MONONOKE

D1711005

Animation: Key Films/Filmmakers

Series Editor: Chris Pallant

PRINCESS MONONOKE

Understanding Studio Ghibli's Monster Princess

Edited by Rayna Denison

BLOOMSBURY ACADEMIC

NEW YORK • LONDON • OXFORD • NEW DELHI • SYDNEY

BLOOMSBURY ACADEMIC
Bloomsbury Publishing Inc
1385 Broadway, New York, NY 10018, USA
50 Bedford Square, London, WC1B 3DP, UK

BLOOMSBURY, BLOOMSBURY ACADEMIC and the Diana logo
are trademarks of Bloomsbury Publishing Plc

First published in 2018
Paperback edition first published 2019

Cover design by Louise Dugdale
Cover image © Chen Hong Lee / Alamy Stock Photo

A catalog record for this book is available from the Library of Congress.

ISBN: HB: 978-1-5013-2976-0
PB: 978-1-5013-5487-8
ePDF: 978-1-5013-2973-9
eBook: 978-1-5013-2974-6

Series: Animation: Key Films/ Filmmakers

Typeset by Newgen KnowledgeWorks Pvt. Ltd., Chennai, India

To find out more about our authors and books visit
www.bloomsbury.com and sign up for our newsletters.

CONTENTS

ILLUSTRATIONS

Figures

Table

ACKNOWLEDGEMENTS

Princess Mononoke has been with me for my whole academic life. I vividly remember queuing to see *Princess Mononoke* in a small cinema in Kanazawa city back in 1997, during my year abroad as an undergraduate student. I was amazed by the crowds (some of whom stood for the entire two-hour plus running time of the film) and by the animation, which was spellbinding. *Princess Mononoke* has stuck with me ever since, inspiring multiple publications over the years, and now, thanks to Chris Pallant's kind invitation, this edited collection. My sincere thanks to Chris and to Katie Gallof and her editorial team at Bloomsbury for helping to make sure that this book became a reality.

Due to the fact that *Princess Mononoke* and I have been travelling through life together for such a long time, there are many people I need to thank. First, of course, I want to extend my deepest thanks and gratitude to my contributors, who have done the impossible by meeting every deadline set with aplomb and good humour. Their work is incredible, showing how much complexity and variety there is in *Princess Mononoke* and how open the film is to differing academic theories and methods.

Given *Princess Mononoke*'s focus on ferocious, talented and kind women, I would like to add my thanks to the women who have inspired and supported me over the years. Four in particular: my mother, Sheila, who is as much my best friend as my mom; my glamorous and wise sister, Ashlie, who always tells me the truth; and, my grandmothers, Hilda Smith and Gladys Denison, who, though no longer with us, have thoroughly shaped who I am today. To these brilliant women, I need to add so many wonderful, talented friends and colleagues who continue to inspire me – Lisa Fearing, Rachel Mizsei-Ward, Melanie Selfe, Emma Pett, Eylem Atakav, Christine Cornea, Sarah Godfrey, Sanna Inthorn, Su Holmes, Hannah Hamad, Yvonne Tasker, Melanie Williams and Alison Winch.

I also wish to acknowledge the generous support of the Great Britain Sasakawa Foundation, which has enabled me to travel to Japan in search of the research materials featured in the introduction to this book.

These thanks, as ever, would not be complete without mentioning my father, Raymond, whose love of sci-fi meant that the popular was always a serious business in our house growing up. And without my fiancé, John, none of this would be possible. John has patiently watched and re-watched every Ghibli film with me over the years, has been there with me for every discovery made during translation work and has supported me regardless of whether the ideas are flowing, or the well has run dry. He is, in my estimation, an even better hero than Ashitaka.

INTRODUCING STUDIO GHIBLI'S MONSTER PRINCESS: FROM *MONONOKEHIME* TO *PRINCESS MONONOKE*

Rayna Denison

When it came out in 1997, Hayao Miyazaki's *Mononokehime* (*Princess Mononoke*) was a new kind of anime film. It broke long-standing Japanese box office records that had been set by Hollywood films, and in becoming a blockbuster-sized hit *Mononokehime* demonstrated the commercial power of anime in Japan.[1] Further, *Mononokehime* became the first of Miyazaki's films to benefit from a 'global' release thanks to a new distribution deal between Disney and Tokuma shoten, then the parent company for Miyazaki's Studio Ghibli. As a result of this deal, *Mononokehime* was transformed through translation: US star voices replaced those of Japanese actors, a new marketing campaign reframed the film for US audiences and famous fantasy author Neil Gaiman undertook a localization project to turn *Mononokehime* into *Princess Mononoke* (1999).[2] As *Princess Mononoke,* it was the first Miyazaki film to receive a significant cinematic release in the United States. In these ways, as *Mononokehime* and *Princess Mononoke,* Miyazaki's film became a 'monster' film event – the source for a long-lasting, wide-spread cultural phenomenon reflective of a general trend towards the globalization of anime.[3]

Globalization had already impacted upon *Mononokehime* before this transformation took place, which is perhaps most obvious at the level of its animated imagery. For, despite Studio Ghibli's reputation for using hand-drawn cel animation, *Mononokehime* included imagery produced using globalized Computer Generated (CG) animation technologies. Miyazaki aligned the use of these new animation techniques with a deepening thematic concern regarding the whole of humanity's relationship with nature. From its animation style and themes to their translation, from its local blockbuster status to its high profile global distribution, therefore, *Mononokehime* was at the vanguard of anime in a period of rapid change. For these reasons and others, twenty years after its initial success, it is worth looking back at how *Mononokehime* marked changes in the Japanese animation industry; at how it shaped, and was shaped, and then reshaped by the cultures with which it came into contact. The essays collected in this volume are therefore intended to reveal just how important *Mononokehime* has been to the history of Japanese, and global, animation.

As this suggests, *Mononokehime* is worth revisiting because of its exceptional status within the *oeuvre* of one of the world's most respected animators: Hayao Miyazaki. Writing in 1999, for *Newsweek*, David Ansen claims that, on watching *Princess Mononoke*, US audiences would 'see why, in animation circles, Miyazaki himself is considered one of the gods.'[4] In the same year, in one of the first extended critical appraisals of Miyazaki's work in English, Helen McCarthy argues that 'Miyazaki now stands at the pinnacle of Japanese artistic achievement. He has helped raise two mass entertainment media, animation and comics, to the status of artistic and literary excellence.'[5] Therefore, as an animator-turned-director, and as an emerging brand name, Miyazaki's style and thematics were already well-established on the release of *Mononokehime*, and his treatment of young female heroines, ambivalent approaches to good and evil, depictions of flight and flying machines and deepening concern about ecological issues were all well-known.[6] However, as McCarthy notes, *Mononokehime* was as much a departure for Miyazaki as it was a distillation of his thematic interests and the style of animation at Ghibli.[7] Shiro Yoshioka argues, in this collection, that Miyazaki adopted a new directorial persona as a public intellectual around the time of *Mononokehime*, turning to scholarly Japanese texts for inspiration and borrowing new theories from history and ecology to deepen the themes of *Mononokehime* (Chapter 1). These themes are most clearly rendered in a newly emergent ambivalence and complexity found within *Mononokehime*'s characterization, something that several of the authors in this collection analyse (for examples see Chapters 5 and 6).

Miyazaki's historical and environmental research also resulted in extreme representations of nature and humanity in *Mononokehime*. Miyazaki has likened *Mononokehime*'s gods to 'living animals, tortured by humans,' and argues that, 'I wanted to show the unbearable existence of these animals. I feel it is impossible to talk about the relationship between humanity and nature unless I depict these aspects of it.'[8] *Mononokehime* is consequently filled with monsters: from the animalized god-monsters who protect the *Shishigami*'s (Deer God) magical forest, to the monstrous human characters bent on its destruction. This is another reason why the title of this collection refers to a 'monster princess'.

There is, however, considerable debate about how to translate the title of Miyazaki's *Mononokehime*. In the English language version of the film, *Princess Mononoke*, part of the Japanese phrasing is retrained, and '*mononoke*' signals US audiences about the film's cultural difference.[9] Jennifer E. Nicholson, for instance, explores how hard it was for US adaptator, Neil Gaiman, to try to incorporate the sense of '*mononoke*' within the English-language version of the film in Chapter 7 of this collection. In more general accounts, Michael Dylan Foster and others have traced the Japanese word *mononoke* at least as far back as *The Tale of Genji*,[10] and argue that it was in common usage in the Heian period of Japanese history (794–1185). Foster translates *mononoke* as a numinous 'thing' that is suspicious or unstable:

> Mono-no-ke phenomena betrayed the instability and mutability of everyday existence, like ripples appearing suddenly in the solid-*seeming* surface of a dark liquid body. They were sudden, unusual, unpredictable – and therefore frightening . . . Perhaps it is helpful to think of the occurrence of mono-no-ke as akin to a crime or an automobile accident – not an everyday occurrence but always a terrible, imaginable possibility capable of rupturing mundane 'reality'.[11]

San, the eponymous princess of *Mononokehime*, displays many of these traits in her uncanny speed, ferocity and unpredictability. However, we have no easy equivalent word in English, which might help to explain why *Mononokehime* became *Princess Mononoke* on its US release. However, given the frightening, unstable and phenomenal aspects of the term, many translate it as 'possessed', 'spirit' or 'monster' (see Chapter 7). Consequently, the word 'monster' is invoked in this collection to signal some of the cultural complexity of Miyazaki's film, as well as its central 'monstrous' gods and indomitable princess. In addition, the translation of *mononoke* as 'monster' also nods to the blockbuster-size of the phenomenon around the film in its local market, and to Miyazaki's new-plumbed thematic extremes.

The use of 'monster princess' in the title of this collection on *Mononokehime* also signals how much Miyazaki's vision for the film changed over time. The original sketches for *Mononokehime* were done by Miyazaki around 1980, shortly after the release of his first film, *Lupin III: Caguriosutoro no shiro* (*Castle of Cagliostro*, 1979). At that time, the imagery for *Mononokehime* shows a Totoro-like bipedal cat character carrying a teenaged girl on his back.[12] Reporting on the subsequent release of this imagery as a storybook in Japan in 1993, a journalist describes the original story as an 'adaptation of *Beauty and the Beast*' that 'resets the work in Japan, telling the story from the perspective of a young girl. Estranged from her father, she is married off to a *mononoke*, or vengeful spectre, and then tries to free her father from evil spirits'.[13] Neither the original look of the characters, nor the story itself, survived to appear in the film version of *Mononokehime*. If anything, these earlier versions indicate how radically Miyazaki changed his core concept before the 1997 film was made. Changing from a Western-style fairy tale to a violent and new kind of *jidaigeki* (period drama) *Mononokehime* reflects Miyazaki's developing seriousness of purpose.

Of this new purpose Miyazaki has said that:

> In fact, [in *Mononokehime*] I meant to state my objection to the way environmental issues are treated. That is, I didn't want to split off the global environment from human beings. I wanted to include the entire world of humans and other living creatures, as well as the global environment, water, and air.

I also wanted to delve into whether people can overcome the hatred that has gradually grown up inside them.[14]

Miyazaki's objection was to the lack of reflexivity in the approach to environmental management and change in Japan, and this is why he has recourse to the Muromachi period (1336–1573) of Japanese history in *Mononokehime*; to a pre-modern setting in which Miyazaki imagines a version of Japan relatively untouched by rice production and deforestation. He uses this loose historical setting to depict a story on the fringes of Japanese history and culture, in which marginalized groups battle with one another over their right to exist. The story centres, not on a princess as the title suggests, but on Prince Ashitaka, a representative of the native, and now lost, Emishi tribe.[15] In a quest narrative, Ashitaka journeys across Japan in an attempt to lift a curse placed on him after a boar god is poisoned by a bullet originating from the guns of an iron-smelting settlement, the Tataraba. On tracing the bullet back to its origins, Ashitaka is thrust into the centre of an on-going conflict between the people of the Tataraba and the animal gods of the nearby forest that the Tataraba is denuding for their iron production.

The animal gods are the clearest indication that *Mononokehime* is an historical fantasy film, but Miyazaki also exaggerates, transnationalizes and invents other aspects of *Mononokehime*'s historical setting to enhance the eco-fable at the heart of his film. Ashitaka's Emishi tribe, for example, are depicted as a pre-modern people on the margins of a Japan's modernizing mainstream, offering another historically fragmented aspect to *Mononokehime*.[16] By contrast, the Tataraba settlement is an invention Miyazaki borrowed and exaggerated from Chinese culture.[17] The settlement, led by a warrior woman, Lady Eboshi, is discussed in Chapter 6 by Alice Vernon, who contends that Eboshi's role as antagonist is ambiguous at best; she is an exaggeratedly human character, filled with obsession and ambition, which is tempered by a protective love for her people that makes them extremely loyal to her. The fact that Eboshi selects her people from amongst some of Japan's most historically marginalized groups, especially lepers and prostitutes, transforms her into a sympathetic character. On the other side of the conflict is San, the '*Mononokehime*', and her wolf god family, who try to protect the *Shishigami*/Didarabotchi from the encroaching human forces that are attempting to hunt and kill it. San is 'othered' repeatedly throughout the narrative. For example, Eija Niskanen argues in Chapter 2 that San's costuming borrows from Japan's ancient past, and is symptomatic of the historical palimpsest at work in *Mononokehime*. As Helen McCarthy shows in Chapter 5, too, San is a one-off female protagonist within Miyazaki's films, as she remains closely tied to the wild and untamed aspects of nature at work in *Mononokehime*, rather than becoming domesticated by love.

The animal gods of *Mononokehime*'s forest, including tribes of wolves, boars and apes, go beyond human history entirely, giving voice to Miyazaki's interpretation of untamed Japanese nature. The animal gods' desperate battle against humanity results in horrifying scenes of war towards *Mononokehime*'s climax. The plight of nature is represented within the *Shishigami*/Didarabotchi, an enigmatic god whose destruction by man creates the film's ambiguous finale. Its dual name reflects its differing day and night forms, whose presence personifies the magic of the untouched natural world, discussed by Tracey-Lynn Daniels and Matthew Lerberg in Chapter 3. The purpose behind the conflict between modernizing humans and the pre-modern magical-natural world is to challenge anthropocentric visions of nature. *Mononokehime*'s ambiguous conclusion, in which a balance of sorts is restored, but most of the magic of nature is lost, suggests Miyazaki's highly ambivalent stance on Japan's approach to environmental matters.

A Monster Hit: Mononokehime's *Blockbuster Status in Japan*

With all of its alterity and new approach to ecology, *Mononokehime* might seem like an unusual example of blockbuster filmmaking. However, the popular anime magazine, *Animēju* (*Animage*), created a promotional set of articles for *Mononokehime*'s release that focus entirely on the film's textual appeals by way of explaining its commercial success. The magazine suggests three main textual appeals for the film. First, the relationship between Ashitaka and San, which *Animage* uses as an opportunity to explore the protagonists' romantic relationship, also providing an interview with San's voice actress, Yuriko Ishida. Their second explanation is that *Mononokehime* offers 'The ultimate in beautiful imagery for Miyazaki's anime', which presages more than half a dozen pages on everything from character design, to background drawings, to the use of CG animation in *Mononokehime*. The third appeal of the film is found in its division between people and the forest in ancient times, which is personified in the difference between the 'violent gods' and the Tataraba's female leader, Eboshi (see Chapter 6).[18] So, *Animage*, and other magazines produced to celebrate the release of *Mononokehime*, suggest that artistry, characterization and the battle between the Tataraba and the animal gods were the primary causes of *Mononokehime*'s success. In essence, *Animage* argues that it was *Mononokehime*'s textual distinctiveness within Japan's crowded anime marketplace that made it a success.

Other commentators differ in their opinions, however. Yasunari Tokuma, the head of Ghibli's then parent company, Tokuma shoten, has suggested that the budget was key to reaping blockbuster rewards from *Mononokehime*: 'There has been two billion yen in direct production costs, and one billion yen of that was used for CG. We spent another one billion yen on advertising too, and if the income and expenditure come out even then it will be a huge success.'[19] The three billion yen budget (roughly US$30 million) was large for anime at that time and made *Mononokehime* into a local equivalent of the 'calculated' blockbuster film.[20] Tokuma's suggestion that breaking even would make

Mononokehime a success is also a sign of how risky the film was perceived to be before its release.

Riskiness and high budgets are at least two factors that mark blockbuster production, and the use of extensive marketing is a third.[21] The large marketing budget provided for *Mononokehime* was a result of Toshio Suzuki's Studio Ghibli advertising system, something discussed by Yoshioka in Chapter 1. Suzuki has said that this system relies on a tripartite advertising strategy: the consistent use of a title logo, the use of a key image and the tag line (in Japanese terminology, the 'catchcopy').[22] This, however, belies the wildly inventive marketing strategy employed by Suzuki for *Mononokehime*, seen in the use of dozens of images in the promotional campaign for *Mononokehime* in Japan.[23] Nevertheless, the prominence of its logo, drawn by Hayao Miyazaki, in combination with its tag-line 'Live' (*Ikiro*), and of a key image of San in front of her wolf-goddess mother, Moro, map closely onto the kinds of promotional imagery seen in blockbuster film promotion elsewhere in the world.[24] This suggests that *Mononokehime* benefited from an increasingly planned system of hit-making at Studio Ghibli, rather than becoming a hit simply thanks to its textual qualities.

Minoru Kikuchi, writing in Japan's *New Media* journal, also notes the presence of a commercial system operating in support of *Mononokehime*'s release.[25] Rather than focusing on budget, though, Kikuchi examines Japan's emerging blockbuster system, noting that Studio Ghibli had an unusual approach to Japan's 'media mix' advertising and merchandizing systems.[26] First, Kikuchi notes that *Mononokehime* was the beneficiary of a promotional and publicity system that Studio Ghibli had been refining since the release of *Majo no takkyūbin* (*Kiki's Delivery Service*, Hayao Miyazaki, 1989; see Chapters 1 and 8). Kikuchi also asserts that Tōei's decision to place *Mononokehime* in some of their major cinemas, rather than in less salubrious circuits usually used for Japanese films, was another contributing factor to its success. But, more than this, Kikuchi argues that:

> While there was media mix style advertising, the queues outside cinemas were mobilized by word of mouth.
>
> Normal hits (making around 2 billion yen at the box office) have a core generational stratum. For *Shitsuraken* [*A Lost Paradise*, Yoshimitsu Morita, 1997] the youngest audiences were people like me, middle and old-aged, and there were many women in particular. On the other hand, for *Shinseiki Evangerion* [*Neon Genesis Evangelion*, Hideaki Anno, 1995–6], the core audience was boys aged between their teens to the first half of the twenties, and I was one of the oldest. However, *Mononokehime* was an unusual film, mixing young and old, men and women.[27]

In this way, Kikuchi posits that the breadth of audiences and word of mouth were ultimately the key to *Mononokehime*'s success in Japan. As these debates suggest, the reasons for *Mononokehime*'s blockbuster success in Japan are many, and, therefore, a holistic view of the film is taken in this collection, giving space to academic approaches ranging from the textual to the contextual, including the film's reception.

Animating the Monster Princess

Interestingly, though, despite many claims made about the quality of *Mononokehime*'s animation, to date there have been few analyses of how the film's animation was produced. Despite the fact that there is considerable work detailing the representational strategies and themes contained within Hayao Miyazaki's films,[28] it is far less common for academics to focus on how his films are animated. In exploring Miyazaki's *Mononokehime*, it is important not to see it as just another hit film, nor to erase its difference from other contemporary anime texts. This is a topic tackled by Julia Alekseyeva in Chapter 4, wherein she analyses the Russian animation influences at work within *Mononokehime* in order to proffer a new transnational theory of anime. As Alekseyeva demonstrates, any understanding of *Mononokehime*'s significance within Japanese animation culture requires an analysis of how the film was made, and its production at the cusp of an industry-wide shift from cel to digital production technologies.

Studio Ghibli, as intimated above, is well-known for its cel animation practices. Typically, cel animation involves using layers of 'celluloid' plastic painted with parts of a scene or of a character, which are then stacked on top of one another and placed on top of background paintings to create images that move when photographed onto film in sequence. Unusually, the high budget for *Mononokehime* allowed the animators to create detailed movements even in ancillary characters and in the details of the natural world and scenery shown in the film. Additionally, huge detail was lavished on *Mononokehime*'s backgrounds, often produced in watercolours.

This division between simplified foreground characters and richly detailed backgrounds is a hallmark of 'limited' animation styles, perhaps especially anime.[29] A good example of this distinction can be seen in the way that the slightly transparent *kodama* tree sprites have less surface detail than the trees they stand on in the *Shishigami*'s forest (see Figure 0.1). In *Mononokehime*, it is the forest scenes that have particularly detailed background paintings, helping to emphasize their beauty and significance within the narrative, which not even the cute *kodama* are allowed to entirely obscure. Added to this, for *Mononokehime*, Studio Ghibli incorporates aspects of CG animation into their 2-dimensional world, adding further complexity to character designs and backgrounds alike. In this way, *Mononokehime* was an experiment that married traditional anime art with newly emergent digital technologies, creating a film that blends old and new styles of animation. Given the focus on character design, backgrounds, colour and the new CG animation style in the promotional materials published in time for *Mononokehime*'s release, these often overlooked aspects of Studio Ghibli's house style will be the focus of this section of the Introduction.

Thomas Lamarre is among those who have attempted to analyse anime's unique qualities. He creates a theory of the animation process, which he calls the 'anime machine', separating it out from other moments in the production, promotion and reception cycle, though he notes how difficult it can be to untangle the highly intertextual worlds of anime.[30] Lamarre argues that the anime machine was once literal, 'The animation stand, for instance, is an apparatus that sets up layers of transparent celluloid with drawings to be photographed.' But, he explains that these final images relate to a more 'abstract' machine of highly diversified artists, painters and designers who produce the images for compilation. He states, 'Such a machine is not, then, a structure that totalizes or totally determines every outcome. It not only comprises the humans who make it and work with it, but also on other virtual and actual machines.'[31] This explanation of the way cel animation is produced offers a window into the world behind the images of Miyazaki's animation, a world whose structures and meanings are vital to an understanding of how *Mononokehime* was made and how the film became meaningful for audiences.

The abstract machine of anime production is constructed of machines and people, and here the focus will be more on the human side of anime's industrial equation, on the people and creative work we can see through the window opened by Lamarre. In taking this side step, we can better see the individuals who have played significant roles in shaping the look and movement of *Mononokehime*. Miyazaki – as the co-founder of Studio Ghibli, as the film's director and as an animator who reportedly drew or altered nearly 80,000 of *Mononokehime*'s

Figure 0.1 *Kodama* tree sprites against a lush painted backdrop in *Mononokehime*.

140,000 cels[32] – is inevitably someone whose history, training and influence are worth analysing. Miyazaki's style of animation has been heavily influenced by his early training at Tōei Dōga, where he began his career in 1963 as a low-ranking in-betweener (someone who draws the animation that takes place in between key frames of action) before working his way up through Tōei Dōga's animation system to become a key animator. Miyazaki's animation style, particularly his character designs, were heavily influenced by Tōei Dōga's style, and especially by Yasuo Ōtsuka, with whom he repeatedly worked while at Tōei, and later at Nippon Animation (see Chapters 1, 2 and 4 on Miyazaki's influences).[33] It is worth noting that Miyazaki's style was in keeping with other contemporary early 'anime'. Miyazaki's character design style – characters with broad faces, often with short hair and relatively simplistic body and limb shapes – has since become a hallmark of the Studio Ghibli house style. However, his character style has become more and more unusual during his career, as Studio Ghibli's character designs have remained comparatively consistent, whereas anime styles have changed and diversified in the rest of Japan's animation industry.

Miyazaki's retention of this character design style goes hand in hand with his assertions about not making 'anime'. He declares that 'The current conditions don't allow decent animated shows to be made' and instead argues that he makes *manga eiga* (manga films).[34] Tōei Dōga's early animated feature films are also often referred to as *manga eiga*.[35] This may help, to an extent, to explain the film-based production model at Studio Ghibli, instead of the more normal specialization in television animation found at other anime studios. It may also help to explain the consistency in Miyazaki's character designs, despite the rapid industrial changes taking place in the rest of Japan's anime industry.

However, Miyazaki's style of animation also owes much to those with whom he has fostered long collaborative relationships. There are several significant moments in Miyazaki's early history that helped to shape Studio Ghibli, and through it, *Mononokehime*. First, from his time at Tōei Dōga Miyazaki began to work with director Isao Takahata, the producer on many of Miyazaki's films and the co-founder of Studio Ghibli. Likewise, it was at Tōei Dōga that Miyazaki first worked with colour designer Michiyo Yasuda, who would go on to design the lush palettes of Ghibli's films. Second, the closure of Topcraft Studio in 1985 meant that, when Studio Ghibli was formed in 1985 for the production of *Tenkū no shiro Rapyūta* (*Castle in the Sky*, Hayao Miyazaki, 1986), it could inherit key animators and other personnel from the defunct studio.[36] This link was crucial, because Topcraft was the studio at which Miyazaki made his first hit film: *Kaze no tani no Naushika* (*Nausicaa of the Valley of the Wind*, 1983). Many of the Topcraft staff members would go on to become permanent staff members Studio Ghibli, perhaps most notably Yoshifumi Kondō the director of Ghibli's *Mimi o sumaseba* (*Whisper of the Heart*, 1995). Third, Miyazaki brought other animators to Ghibli from his television productions, for instance female animator Makiko Futaki, who first worked with Miyazaki on *Meitantei Holmes* (*Sherlock Hound*, 1984). While Studio Ghibli's early status was tenuous and staff were hired on a contract-by-contract basis,[37] by the early 1990s they were in a position to make staff permanent.[38] This has meant that, unlike other anime studios where staff turnover is high, Studio Ghibli has been able to develop a relatively stable roster of key staff members, many of whom have previous experience working for Miyazaki.[39] This has also helped to produce a consistent 'house style' of animation at Studio Ghibli.

Miyazaki contends that the 'major characteristic of Studio Ghibli – not just myself – is the way we depict nature'.[40] Images of nature, animal characters and weather events are all notable characteristics of Studio Ghibli's house style. One of the most important aspects of this style is the way Ghibli animators present the details of the natural world. Kazuo Oga, one of *Mononokehime*'s art directors, claims that

> Even though we were aiming at realistic backgrounds, I think that it would be bad if we went that far. While wanting to try for 'simplicity within the detail', for me, it becomes art as I draw the fine detail unconsciously . . . However, the thing that makes Miyazaki most angry are images that are strangely shoddy and shallow. Even though it takes time, the pictures that I have taken trouble over have more importance in themselves, and have power. The ones that are shallow, the ones that cut corners, are the one he dislikes the most.[41]

Ghibli's approach to aestheticizing the natural world is sketched by Oga in this quotation, with Miyazaki acting as the final arbiter of animation quality at Ghibli. Oga notes that the aim is not to reproduce nature precisely, but rather to simplify and caricature nature's essential meanings. It is this hyper-realistic aestheticization of nature that leads to observational moments of quiet reflection in *Mononokehime*, from a kingfisher taking flight at the side of a river, to the first drops of rain darkening a path, to the wind bending the stalks of grass in a field as Ashitaka makes his journey to the *Shishigami*'s forest. Depicting nature, therefore, is not just about the level of realism in background paintings or moving images for Ghibli, but is as much a product of the time given over to observing moments from the natural world.

For *Mononokehime*, certain key Studio Ghibli staff members were emphasized repeatedly through appearances in promotional magazine coverage. These appearances also reveal how Studio Ghibli's house style has been expanding and developing. For example, *Animage* magazine relates that there were five animation art directors for *Mononokehime*: Kazuo Oga, Nizō Yamamoto, Naoya Tanaka, Satoshi Kuroda and Yōji Takeshige. The author claims: 'Putting five people in charge of the art in this one film is more than a luxury, it is unheard of. However, there is an example in Ghibli films: *Castle in the Sky* (with art direction by two people, Toshio Nozaki and Nizō Yamamoto), but this time the art direction line-up has increased still further.'[42] Hinting at the large scale of the production, this article highlights a particular kind of animator, the animation art director, as key to the scale and success of *Mononokehime*. The article goes on to note that the film was essentially parcelled up, with different art directors taking charge of specific types of scene and shots. Quoting Sengi Tanaka (part of the distribution and promotional team for *Mononokehime*), the article claims that there is 'a method for dividing it up – the art of the daytime in Ashitaka's village at the beginning is all Oga, the nights are Yamamoto'.[43] Comic Box's promotional magazine, *Mononokehime o yomitoku* (*Reading Mononokehime*), confirms this analysis. The first question asked in the interview with Nizō Yamamoto is about his experience of working with the four other art directors. He replies that there were some scenes everyone wanted to do, but that they made pragmatic decisions in consultation with one another in order to keep *Mononokehime* on track.[44] Despite Miyazaki's claim to personal involvement in most of the production then, these articles suggest that tasks were delegated at Studio Ghibli, and that animators were encouraged to specialize in order to create consistency in the animation for *Mononokehime*.

Nevertheless, these art directors also routinely discuss their relationship to Miyazaki. For example, when interviewed for respected film magazine, *Kinema Junpo*, Yamamoto tells the interviewer that, of the 340 or so shots in the *Shishigami's* forest, he was responsible for about 150. Yamamoto goes on to say that:

> Miyazaki instructed us about how he wanted us to express ourselves, about the grace of the ancient forest, its appearance and the mood of that period. Within those artistic limits I responded to the best of my ability. My ideas were not perfectly expressed through . . . Even though I was paying careful attention to the progress of my work, the director did not easily give me the 'OK'.[45]

In saying this, Yamamoto stresses the importance of quality and of serving Miyazaki's vision for *Mononokehime*. However, Yamamoto's comments also reflect a certain amount of autonomy enjoyed by animators at Ghibli, with work only corrected or critiqued towards the end of the production process.

Colour designer Michiyo Yasuda, tells a different story about working with Miyazaki on *Mononokehime*. Her interview with *Kinema Junpo* begins with statements about her working relationship with Miyazaki and with an assessment of *Mononokehime*'s quality. 'We've been working together for thirty years. Whenever I think about Miyazaki it's interesting . . . This is a new kind of film for Miyazaki, and I feel that it is a more advanced world than in his films up to now'.[46] Yasuda's story of working with Miyazaki on *Mononokehime* is distinct from Yamamoto's in the greater freedom (and anxiety) it provoked. Yasuda says that there were 'no instructions about what kinds of colour to use', after declaring that, 'when I was deciding about the colour for the Didarabotchi and *Shishigami*, I was worried and didn't really know if it was ok. I do consult with Miyazaki when deciding on the colours, but because it's not about the exact colours, I worry right up until the final rushes'.[47] Yasuda's relative autonomy in selecting the varied colour schemes of *Mononokehime* – including the lush greens of the *Shishigami*'s forest, the earthy browns of the Tataraba ironworks and the night-time greys and blues of the Didarabotchi's visitations – became a source of anxiety for her, as did Miyazaki's lack of supervision.

Additionally, Yasuda's narrative, and others from *Mononokehime*'s promotion, work to signal the newness, perceived riskiness and high stakes of the production. They also repeatedly provide evidence of a machinery at work in Studio Ghibli, with experienced personnel working with relative autonomy in familiar roles to enhance the quality of production. In these accounts, Miyazaki becomes the unpredictable visionary core of the production, whose complex imagination for *Mononokehime* drove one of his staff members to say: 'I'm exhausted! One more film like that, and I'll go mad!'[48]

Ghibli's famed nature imagery was further enhanced within *Mononokehime* through the creation of the studio's new 'CG Room' (*CG shitsu*), a new area of, and department within, the studio specifically created for the CG animation team at Ghibli. Most obviously, the *tatarigami*, or cursed boar-god, who attacks Ashitaka's village at the beginning of *Mononokehime* is covered in writhing, computer-generated worms (Figure 0.2). The new head of the CG Room, Yoshinori Sugano, told one interviewer: 'It was Miyazaki's request to make the *tatarigami* in 3D . . . While making the best use of cel animation know-how we pinned that to 3D movement. Finally, we finished it with Toon Shader, and the process was composited and completed.'[49] The early decision to include CG animation is significant, allowing *Mononokehime*'s animation to be produced as a mixture of 2- and 3-dimensional images. *Mononokehime*'s theatrical pamphlet reveals that five different kinds of CG processes were used to enhance the film's imagery. These can be roughly divided into three types of animation technique. First was the use of digital paint to colour the images. Second, CG processes were used to create digitally layered images that could increase the depth of *Mononokehime*'s imagery; for example, taking hand-drawn images and placing them within three-dimensional environments. These were sometimes entirely digitally created, and at others were a mixture of hand-drawn and CG animation technologies. Third, a set of processes was used to add extra details and smooth transitions, like particles that swirl in the air or inside characters (Figure 0.3), and characters who morph from one creature into another.[50]

The attempt to make this imagery fit with Studio Ghibli's existing 2-dimensional 'anime' aesthetic is demonstrated in Sugano's comments. He notes that the most complex images were those where CG techniques were used to hide the joins between original work in cel animation and the new computer animation. This can also be seen, for example, when the Didarabotchi sheds 'particles' created using CG animation (Figure 0.3), or when the flowers that bloom after the death of the *Shishigami* are created through a composite of computer and hand-drawn animation. Significantly, these moments of CG-produced difference are linked to spectacle in *Mononokehime* and are centred on the characters most closely associated to fantasy; namely, on the *Shishigami/ Didarabotchi* and the cursed *tatarigami* gods of *Mononokehime*.

Figure 0.2 The CG animated *tatarigami*.

Figure 0.3 Didarabotchi contains and sheds computer-generated particles.

Although the theatrical pamphlet for *Mononokehime* makes it clear that only about five minutes of the total screen time was entirely digitally produced, there was a further ten minutes of composite CG and hand-drawn footage, making about a ninth of the total film computer-generated.[51] Sugano notes a surprisingly pragmatic foundation for Ghibli's increasing use of CG animation in *Mononokehime*, one that has nothing to do with animation spectacle:

> It wasn't the case that we gathered people together to discuss the future of CG, but I think that the main producer was thinking about such things. At

any rate, not only was the domestic provision of cels dying out, but the [cel] paints were not available domestically any longer, [and] this was all clear before we began the *Mononokehime* project.[52]

Pragmatism, not just artistry, therefore, drove Ghibli's decision to shift towards the use of computer animation. With its pragmatic foundations and attempts to mask the joins between CG animation and hand-drawn animation, *Mononokehime* may have utilized CG animation for fantasy creatures, but the studio's larger aims seem far more prosaic. Within the discourses of quality and art sketched above, therefore, the machinery of Studio Ghibli is also made visible, and the highly diversified, collaborative and composite processes used to animate *Mononokehime* are revealed. Combined together with the scale of production and the film's large budget, these discourses about *Mononokehime*'s creation suggest that the film was at the cutting edge of technical possibility in anime, once more suggesting a monstrously large, cutting edge film production.

Becoming Princess Mononoke

The importance of the animation is thrown into relief when considering the fact that the animation of *Mononokehime* became one of the few unchanging aspects of the film as it travelled beyond Japanese borders. As the film travelled to Asia, the United States, Europe and elsewhere, it became appended with new subtitle tracks, new voice casts and new advertising campaigns (see Chapters 7 and 8). Each new iteration added meanings, not least in attempts to explain *Mononokehime*'s culturally specific historical and fantasy elements. However, *Mononokehime*'s global distribution was more planned than this suggests. There were, initially, two major global circuits through which *Mononokehime* travelled. The first began in Japan, where distributor-studio Tōhō retained control of *Mononokehime*'s Asian releases.[53] However, in the second circuit, Miyazaki's film was put into the hands of a Disney subsidiary, Miramax, for distribution in the United States and much of the rest of the world, including its eventual re-distribution back to Japan as *Princess Mononoke*.

This dual release circuit was the product of what is colloquially known as the Disney-Tokuma deal of 1996, in which Buena Vista International secured distribution rights for Miyazaki's films in the United States and beyond. Speaking to the *Yomiuri Newspaper* in 1997, Miyazaki said:

This agreement was reached between Tokuma, one of the producing companies, and Disney practically before we realized what was happening. But Disney is quite a severe taskmaster, so if the film doesn't do well commercially, I'm sure they'll quickly pull out. This shouldn't be seen as that big of a deal, just as with the delusion that 'Japanimation' is foremost in the world.[54]

Although Miyazaki may have been trying to manage Japanese expectations regarding *Mononokehime*'s potential for global success, the deal between Buena Vista International (for Disney) and Tokuma shoten was 'a big deal'. It provided a large-scale global release for *Mononokehime* under the auspices of one of the United States' most powerful media conglomerates. But perhaps even more importantly, *Mononokehime* was given a new, globalized identity and a new advertising campaign to go with it, transforming the film from a Japanese blockbuster into the art house film *Princess Mononoke*.

Miramax's treatment of *Princess Mononoke* was unusual at the time, and set the tone for many subsequent releases of Miyazaki's animated films in the United States. As Jennifer E. Nicholson argues in this collection, it was a significant departure from the treatment of most anime releases. In particular, its translation was undertaken not by a screenwriter, but by a famous novelist and comic book writer, Neil Gaiman (Chapter 7). Gaiman worked with the existing animation to localize and explain *Mononokehime*'s more culturally distant elements for US audiences; for example, adding explanatory dialogue when characters' faces are out of view. Gaiman's involvement also allowed Miramax to use his existing star power to draw across fandoms from comic books into animation.

However, the localization process extended further than this suggests. *Mononokehime*'s reproduction for the United States also notably included famous film and television stars like Claire Danes, Billy Bob Thornton, Gillian Anderson, Minnie Driver and Jada Pinkett-Smith, whose presences in the voice cast worked to bring a range of US and European accents into the soundscape of the new *Princess Mononoke*.[55] As with Gaiman's presence, these stars had a promotional value to *Princess Mononoke*, appearing on posters in the United States as well as at premiere events, something that Laz Carter discusses in Chapter 8. In addition, though, they helped to signal a distinction drawn between *Princess Mononoke* and other anime releases in the United States. Instead of utilizing the existing anime voice acting companies in the United States, using star voices placed *Princess Mononoke* into a new category of US animation that was making heavy use of star voices. As Laz Carter argues in Chapter 8, the reproduction of *Mononokehime* into *Princess Mononoke* thereby suggests that Miramax hoped to place Miyazaki's film somewhere between art house cinema and mainstream US blockbuster status.

However, the challenges in crossing between the art house and mainstream at the time of *Princess Mononoke*'s US release are clear from its initial reception. *Princess Mononoke* was released in the United States in 1999 to critical acclaim – and some consternation. Roger Ebert, one of the most famous US film critics of the time, reviews *Princess Mononoke* with considerable positive hyperbole, including its new voice cast in his praise. He ends his review by commenting that: 'There is a remarkable scene where San and Ashitaka, who have fallen in love, agree that neither can really lead the life of the other, and so they must grant each other freedom, and only meet occasionally. You won't find many Hollywood love stories (animated or otherwise) so philosophical. *Princess Mononoke* is a great achievement and a wonderful experience, and one of the best films of the year.'[56] Here, the film's difference to local films becomes a positive, and Ebert asserts that it should be read in comparison to live action and not just animated films.

The *New York Times*, on the other hand, writes that 'Miramax will need all the marketing help the star names can provide: while it may prove an animation masterpiece, *Princess Mononoke* will probably be a hard sell in the United States. Set in 15th-century Japan, it features no chirpy musical numbers or wacky jabber-jawed comic-relief characters in the manner of recent Disney crowd-pleasers.'[57] While Ebert proclaims that *Princess Mononoke* deserves to be read in relation to live action films, Tucker finds fault with *Princess Mononoke* because of its difference to the United States' dominant style of animation: Disney. From the outset, therefore, *Princess Mononoke*'s difference to local animated block-busters in the United States was a problem for its US distributors, not least because of their own association with Disney. This shifting reception is something that Emma Pett traces across the history of *Princess Mononoke* in the United States and Europe within this collection as she examines the continual reappraisal of Miyazaki's film by audiences outside Japan (Chapter 9).

This continual reappraisal applies to fans too. As Kikuchi noted above, *Mononokehime* was a significant cultural phenomenon on its release in Japan. The making-of video, *Mononokehime wa kōshite umareta* (*This is How Mononokehime was Born*, 2000), contains scenes of long queues stretching outside of cinema venues, and shows audience members standing throughout screenings.[58] The marketing in Japan reflected this audience enthusiasm, with the newspaper advertisements for *Mononokehime* declaring its shifting status from *daihitto* (big hit) to record breaker and giving a running audience total until admissions topped ten million people.[59] Aligned to this phenomenology was the production of a large amount of merchandise. This merchandise included tie-in specialist magazine coverage, as well as things like *kodama* and *tatarigami* plush toys and even a replica of San's mask that sold for just over 39,000 yen (approximately US$350, see Figure 0.4). However, in the years that have followed, *Mononokehime* has become a far less significant feature of on-going Ghibli merchandising, dwarfed in importance by child-friendly characters like Totoro or Jiji, the black cat from *Majo no takkyūbin*. In sum, this suggests a phenomenology not unlike that witnessed for blockbuster films in the United States: an initial, large-scale cultural phenomenon that is relatively short-lived and replaced by the next in a series of bigger and bigger hits, as was the case for Miyazaki's next film, *Sen to Chihiro no kamikakushi*, or *Spirited Away*, in 2001.[60]

For audiences in the United States the phenomenology surrounding *Princess Mononoke* was far more restricted. On the one hand, the Disney-Tokuma deal did not include merchandising rights, meaning that any merchandise made available to fans in the United States had to be imported. On the other hand, the

Figure 0.4 *Kodama* merchandise (personal photograph).

relatively small numbers of cinemas screening *Princess Mononoke* in the United States meant that the film did not have the same kind of cultural profile or ubiquity as seen in Japan. Some audience members made a virtue of this scarcity, claiming fan status online by talking about the sacrifices they made to see the film in the United States.[61] For example, several fans used the distance driven, or time spent travelling to cinemas, as a badge of honour.[62] As this kind of fan discourse suggests, *Princess Mononoke* has become a cult object over time.

Fans now routinely perform their relationship with *Princess Mononoke* through a variety of activities including creative acts like cosplay and fancrafting.[63] This kind of creative fan art, from ephemera like *Princess Mononoke* cakes to more lasting objects like jewellery or the forthcoming *Wolf Girl* (Nate Drake), which promises to be a short, live action fan film funded on Kickstarter, have provided Miyazaki's film with an extended cultural life that continues to the present day. Even as *Mononokehime* goes past its twentieth anniversary, therefore, it remains a lasting source of creative inspiration to fans from around the world. Becoming *Princess Mononoke*, therefore, has helped to ensure that Miyazaki's 1999 film has a lasting global cultural presence.

The chapters in this collection have been selected to showcase the verdant and varied cultural legacy and history of *Mononokehime*. Split into three parts, this collection explores some of the crucial features of *Mononokehime*'s textual characteristics, while also investigating the contexts of its production and reproduction, thinking about what the film has meant for its director and studio. To this end, the chapters in Part 1 analyse the impact that *Mononokehime* had on its director, Hayao Miyazaki, and his stance on Japanese ecology. Shiro Yoshioka begins the collection with an examination of how *Mononokehime* allowed Miyazaki to become a public intellectual in Japan, contrasting popular filmmaking with a seriousness of intent. In Chapter 2, Eija Niskanen analyses the ancient Japanese cultural places and artefacts that influenced *Mononokehime*'s aesthetics, linking these to Miyazaki's concerns about the environment. Tracey Daniels-Lerberg and Matthew Lerberg take this assessment of Miyazaki's environmental themes further in Chapter 3 in order to theorize his approach to environmental balance. Through their investigations, these contributors show a fundamental shift in both Miyazaki's public persona and his filmmaking at the time of *Mononokehime*.

Part 2 takes a closer look at another theme that has gained importance over time: feminism. Emma Pett shows in Chapter 9 that *Mononokehime* has shifted meanings from monstrous princess to become highly regarded as a 'feminist' animated film. Julia Alekseyeva, as well as producing a theory of transnational anime, addresses a key influence on *Mononokehime*'s female characters: Russian director Lev Atamanov's *Snezhnaya Koroleva* (*The Snow Queen*, 1957). She traces Eboshi, San and other representations from *Mononokehime* back to the character designs of this Russian animation, showing important links between the two. By contrast, Chapters 5 and 6 take a deeper and closer look at *Mononokehime*'s female characters and Miyazaki's relationship to feminism and (anti-)heroism. In Chapter 5, Helen McCarthy reconsiders Miyazaki's representations of female empowerment in *Mononokehime* in a comparative analysis that relates San to other Miyazaki heroines. McCarthy argues that San is unique within Miyazaki's oeuvre, marking a high point for his representation of female freedom and empowerment. In Chapter 6, Alice Vernon focuses on the Tataraba's leader, Lady Eboshi, considering her significance in a medium that is otherwise dominated by youthful girls and boys. Women's aging and empowerment within Miyazaki's cinema thereby form the foci of this second Part. Each of the authors uses gender representation to illustrate the diversity of influences and connections at work in Miyazaki's *Mononokehime*.

The final Part is devoted to the translation, adaptation and reception of *Mononokehime* in its guise as *Princess Mononoke*. In this Part, each of the chapters shows how the film's initial success was expanded upon by the efforts of those taking it from Japan to the rest of the world. In Chapter 7, Jennifer E. Nicholson queries the roles of translation and adaptation in making *Mononokehime* legible for an international audience. She contends that this process is fraught with potential for cultural misunderstanding, obfuscation and appropriation. Laz Carter, similarly, in Chapter 8, analyses the 'paratextual' marketing created to sell US audiences on *Princess Mononoke*. He shows how the film's promotional imagery worked to de- and re-contextualize the film, selling US stars as much as Japanese animation. In the final chapter, Emma Pett analyses the success of these marketing and adaptation efforts, reading their efficacy through *Princess Mononoke*'s reviews and news coverage over the twenty years that it has been circulating in US and European culture. Pett's findings offer an insightful conclusion to this collection, noting that what was once a challenging film text has now become an animation classic.

Mononokehime's cultural monstrosity may well be most visible in this shift: beginning as a film that was challenging, difficult, cutting edge and full of potential 'monsters' and later becoming normalized as a classic of its medium and genre. Within Miyazaki's worlds, *Mononokehime* remains as a standout and standalone endeavour. It still contains a unique visual and narrative landscape in which monsters clash with humans, and good and evil commingle to allegorize a dangerous moment in humanity's relationship to the natural world. These ambiguities go beyond the text as well, showing in the way that *Princess Mononoke* presented a new kind of animation to Japanese and US audiences alike, aligned with new trends in technologies and voice casting, but aimed at a more grown-up audience than was normal for US audiences. Ebert's comments are salient in this regard, because *Princess Mononoke*'s distribution by Miramax was marked by the attempt to orchestrate a new market for animation in the United States, one which asked audiences to accept more adult, more complex and more ambiguous animated films. Even twenty years after its release, therefore, the continuing cultural life of Miyazaki's *Mononokehime* is a testament to the global importance of this Japanese animated classic.

Notes

1 Rayna Denison, 'The Language of the Blockbuster: Promotion, *Princess Mononoke* and the *Daihitto* in Japanese Film Culture' in Leon Hunt and Leung Wing-Fai (eds), *East Asian Cinemas: Exploring Transnational Connections on Film* (London and New York, NY: I. B. Tauris, 2008), pp. 103–22.

2 In this introduction chapter, I will use *Mononokehime* to differentiate between the Japanese release and the subsequent translation, but the collection will normally refer to this film, and all others, by their English language titles, after an initial introduction that includes both the English and the Japanese. The original *Princess Mononoke* character names are used throughout, rather than their translations. Japanese names are given in the Euro-American name order, forename followed by surname. In these footnotes, translated titles in English are used except where doing so would create confusion.

3 Joseph Tobin, ed, *Pikachu's Global Adventure: The Rise and Fall of Pokémon* (Durham: Duke University Press, 2004).

4 David Ansen, '"Princess" Ride', *Newsweek*, vol. 134, no. 18, 1 November 1999, p. 87.

5 Helen McCarthy, *Hayao Miyazaki: Master of Japanese Animation* (Berkeley, CA: Stone Bridge Press, 1999), p. 48.

6 See: Patrick Drazen, *Anime Explosion! The What? Why? & Wow! of Japanese Animation* (Berkeley, CA: Stone Bridge Press, 2003); McCarthy, *Hayao*

Miyazaki; Susan J. Napier, 'Vampires, Psychic Girls, Flying Women and Sailor Scouts: Four Faces of the Young Female in Japanese Popular Culture' in Dolores P. Martinez, ed., *The Worlds of Japanese Popular Culture: Gender, Shifting Boundaries and Global Cultures* (Cambridge: Cambridge University Press, 1998), pp. 91–109

7   McCarthy, *Hayao Miyazaki*, pp. 201–3.

8   Hayao Miyazaki, *Turning Point 1997-2008*, trans. Beth Cary and Frederik L. Schodt (San Francisco, CA: VIZ Media 2014 [2009]), p. 31.

9   Denison, 'The Language of the Blockbuster'.

10   Murasaki Shikibu, *The Tale of Genji*, trans. Edward G. Seidensticker (New York: Knopf, 1008 [1985]).

11   Michael Dylan Foster, *Pandemonium and Parade: Japanese Monsters and the Culture of Yōkai* (Berkeley, CA: University of California Press, 2009), pp. 6–7, emphasis in original.

12   Hayao Miyazaki, *Princess Mononoke: The First Story*, trans. Jocelyne Allen (San Francisco, CA: VIZ Media, 2014 [1993]).

13   Hayao Miyazaki, *Starting Point 1979-1996*, trans. Beth Cary and Frederik L. Schodt (San Francisco, CA: VIZ Media, 2009 [1996]), p. 410.

14   Miyazaki, *Turning Point*, pp.85–6.

15   John A. Tucker, 'Anime and Historical Inversion in Miyazaki Hayao's *Princess Mononoke*', *Japan Studies Review*, vol. 7, no. 1 (2003), pp. 65–102.

16   Tucker, 'Anime and Historical Inversion', pp. 65–102.

17   Miyazaki, *Turning Point*, p. 64.

18   *Animage*, 1997, pp. 6–31.

19   Quoted in Hidetada Udagawa, '*Mononokehime sekai dōji kōkai no ōshōbu*' [The Great Game of *Princess Mononoke*'s Simultaneous Worldwide Release], *The Weekly Toyo Keizai*, 13 April 1996, p. 26.

20   Chris Berry, ' "What's Big about the Big Film?": "De-Westernizing" the Blockbuster in Korea and China' in Julian Stringer (ed.), *Movie Blockbusters* (London: Routledge, 2003), pp.217–30; Thomas Schatz, 'The New Hollywood' in John Collins, Hilary Radner and Ava Preacher Collins (eds), *Film Theory Goes to the Movies* (New York: Routledge, 1993), pp. 8–36.

21   Julian Stringer, ed., *Movie Blockbusters* (London: Routledge, 2003).

22   Toshio Suzuki, *Eiga Dōraku* [*My Film Hobby*] (Tokyo: Pia, 2005), p. 122.

23   Studio Ghibli, *Naushika no 'shinbun kōkoku' tte mitakoto arimasuka: jiburi no shinbun kōkoku 18 nenshi* [*Have You Seen the Newspaper Advertisements for Nausicaä?: The 18 Year History of Ghibli's Newspaper Advertisements*] (Tokyo: Tokuma shoten, 2002).

24   Justin Wyatt, *High Concept: Movies and Marketing in Hollywood* (Texas: University of Texas Press, 1994).

25   Minoru Kikuchi, '*Sūpāburando toshite no Miyazaki anime: naze Mononokehime genshō*' [Miyazaki Anime as a Super Brand: Why Has *Princess Mononoke* Become a Phenomenon?], *New Media*, no.180, September 1998, pp.46–50.

26   Marc Steinberg, *Anime's Media Mix: Franchising Toys and Characters in Japan* (Minneapolis, MN: University of Minnesota Press, 2012).

27   Kikuchi, 'Miyazaki Anime as a Super Brand', p.47.

28   Christine Hoff Kraemer, 'Between Worlds: Liminality and Self-Sacrifice in *Princess Mononoke*', *Journal of Religion and Film*, vol. 8, no. 2 (2004),

Article 1. http://digitalcommons.unomaha.edu/jrf/vol8/iss2/1/ (accessed 15 April 2017); Susan J. Napier, 'Confronting Master Narratives: History as Vision in Miyazaki Hayao's Cinema of De-assurance', *East Asian Cultures Critique*, vol. 9, no. 2 (2001), pp.467–93.

29   For more see: Rayna Denison, *Anime: A Critical Introduction* (London: Bloomsbury, 2015); Thomas Lamarre, *The Anime Machine: A Media Theory of Animation* (Minneapolis, MN: University of Minnesota Press, 2009); Paul Wells, 'Smarter Than the Average Art Form: Animation in the Television Era' in Carole A. Stabile and Mark Harrison (eds), *Prime Time Animation: Television Animation and American Culture* (London: Routledge, 2003), pp.15–32.

30   Lamarre, *The Anime Machine*, p. xiv.

31   Lamarre, *The Anime Machine*, p. xxvi.

32   David Chute, 'Organic Machine: The World of Hayao Miyazaki,' *Film Comment*, vol. 34, no. 6 (1998), pp. 62–5.

33   Jonathan Clements, *Anime: A History* (Basingstoke: Palgrave Macmillan, 2013); Rayna Denison, 'Before Ghibli Was Ghibli: Analysing the Historical Discourses Surrounding Hayao Miyazaki's *Castle in the Sky* (1986)', *East Asian Journal of Popular Culture*, vol. 4, no. 1 (2018).

34   Miyazaki, *Turning Point*, p. 77.

35   Clements, *Anime*.

36   Denison, 'Before Ghibli Was Ghibli'.

37   Denison, 'Before Ghibli Was Ghibli'.

38   Suzuki, *My Film Hobby*.

39   McCarthy, *Hayao Miyazaki*.

40   Miyazaki, *Turning Point*, p.90.

41   Quoted in: *Mononokehime o yomitoku* [*Reading Princess Mononoke*], Comic Box, 2 (August 1997), p.109.

42   *Animage*, 225, March 1997, p.16.

43   *Animage*, 225, March 1997, p.16.

44   *Mononokehime o yomitoku*, p.111.

45   Shunji Ōmori, '*Sutaffu intabyū bijutsu Yamamoto Nizō ni kiku: kuraku shizunda minasoko to akarui midori no koke wo egaku no ga muzukashikatta*' [Staff Interview: Nizō Yamamoto: It Was Difficult to Draw the Depths of a Dark River Bed and Bright Green Moss], *Kinema Junpo*, no. 1233 (1997), p. 83.

46   Shunji Ōmori, '*Sutaffu intabyū Yasuda Michiyo-shi ni kiku: Miyazakisan no mezasu sekai wo hageshiku, yasashiku, "iro" de sasaeru*' [We Talk to Colour Designer Michiyo Yasuda: The World That Miyazaki Is Aiming For Is Supported by Colour, Intensely, Gently], *Kinema Junpo*, no. 1233 (1997), p. 92.

47   Ōmori, 'We Talk to Colour Designer Michiyo Yasuda, pp. 91–2.

48   Yamamoto, quoted in *Mononoke wo yomitoku*, p.110.

49   Tomio Shimamura and Yoshinori Sugano, '*Honkakuteki dejitaruka ni idonda Mononokehime no CG genba kara*' [From the site of *Princess Mononoke*'s CG which defied standard digitalization], *Kinema Junpo*, no. 1233 (1997), p. 80.

50   *Mononokehime Pamfuletto* [*Princess Mononoke Theatre Programme*] (Tokyo: Tokuma shoten, 1997), pp. 29–30.

51   *Mononokehime Pamfuletto*, p. 30.

52   Shimamura and Sugano, 'From the site of *Princess Mononoke*'s CG', p. 77.

53 Rayna Denison, 'Cultural Traffic in Japanese Anime: The Meanings of Promotion, Reception and Exhibition Circuits in *Princess Mononoke*' (PhD thesis submitted to the University of Nottingham, 2005).

54 Miyazaki, *Turning Point*, p. 70.

55 Rayna Denison, 'Disembodied Stars and the Cultural Meanings of *Princess Mononoke*'s Soundscape'. *Scope: An Online Journal of Film Studies*, vol. 3, no. 1 (November 2005). http://www.nottingham.ac.uk/scope/documents/2005/october-2005/denison.pdf (accessed 30 January 2017).

56 Roger Ebert, 'Drawing Success', *Chicago Sun-Times*, 6 September 1999.

57 Ken Tucker, 'Cute Characters, But No Comic Relief', *New York Times*, 12 September 1999, p. 46.

58 Denison, 'Cultural Traffic in Japanese Anime'.

59 Studio Ghibli, *Have You Seen the Newspaper Advertising*? pp. 366–88.

60 Kevin S. Sandler and Gaylyn Studlar, eds, *Titanic: Anatomy of a Blockbuster* (New Brunswick, NJ: Rutgers University Press, 1999).

61 Matt Hills, *Fan Cultures* (London: Routledge, 2002).

62 Denison, 'Cultural Traffic in Japanese Anime'.

63 James Rendell, 'Bridge Builders, World Makers: Transcultural Studio Ghibli Fan Crafting', *East Asian Journal of Popular Culture*, vol. 4, no. 1 (2018).

Part 1

INTELLECTUALIZING MIYAZAKI: POLITICS, RELIGION
AND THE ENVIRONMENT IN *PRINCESS MONONOKE*

Chapter 1

PRINCESS MONONOKE: A GAME CHANGER

Shiro Yoshioka

If we were to do an overview of the life and works of Hayao Miyazaki, there would be several decisive moments where his agenda for filmmaking changed significantly, along with how his films and himself have been treated by the general public and critics in Japan. Among these, *Mononokehime* (*Princess Mononoke*, 1997) and the period leading up to it from the early 1990s, as I argue in this chapter, had a great impact on the rest of Miyazaki's career. In the first section of this chapter, I discuss how Miyazaki grew sceptical about the style of his filmmaking as a result of cataclysmic changes in the political and social situation both in and outside Japan; in essence, he questioned his production of entertainment films featuring adventures with (pseudo-)European settings, and began to look for something more 'substantial'. The result was a grave and complex story about civilization set in medieval Japan, which was based on academic discourses on Japanese history, culture and identity.

As I detail in the second section of this chapter, before *Princess Mononoke*, Miyazaki's vast amount of general knowledge was already visible in various interviews and essays, as well as his films, and he was regarded as a kind of *bunkajin* (a man of culture) who can comment intellectually on social, cultural and environmental issues from the perspective of a creator. But in *Princess Mononoke*, he explicitly engaged with academic discourses on Japanese historical and cultural identity, most notably with historian Yoshihiko Amino's view of history. As a result of this association of the film and Miyazaki himself with academics and other *bunkajin*, such as novelist–critics Ryōtarō Shiba and Yoshie Hotta, Miyazaki and his films came to be viewed as something (semi-) highbrow, rather than 'lowbrow popular culture' (*tsūzoku bunka*) as Miyazaki always insisted.

It is not simply the theme of *Princess Mononoke* and Miyazaki's approach to filmmaking that changed and put him in the position of *bunkajin*. As discussed in the final section of this chapter, the very fact that *Princess Mononoke* had unprecedented levels of success is also important. We have to note, however, that this success is not simply because of the superb technical and textual quality of the film, but is a combination of his track record as a creator of animation for general audiences and also rigorous, and extensive, promotion coordinated by Toshio Suzuki, the producer at Studio Ghibli. Until late 2016, when Makoto Shinkai's *Kimi no na wa* (*Your Name*, 2016) became a smash hit and finally broke the record set by *Hauru no ugoku shiro* (*Howl's Moving Castle*, Hayao Miyazaki, 2004) pushing *Gake no ue no Ponyo* (*Ponyo*, Hayao Miyazaki, 2008) out of the top-ten list, all of the films Miyazaki created after *Princess Mononoke* were among the ten most successful films released in Japan, apart from *Kaze tachinu* (*The Wind Rises*, Hayao Miyazaki, 2013). *Sen to Chihiro no kamikakushi* (*Spirited Away*, Hayao Miyazaki, 2001) was (and is at the time of writing) at the top of the chart, followed by *Howl's Moving Castle* at fifth, *Princess Mononoke* at sixth and *Ponyo* at tenth.[1] Instead of simply lauding the quality of these films, however, we need to contextualize their popularity taking a number of other factors into consideration.

One significant change *Princess Mononoke* caused was that it enabled anime to become the subject of critical and academic discussion within Japanese *rondan* (the arena of literary, social and cultural criticism). While Miyazaki himself came to be associated with academics and critics, they, in turn, began to analyse and discuss anime texts in order to reflect on their own agendas and academic interests. Together with *Shin seiki Evangerion* (*Neon Genesis Evangelion*, Hideaki Anno, 1995), *Princess Mononoke* can be regarded as a catalyst for the shift of the position of anime from something to be consumed by children and hardcore fans to a form of 'art' that is worthy of critical attention.

This chapter demonstrates the significance of *Princess Mononoke* by going through these points in three sections. The aim of this chapter is not so much to analyse or discuss the film text for its superb quality, but to present the significance of the film in terms of its impact on Miyazaki and anime in general.

The Road to Mononoke

The early 1990s was the period when Miyazaki's policy of filmmaking changed significantly, reflecting cataclysmic change in political and social situation in the world, especially the Gulf War in 1991, the end of the Cold War and the ensuing ethnic conflict in Yugoslavia. These events deeply angered and disappointed Miyazaki. In an article that appeared in a weekly magazine in 1991, Miyazaki stated critically that the Gulf War lacked cause and the Japanese government's decision to support the Coalition Forces was 'solely out of a desire to do business with and be "good neighbors" to our allies.'[2] The Gulf War was a pivotal moment in post-war Japanese history because, as a result of criticism from the international community for simply contributing funds but not sending any troops, the Japanese government, for the first time, decided to send the Self-Defense Forces abroad.[3] The decision was controversial because Article 9 of the Japanese Constitution states that the country renounces war as a means to solve international conflicts. In accordance with this position, in the article cited earlier, Miyazaki suggests that the operation was in breach of the Constitution and states that he 'want[s] to find something that can become our core principles'.[4]

The collapse of communist regimes and the end of the Cold War also tormented Miyazaki in several ways that relate to his core principles. First, he was bitterly disappointed by the fact that the end of the Cold War led to resurgence of ethnic conflicts. He found the civil war in Yugoslavia (1991–2001) particularly shocking. The area of the Adriatic Sea was exactly where his *Kurenai no buta* (*Porco Rosso*, 1992) was set, which was in production then. Miyazaki was also dismayed because it appeared to him as if history was repeating, replaying what happened before World War I.[5] He also felt apprehensive about the demise of communist states. In an interview in 1992, coinciding with the release of *Porco Rosso*, Miyazaki said that the collapse of the Soviet Union itself meant nothing to him because he thought it simply followed classic examples in history where people stood up against oppression.[6] Miyazaki also confided that while he had, for a long time, no illusions about communism as a political and social system, he still had some hope in socialism because, in his view, at the core of socialism was respect for dignity of people.[7] For Miyazaki, such socialistic ideals were his 'starting point', or a 'major pillar', when he formed his identity in his youth.[8] However, he now realized that such an ideal is a 'horizon that can be never reached' and even after socialism, which he thought could be a bridge to such an ideal state, had collapsed he stated that one had to 'keep walking'.[9] In the same interview, he called *Porco Rosso* a 'moratorium' before tackling various problems in the 1990s.[10] Consequently, Miyazaki believed that in future he had to create a more 'substantial film' (*honshitsuteki na eiga*).[11] Although Miyazaki said he was not sure what a 'substantial film' was, one thing he was sure was that he would no longer create films set outside Japan.[12]

Another interview in the same year offers a clue to understanding what a substantial film might be. In the interview, Miyazaki again made references to the global political situation including the civil war in Yugoslavia. He said that in the 1980s, people in Japan generally seemed to believe that one day the world would come to an abrupt end for such reasons as natural disaster.[13] However, Miyazaki also stated that as he was creating *Porco Rosso*, he reached a certain realization. Asked what it was, he replied: 'Put quite simply, that "no matter how messy things get, we have no choice but go on living."'[14] Miyazaki also said that 'Heading into the twenty-first century, nothing's been resolved. Everything's being dragged into the new era, so we'll just have to go on living, repeating the same stupid mistakes over and over again.'[15] In short, the realization is that one has to confront the reality of the present and also look towards the future, however gloomy and pessimistic it is. To depict such a realization in the form of a 'substantial film', Miyazaki had to abandon his previous philosophy of animation.

Up to the late 1980s, at the core of Miyazaki's approach was that animation should be based in lowbrow popular culture. In a lecture given in 1988, Miyazaki stated that for a film belonging to 'lowbrow popular culture', '[w]hat's important . . . is not whether the film has some sort of permanent artistic value'. Instead, 'even if they are lightweight in nature, the more popular and common films still must be filled with a purity of emotion' and, as such, the film should 'invite anyone in' with few barriers to entry into it yet 'the barriers to exit must be high and purifying'.[16] By 'purifying', Miyazaki suggests the power of such a film to allow its audience to temporarily forget about reality, and to feel refreshed and liberated before returning to reality.[17] Characteristics of Miyazaki's works before *Mononoke* – straightforward adventure stories rather than ones with complicated storyline and subtle themes – derive from this principle. Miyazaki's proposals regularly state that the film is an 'entertainment film' or 'enjoyable film' (*My Neighbor Totoro, Kiki's Delivery Service, Porco Rosso* and *Ponyo*). The proposals also often proclaim that the key concept of the film is *risō*, or 'ideal' (*Castle in the Sky, Whisper of the Heart*), *shiawasena*, or 'happiness' (*Totoro, Kiki*), *ai*, or 'love' (*Porco, Ponyo*), *kibō*, or 'hope' (*Nausicaa of the Valley of Wind*), and also *ikiru koto no subarashisa*, which translates as the 'joy or worthiness of life' (*Whisper of the Heart*). The proposal for *Mononoke* also features a similar phrase, *ikiru ni atai suru* or '[There are] things that [are] worth living for [even in a world full of chaos and vice]'. The fantastic settings of his films, including the choice of locales modelled on Europe (*Kiki, Porco*), Central Asia (*Nausicaa*) and a bucolic Japan of the past (*Totoro*), may well also reflect this principle.

Miyazaki's idea that fantasy should allow the audience to forget about reality and give them the power to return to reality is clearly escapist. Isao Takahata, a long-time colleague, friend and arch-rival of Miyazaki has asserted that the worlds in Miyazaki's films are not on the same plane as the real world. He has also stated that the fantasies depicted in Miyazaki's films, against Miyazaki's intentions, do not prepare the audience to return to reality because fantasy in Miyazaki films is self-contained within the film and not compatible with the reality confronting the audience. In Takahata's view, the audience of such films simply indulge themselves in fantasies that are realistically and superbly depicted in Miyazaki's films, rather than returning to their own reality.[18]

As a result of the realization of the need to confront and accept the reality of the present and the future, however grim it is, Miyazaki turned to the past of Japan. He abandoned his principle of 'lowbrow popular culture' and began to make a substantial films based on academic discourse about Japanese medieval history. His divorce from the principle of 'lowbrow popular culture' and explicit association with more highbrow culture, especially academia, eventually changed Miyazaki's own status significantly.

Japanese History in Princess Mononoke

Miyazaki was interested in creating stories set in pre-modern Japan from the early stages of his career. But the focus of interest changed significantly between then and the time of *Princess Mononoke*. In his childhood and youth, Miyazaki has said that he hated Japanese history, culture and his own Japanese identity because of the sense of guilt caused by the fact that his family ran a war-related business during World War II and the family was well off even at the height of the war.[19] However, as a result of an encounter with the concept of 'evergreen forest culture theory' (*shōyō jurin bunka ron*), which emphasizes botanical and cultural links between Japan and South East Asia such as Bhutan, Nepal and Yunnan, Miyazaki was able to see Japan and himself as part of Asia.[20] In an interview in 1988, Miyazaki recalls:

> I felt so liberated and so pleased when I found out that what flowed inside me was connected to the broadleaf evergreen forest. My culture went far beyond the idiotic Japanese who started the war, beyond Hideyoshi Toyotomi [a samurai from the sixteenth century who unified Japan for the first time and also] who invaded Korea, and beyond *The Tale of Genji* that I detested.[21]

Notable here is Miyazaki's distaste for stereotypical Japanese historical and cultural icons such as samurai and Heian period literary classics. Interestingly, however, in another interview in 1985, Miyazaki mentioned his interest in creating a film set in medieval Japan. After referring to his desire to create a 'heroic period play' (*sōretsu na jidaigeki*) that is 'totally different from any [conventional] period drama or folktales yet the setting is clearly Japanese', Miyazaki said that the best protagonists Japan could offer were samurai.[22] However, he was quick to add that the image of samurai he had in his mind was not that of the Tokugawa period. In his view, in the Tokugawa period, the image of the samurai was deformed when such ideas as serving his lord, or the idea of the way of the warrior (*bushidō*), 'clung to it' (*gusha gusha to kuttsuite kita*).[23] Miyazaki maintained that, in reality, originally it was only the samurai who could decide his own fate with his own wisdom and strength. Miyazaki continued by stating that such an idea disappeared after World War II, and instead, texts that analysed samurai from the perspective of the 'salary man' or evaluated Ieyasu Tokugawa (the shogun who established the Tokugawa shogunate in 1603, marking the beginning of the Tokugawa period that continued for the next 250 years) from the perspective of business owners became popular.[24] Although he seemed to be unsure exactly what kind of story he had in his mind at this point, Miyazaki said, 'I hope I can create a magnificent story that is set in Japan when things were still rough, together with a touch of Science Fiction-like taste.'[25]

One year later, in a lecture given in 1986 where Miyazaki talked about the possibility of 'creating a classic adventure story in contemporary Japan', in response to a question from the audience suggesting he make a film with a samurai as the protagonist, Miyazaki repeated what he said in the 1985 interview and then spoke about his view of Japanese history at length. He said:

> Unless [the creators] realize for themselves that Japanese history is probably different from [what they read] in textbooks, hear [from others], or see in

period dramas and in reality it is far more diverse, deep and about various vivid lives of people, there won't be interesting period dramas.

However, as various things such as folk studies, history of agriculture and archaeology change, the way people think about Japanese history is recently being broadened. [They now pay attention to] history beyond that of great historical figures and heroes found in historical records and [are interested in] the life of ordinary people and also people who lived in [remote] mountains. [In such alternative views of history] we can find complexity and richness that cannot be simply placed under the banner of single-race state (*tan'itsu minzoku kokka*).[26]

As presented here by Miyazaki, this issue of diversity in Japanese history is clearly influenced by historian Yoshihiko Amino. Since the late 1970s, Amino has presented a view of medieval Japan that focuses on the significance of people who were neglected in conventional research on Japanese history such as women, artisans, performers, craftsmen and outcasts.[27] Notably, when *Princess Mononoke* was released, Amino provided a commentary for the theatre programme.[28] Miyazaki later said that in reading Amino's books, 'I came across many explanations of history that seemed convincing to me.'[29]

The influence of 'evergreen forest culture theory' and Amino is observable in the setting of *Mononoke*. Miyazaki revealed that the costume of the girls of Ashitaka's village were modelled on those of people living in mountainous areas in Bhutan and Thailand.[30] Women play significant roles in operation of the ironworks, which is also run by a woman, Eboshi. In his commentary, Amino pointed out that judging from her costume she probably is a type of courtesan called *shirabyōshi* who danced and sang in male outfits in medieval Japan.[31]

Apart from specific Japanese history, Miyazaki's view of religion also affiliated *Princess Mononoke* and Miyazaki with academia. The killing of the deities of the forest, a central theme of the film, is strongly influenced by a play called *Girugameshu* (*Gilgamesh*, 1988) by Takeshi Umehara, a scholar, critic and author known for nationalistic *Nihonjinron*-style writings on Japanese cultural identity that often stress cultural uniqueness or even Japanese superiority, especially vis-à-vis the West. After *Gilgamesh* was published in 1988, Umehara sent the play to Miyazaki for possible adaptation into anime, only to be politely rejected.[32] Ten years later, Umehara was asked to write a review of a film called *Mononokehime*. He was annoyed to see the film because, for him, *Mononoke* had exactly the same theme as the play that Miyazaki had declined to adapt – the killing of the deities of the forest. Umehara did see that the film was totally different from his play in terms of setting and plot, and he commented that 'a word could have been said to me about it'.[33] The grudge was solved when he met Miyazaki for a roundtable discussion where Umehara told Miyazaki about the course of events as seen from his perspective, and Miyazaki indirectly apologized by saying, 'In the process of making the film, I realized that I had included some of my interpretations of your *Gilgamesh*.'[34]

Besides the idea of 'killing the deities', *Princess Mononoke* and Miyazaki also seem to share another important concept with Umehara: awe for nature as the core of Japanese cultural identity. In an interview in 1997, Miyazaki said that what is now called 'nature' in Japan is actually a result of total destruction of the original Japanese landscape filled with deep and forbidding forest. The image of such pristine land with untouched forest and clean water and the idea that deities live there, in his view, still resides deep within the consciousness of Japanese people even today. He argues that it can be seen in the Japanese gardens that attempt to recreate remote mountains and steep valleys. In the ancient past, Japanese people had fear and awe for such nature, but out of necessity they cut down trees, begging the deities for their forgiveness. Yet, according to Miyazaki, recently such understanding of nature has been lost and Japanese people now seem to think that 'all pieces of land have price tags and [a few] other places are either under control of the government or destined to be golf courses'.[35] He continued by saying that the only way to protect the natural environment in contemporary Japan was to make every mountain and river in the country into a Shintō shrine because even today Japanese people retain the animistic belief that deities dwell in nature and they can deliver divine punishment if they are treated badly.[36] The image of the forest in *Princess Mononoke* seems to reflect the 'true' nature that still lurks in the cultural identity of Japanese people and the ending of the film where mountains that once went bald are covered with greenery can be interpreted as arrival of a new form of 'nature' that continues to this day.

Umehara has made very similar remarks. He has claimed that in the ancient Jōmon period (14,000–300 BC), Japanese people regarded trees as deities and the idea was passed down to Shintōism in the form of forests accompanying shrines. But, Umehara argues, later Shintōism was deformed, especially since the Meiji period, when it was linked with nationalism. As a result, such animistic belief was obscured.[37] Umehara also shares with Miyazaki the essentialist idea that at the bottom of contemporary Japanese cultural identity is the 'spirit' of the ancient Jōmon period.[38] Thus *Princess Mononoke* not only deals with an alternative view of Japanese history, but it also resonates strongly with *Nihonjinron*-style essentialist academic discourse in Japan.[39]

Before *Princess Mononoke*, Miyazaki already was asked to comment on the natural environment in interviews, essays and roundtable discussions, especially in relation to his earlier film, *Nausicaa*. The interviewers/discussants include American author Earnest Callenbach, who wrote *Ecotopia: The Notebooks and Reports of William Weston*, a popular novel that greatly influenced development of counterculture and green movement in the 1970s and Shin'ichirō Inaba,[40] one of the first academics in Japan to write a monograph on Miyazaki.[41] Miyazaki also met with literary figures such as Science Fiction novelist Baku Yumemakura[42] and novelist Ryū Murakami.[43] Most importantly, in 1992 Miyazaki met authors, novelists and critics Ryōtarō Shiba and Yoshie Hotta, who are known nationally for their writings on Japanese history and culture. It was through this encounter with them, where Miyazaki saw them matter-of-factly accept the idea that 'people are irredeemable' and simply laughed at it, that Miyazaki reached the realization mentioned at the end of the previous section.[44] The articles containing these interviews and discussions mainly appeared in mainstream weekly magazines or anime magazines, especially *Animage* published by Tokuma shoten, which has had strong links with Miyazaki and Studio Ghibli since the 1980s.

Following *Princess Mononoke*, however, established academics and critics began to be more frequently featured as interviewer/discussant in these publications. This is readily observable in the interviews and discussions found in *Turning Point*, a collection of essays and interviews by Miyazaki since 1997. The section on *Princess Mononoke* in the book features discussions between Miyazaki and Amino;[45] Yoshio Nakamura, a professor emeritus at Tokyo Institute of Technology specializing in landscape engineering;[46] Tadao Satō, one of the most prominent film critics in Japan[47] and American film critic Roger Ebert.[48] The panel at the aforementioned roundtable with Umehara also includes Amino, Seiryū Kōsaka, a Buddhist monk and artist, and Keiichi Makino, a manga artist and a professor emeritus of Kyoto Seika University.[49] The venues for these publications also expanded beyond conventional mainstream media. While interviews with the critics appeared in major film magazines or publications by publishing conglomerate Tokuma shoten mainly targeting fans of anime, other interviews were published in more niche media aimed at specialist readers such as academics and professionals.

In addition to interviews and discussions, writings by academics also appeared *en masse*. One example is a special issue of monthly magazine called *Yuriika* (*Eureka*). The literary magazine had previously published some special issues related to manga, anime and videogames. Yet in August 1997 an entire issue of the magazine was dedicated to analysis and criticism of *Princess Mononoke* and other films by Miyazaki. The contributors included Japanese historians, anthropologists, poets, literary critics, screen playwrights, authors of children's stories, psychiatrists, art historians, film directors and critics.

One obvious reason for the surge of academic and critical interest in the film and Miyazaki is the affinity between the themes of *Princess Mononoke* and academics, as discussed above using Amino and Umehara as examples. The issues, such as cultural diversity in medieval Japan and animism as a central idea of Japanese cultural identity, were 'easy topics' for academics to write about and appropriate topics for media especially because of the complex setting and storyline, which were so unlike previous Miyazaki films. However, that is not necessarily the only reason. There also are other factors that we need to consider. Miyazaki, although not to the same degree as after *Princess Mononoke*, has, since the 1980s, been regarded as an intellectual auteur who creates very high quality animation with deep messages about the environment, civilization and society that appeal to wide range of audiences, rather than just children or fans of anime. Therefore, Miyazaki becomes 'suitable' for appearances in mainstream media making comments or having discussions with intellectuals on such topics. In other words, by 1997, Miyazaki already had a 'track record' as a quasi-*bunkajin*. Therefore, when *Princess Mononoke* came out, replete with themes attractive to Japan's mainstream media, academics and critics alike, and Miyazaki extensively commented on them, he and the film attracted critical and academic attention. However, there are still two other factors we need to pay attention to: the phenomenal commercial success of *Princess Mononoke* and a 'trend' in Japanese *rondan* for discussing anime, triggered by popularity of *Neon Genesis Evangelion*.

General and Academic Popularity of Princess Mononoke

As mentioned at the beginning of this chapter, *Princess Mononoke* is one of the most successful films released in Japan so far. Miyazaki was already well-known, thanks to the success and popularity of his previous films, but the level of success *Princess Mononoke* achieved was far greater than that of his previous works. Even *Porco Rosso*, the most successful Miyazaki film before *Princess Mononoke*, earned no more than 2.7 billion yen while *Princess Mononoke*'s revenue reached a staggering 11.3 billion yen.[50] The success, however, is not simply owing to technical and textual quality of the film. Instead, it greatly owes to promotional strategies devised by Toshio Suzuki, the producer of Studio Ghibli.

Before *Princess Mononoke* was released, it was already mandatory for the film to be more successful than *Porco Rosso* or even *Nankyoku monogatari* (*Antarctica*, Koreyoshi Kurahara, 1983), the most successful Japanese film at the time, to cover the high cost of production (over 2 billion yen, approximately US$20 million).[51] By the time of *Princess Mononoke*, Suzuki had already established a method to promote films by Ghibli making full use of a collaborative network of media such as TV and magazines, as well as massive campaigns involving sponsor(s) of Ghibli films. For example, in the case of *Porco Rosso*, Japan Air Lines, the sponsor of the film, cooperated in promoting the film by printing *Porco Rosso*'s characters on its flight timetables, which were distributed at airports and travel agencies. In addition, in-flight magazines carried articles on the film, giving postcards and other promotional materials including discount coupons for cinema screenings to the passengers and even flying an airship with the title of the film and face of the protagonist on it.[52] For *Porco Rosso*, Suzuki also organized a number of previews for audiences chosen by lottery. Suzuki regarded these previews as significant because advertising them on TV and magazines contributed to further promoting the film, and they were also useful to spread word of mouth.[53]

Suzuki used the same strategy for *Princess Mononoke* but on a larger scale: a total of 70 previews were organized compared with 23 for *Porco Rosso*.[54] More significantly, thanks to his connection with Fumio Nishino, who was responsible for booking of cinemas at the distributor Tōhō's chain, Suzuki succeeded

in releasing the film in as many prestigious cinemas in Japan as possible, allowing *Princess Mononoke* to compete against Steven Spielberg's *Jurassic Park*
(1993), which was released in Japan at the same time as *Princess Mononoke*.[55]
Miyazaki's reputation also helped because by the mid-1990s cinema multiplexes
were increasing throughout the country. In these newer cinemas, unlike conventional Japanese ones, programming was not under the control of film distribution companies. Therefore, the owners of the cinema complexes, among
whom were many fans of Miyazaki films, they could offer to show his latest
film *Princess Mononoke*.[56] Eventually *Princess Mononoke* was released in 260
cinemas out of 1,800 in Japan at the time.[57]

The extensive promotion using a variety of media, and also the inclusion
of *Princess Mononoke's* most shocking scene in the trailer – graphic violence
that was absent from previous Miyazaki films – helped to indicate that *Princess
Mononoke* would be very different from Miyazaki's previous works (for more
on the film's marketing, see Chapter 8). In addition, Miyazaki's suggestion that
this could be his last film raised levels of public interest in *Princess Mononoke*,
which were already surging before the film was actually released. In an interview, Mieko Hara, a designer at Tōhō working on the newspaper advertisements for *Princess Mononoke* stated that she received phone calls from cinemas
in the evening immediately before the opening saying there were already long
queues outside the cinemas for advance tickets even shortly before the box
offices were due to be closed, which was something never happened before.[58]

The content of the film itself, of course, contributed to the success. The very
fact that the film, unlike previous Miyazaki films, has complex settings and a
plot with references to Japanese history and culture apparently helped to boost
the audience figures. According to Masaru Yabe, a producer at Tōhō responsible for advertisements and promotion of the film, it was 'famous' (*hyōban ni
nattemashita*) within the company that there seemed to be a number of audience members who saw the film repeatedly.[59] Thanks to the thematic complexity, the film had enough enigmatic allure to get the audience talking about it.
Noriko Aonara, colleague of Yabe's, remembers seeing many people discussing
what they have just seen in *Princess Mononoke* in a café in central Tokyo near a
large cinema where the film was shown.[60]

The urge to discuss the film was not confined to the audience. The media
extensively reported the popularity of the film often with comments by academics. For example, an article in the *Nikkei*, or as it was at the time, *Japan
Economics Newspaper*, attempted to analyse why the film was so popular after
informing the readers that the film had already by then broken records for
audience numbers and box office revenue and was to be released in the United
States distributed by Disney. The article claims that the popularity of the film
can now be called a 'social phenomenon' (*shakai genshō*) mainly owing to
young people in their teen and twenties.[61] The article presents some examples of reactions by young audience members that all emphasize how the film
made them feel that they should live despite difficulties they are facing such

as bullying or 'feeling that life is nothing but hard because of sense of anxiety and isolation without any specific reason'.[62] One of the respondents told the reporter that he saw the film no less than nine times, attesting to Yabe's remark above.[63] Then the article turns to academics for comments and explanations. Tatsuya Yumiyama, a lecturer in religious studies at Kokugakuin University at the time pointed out that the film worked as a therapy for young people in contemporary Japan who had very low image about themselves. Rika Kayama, a psychiatrist, is reported to be against the idea because she believes that the reaction by the youth audience is mere self-satisfaction because they are simply picking what suits their needs out of the film within a context irrelevant to the 'original intention of the work' and interpreting them selfishly. Masachi Ōsawa, then an assistant professor in sociology at Kyoto University, by contrast, is quoted as having said that he saw hope in *Princess Mononoke* because the film reflects the situation in *fin-de-siècle* Japanese society where people cannot talk about their own dreams and ideals even cynically, and presents a message that they still have to live positively.[64]

This type of 'analysis' is not actually unusual for Japanese mainstream media when they report on the popularity of anime or manga. In the case of *Princess Mononoke*, however, we should note the context. As another article on *Asahi Newspaper* states, it was 'trendy' in Japanese *rondan* at the time to discuss the '*Mononoke* phenomenon'.[65] The reporter, however, discusses the academic popularity of *Princess Mononoke* in tandem with another anime text: *Neon Genesis Evangelion*. The highly popular anime television series was originally broadcast in October 1995. Similarly to *Princess Mononoke*, it attracted academic interest because of its complex and mysterious plot and settings laden with references and allusions to topics in the realms of developmental psychology, theology and religion through to science fiction, anime and Japanese monster films. Just as for *Princess Mononoke*, the media turned to academics for explanations about the popularity of *Neon Genesis Evangelion*. *Mainichi Newspaper*, on 28 November 1996, for example, carried an essay by Takahiro Ōtsuki, then an assistant professor in folk studies at National Museum of Japanese History, who criticized *Evangelion* for its 'autistic' nature. *Asahi Newspaper*, on 12 April 1997, carried an article on the series where intellectuals of the same age as its director Hideaki Anno, including Toshiya Ueno, then an assistant professor at Chūbu University, commented on the text.[66] In short, *Mononoke* was released in a climate where anime texts and their popularity was in the limelight as a subject for potential academic and critical discussion as a representation of contemporary Japanese society.

In the case of *Princess Mononoke*, the affinity with academia, as examined in the previous section, was even stronger than for *Evangelion* because Miyazaki, unlike Anno whose works were popular among hardcore fans of anime but not necessarily well-known beyond them, already had a 'track record' both as an animator and quasi-intellectual. When *Princess Mononoke* was released in such a climate and became a phenomenal success, Miyazaki and his works were labelled as something suitable for academic and critical discussion. His next film, *Spirited Away*, also attracted similar academic interest represented by another special issue of *Eureka* and similar materials carrying columns and essays on the film and its context by academics and various critics.[67] Thus, Miyazaki and his films were firmly established as a subject of academic discourses.

Conclusion

Seen retrospectively, *Princess Mononoke* might be viewed as a blessing and a curse for Miyazaki. On the one hand, *Princess Mononoke* made Miyazaki a global icon of contemporary Japanese cinema once it was released outside Japan. The same process of making him into *bunkajin* was apparently repeated when he was interviewed by foreign media. Roger Ebert told Miyazaki that 'some of the images [in *Princess Mononoke*] reminded me of Japanese art from two hundred years ago' and hailed him as Japanese 'national treasure.'[68] At the Berlin Film Festival to which *Princess Mononoke* was invited, Miyazaki had press conferences over five days with representatives from more than twenty publications every day.[69] In the conferences, the media asked a number of questions on the relationship between *Princess Mononoke* and Japanese history and culture as well as environmental issues.[70] Miyazaki's reputation was firmly established when he later won the Academy Award and the Gold Bear for *Spirited Away* at Berlin.

The fame, on the other hand, might also have impacted less positively on his subsequent films. After *Princess Mononoke*, Miyazaki never returned to his earlier entertaining adventure stories. Although in *Ponyo* he seems to have tried to return to a simple story for children, he chose to put an end to his career by creating a film that was essentially about himself and his family – *The Wind Rises*. As I tried to show in this chapter, the shift to more 'fundamental' film was Miyazaki's reaction to what he saw as cataclysmic political and social change in the early 1990s. Yet, his words in the statement announcing retirement – 'I am free' (*Boku wa jiyū desu*) – and his remark in the ensuing press conference that he does not want to be a *bunkajin,* but rather wants to be 'a chap who owns a small independent factory in town' (*machi kōba no oyaji*) seem to suggest that only by retirement could Miyazaki free himself from the 'curse' of *Princess Mononoke* that bound him into the seat of a *bunkajin*.[71]

Notes

1 Kōgyō tsūshinsha, '*Rekidai ranking*' [Historical Rankings], *CINEMA Ranking Tsūshin*, 2016. http://www.kogyotsushin.com/archives/alltime/ (accessed 11 May 2016).

2 Hayao Miyazaki, *Starting Point 1979-1996*, trans. Beth Cary and Frederik L. Schodt (San Francisco, CA: VIZ Media, 2009 [1996]), p. 147.

3 For more details on Article 9, the Japanese Self-Defense Forces and development after the 1990s, see Jeff Kingston, *Contemporary Japan: History, Politics and Social Change since the 1980s* (London: Wiley Blackwell, 2013), pp. 115-35.

4 Miyazaki, *Starting Point*, p. 147.

5 Hayao Miyazaki, *Kaze no kaeru basho* [*The Place Where the Wind Returns to*] (Tokyo: Rokkingu on, 2002), p. 95.

6 Miyazaki, *The Place Where the Wind Returns to*, p. 95.

7 Miyazaki, *The Place Where the Wind Returns to*, p. 110.

8 Miyazaki, *The Place Where the Wind Returns to*, p. 109.

9 Miyazaki, *The Place Where the Wind Returns to*, p. 110.

10 Miyazaki, *The Place Where the Wind Returns to*, p. 94.

11 Miyazaki, *The Place Where the Wind Returns to*, p. 122.

12 Miyazaki, *The Place Where the Wind Returns to*, p. 122.

13 Miyazaki, *Starting Point*, p. 386-7.

14 Miyazaki, *Starting Point*, p. 386.

15 Miyazaki, *Starting Point*, p. 388.

16 Miyazaki, *Starting Point*, p. 71-2.

17 Miyazaki, *Starting Point*, p. 71.

18 Isao Takahata, 'Rongu intabyū: Takahata Isao' [Long Interview: Isao Takahata], *Hōhokekyo tonari no Yamadakun o yomitoku!?* [*Reading My Neighbors the Yamadas*], Comic Box (1999), pp. 20-2.

19 Hayao Miyazaki, *Shuppatsu ten* [*Starting Point*] (Tokyo: Tokuma shoten, 1996), pp.265-6.

20 For more details on this theory, see: Sasuke Nakao, *Saibai shokubutsu to nōkō no kigen* [*The Origins of Cultivate Plants and Farming*] (Tokyo: Iwanami shoten, 1966); and, Kōmei Sasaki, *Shōyō jurin bunka towa nanika* [*What Is Evergreen Forest Culture?*] (Tokyo: Chūō Kōron Shinsha, 2007).

21 Miyazaki, *Starting Point*, p. 358.

22 Miyazaki created storyboards under the title of *Mononokehime* in 1980. Although the project never materialized, they were later published as a picture book in 1993. This is totally different from *Mononokehime* as we know today: it is about a girl whose father, a samurai, was possessed by an evil spirit, and a monster resembling the Cat Bus in *Totoro*. The girl offers to marry the monster if he could help her father by defeating the spirit. After a long journey the duo confronts the father, defeats the spirit and saves him. In the final battle at the end of the story, the father dies after the spirit leaves his body, and the people of the town governed by the father stand up against the oppression they suffered while the father was under control of the spirit. The city and the castle burst into flame, and the monster, with the girl, leaves for its den. Interestingly, the story rather seems to be more like a mixture of period drama, fantasy and folktale. (Also note the idealistic image of people standing up against oppression.)

23 Hayao Miyazaki and Yasuo Ōtsuka, 'Ikihaji o sarashite ikiru otoko to shite no rupan' [Lupin is a man who is Living in Disgrace] in *Animēju* (*Animage*) (ed.), *Eiga Tenkū no shiro Lapyuta Guide Book* [*Castle in the Sky Guide Book*] (Tokyo: Tokuma shoten, 1986), p. 195.

24 Miyazaki and Ōtsuka, 'Lupin is a man', p. 195.

25 Miyazaki and Ōtsuka, 'Lupin is a man', p. 195.
26 Hayao Miyazaki, '*Gendai ni oite kotenteki bōken katsugeki wa ariuruka*' [Are there Classic Adventure Stories Today?], *Yuriika* [*Eureka*], August 1997, p. 148.
27 For details of Amino's view of medieval Japanese history, see: Yoshihiko Amino, *Nihon no rekishi o yominaosu (zen)* [*Rewriting the History of Japan (Complete)*] (Tokyo: Chikuma shobō, 2005).
28 Yoshihiko Amino, '"*Shizen*" to "*ningen*," 2 tsu no seichi ga shōtotsu suru higeki' [Nature and Humanity: The Tragedy When Two Sacred Places Collide] in *Mononokehime Pamfuletto* [*Princess Mononoke Theatre Programme*] (Tokyo: Tōhō, 1997), p.15.
29 Hayao Miyazaki, *Turning Point 1997–2008*, trans. Beth Cary and Frederik L. Schodt (San Francisco, CA: VIZ Media, 2014 [2009]), p. 97.
30 Miyazaki, *The Place Where the Wind Returns to*, p. 166.
31 Amino, 'Nature and Humanity', p.15.
32 Miyazaki, *Turning Point*, p. 96.
33 Miyazaki, *Turning Point*, p. 96.
34 Miyazaki, *Turning Point*, p. 97.
35 Hayao Miyazaki, '*Mori to ningen*' [The Forest and the Human-Being], *Mononokehime o yomitoku* [*Reading Princess Mononoke*], Comic Box, 2 (August 1997), p. 78.
36 Miyazaki, 'The Forest and the Human-Being', pp. 77–9.
37 Takeshi Umehara, '*Mori no shisō' ga jinrui o sukuu*' [*Forest Ideology Will Save Mankind*] (Tokyo: Shōgakukan, 1991), pp. 12–19, 36, 206.
38 Takeshi Umehara, '*Nihon no shinsō*' [The Depth of Japanese Ideology] in *Umehara Takeshi choaskushū* [Collected Works of Hiroshi Umehara], no. 6 (Tokyo: Shōgakukan, 2000), p. 35.
39 Miyazaki has been also long fascinated with the Jōmon period because of its cultural richness and peacefulness (as he so believed based on books by archaeologist Ei'ichi Fujimori). See Miyazaki, *Turning Point*, pp. 293–7. The *nihonjinron*-style view of cultural identity is important in thinking about theme of *Princess Mononoke* and also *Spirited Away*. For full discussion of Miyazaki's idea of essentialist 'unconscious memory' inherited among Japanese people since immemorial past and comparison with essentialist cultural discourse among liberal and conservative Japanese scholars including Umehara, Shunpei Ueyama, Shūichi Katō and Masao Maruyama, see Chapters 6 and 7 in: Shiro Yoshioka, 'Memory, Nostalgia and Cultural Identity in the World of Miyazaki Hayao' (PhD Thesis submitted to the International Christian University, 2009).
40 Miyazaki, *Shuppatsu ten*, pp.334–42.
41 Shinichirō Inaba, *Naushika kaidoku: Yūtopia no rinkai* [*Deciphering Nausicaä: A Critique of Utopia*] (Tokyo: Madosha, 1996), pp. 190–218.
42 Miyazaki, *Shuppatsu ten*, pp. 354–63.
43 Miyazaki, *Shuppatsu ten*, pp. 353–64.
44 Miyazaki, *Starting Point*, p. 207.
45 Miyazaki and Amino in: Miyazaki, *Turning Point*, pp. 60–9.
46 Yoshio Nakamura, a professor emeritus at Tokyo Institute of Technology specializing in landscape engineering, Miyazaki, *Turning Point*, pp. 135–49.
47 Tadao Satō, one of the most prominent film critics in Japan, in: Miyazaki, *Turning Point*, pp. 42–59.

48 Roger Ebert in: Miyazaki, *Turning Point*, pp. 184–9.

49 Miyazaki, *Turning Point*, pp. 94–121.

50 Studio Ghibli, '*Sutajio jiburi monogatari: Mizou no taisaku "Mononokehime"*' [The Story of Studio Ghibli: The Unprecedented Masterpiece *Princess Mononoke*] in Studio Ghibli and Bunshun bunko (eds.), *Jiburi no kyōkasho 10: Mononokehime* [*Ghibli Textbook 10: Princess Mononoke*] (Tokyo: Bungei shinjū, 2015), pp. 30, 49.

51 Toshio Suzuki, '*Chie to dokyō no ōbakuchi! Mizou no "Mononokehime daisakusen"*' [A Huge Gamble Taking Real Courage and Wisdom!: The Epic 'Operation Mononoke'] in Ghibli and bunko, *Jiburi no kyōkasho 10* p. 59.

52 '*Senden keikakusho*' [Advertising Plan] in Studio Ghibli (ed.), *Sutajio jiburi sakuhin kanren shiryōshū IV* [*Collection of Supplementary Materials on the Works of Studio Ghibli IV*] (Tokyo: Tokuma shoten, 1996), p. 49.

53 Suzuki, 'A Huge Gamble Taking Real Courage and Wisdom!', p. 54.

54 Seiji Kanō, *Miyazaki Hayao zensho* [*The Complete Hayao Miyazaki*] (Tokyo: Firumu āto sha, 2006), p. 210; '*Senden keikakusho*', p. 49.

55 Suzuki, 'A Huge Gamble Taking Real Courage and Wisdom!', pp. 69–70.

56 Hideyuki Takai, Masaru Yabe, Minami Ichikawa, Shinpei Ise, Seiji Okuda and Toshio Suzuki, '*Tokushū "Jiburi no dai hakurankai Tōhō no rekidai purodūsā ga ōi ni kataru*', [Special Feature: The Great Ghibli Exhibition: Current and Previous Producers of Tōhō Tell Everything about Their Work], *Neppū*, vol. 13, no. 9 (September 2015), p. 13.

57 Kanō, *The Complete Hayao Miyazaki*, p. 211.

58 Studio Ghibli, *Naushika no 'shinbun kōkoku' tte mitakoto arimasuka: jiburi no shinbun kōkoku 18 nenshi* [*Have You Seen the Newspaper Advertisements for Nausicaä?: The 18 Year History of Ghibli's Newspaper Advertisements*] (Tokyo: Tokuma shoten, 2002), p. 345.

59 Studio Ghibli, *Have you Seen the Newspaper Advertisements*, p. 346.

60 Studio Ghibli, *Have you Seen the Newspaper Advertisements*, p. 346.

61 Midori Shiraki, '*Kyokō no jidai ni michisuji shimesu: messēji "ikiro" ni wakamono han'nō*' [Showing the Path to a Fictional Age: Young People's reactions to the message to 'Live'] in Ghibli and bunko, *Jiburi no kyōkasho 10*, p. 176.

62 Shiraki, 'Showing the Path to a Fictional Age', p.176.

63 Shiraki, 'Showing the Path to a Fictional Age', p.176.

64 Shiraki, 'Showing the Path to a Fictional Age', pp. 178–9.

65 Tateo Nishijima, '*Anime: Gendai no shin'wa: Nazo ga umidasu kaishaku no kōzui*' [Anime: Modern Myths: Mysterious Stories and SettingsThat Create A Flood of Interpretations], *Asahi shimbun*, 16 August 1997 (morning issue), p.11.

66 '*Nazo no monogatari ninki no nazo*' [The Mystery of the Popularity of Mysterious Stories], *Asahi Shimbun*, 12 April 1997 (morning issue), p. 18.

67 *Yuriika* [*Eureka*], vol. 33, no. 7, August 2001, *Chihiro to Fushigi no machi: Sen to Chihiro no kamikakushi tettei kōryaku gaido* [Chihiro and the Strange Town: the Ultimate guide for Understanding *Spirited Away*] (Tokyo: Kadokawa shoten, 2001) and '*Sen to Chihiro no kamikakushi' o yomi 40 no me* [40 Viewpoints to Read *Spirited Away*] (Tokyo: Kinema junpōsha, 2001) are typical examples. The former has a column by Terunobu Fujimori, an academic known for his research on pseudo-western style buildings in pre-war Japan. The latter has interviews with Takashi Tachibana, a critic known for a number of non-fiction works on a range of subjects ranging from post-war Japanese politics to neuro science and Takeshi

Yōrō, an anatomist famous for a string of popular books on human body, brain and civilization. Tachibana mentions possible link between the film and ancient Japanese myths as observable in names of the characters while Yōrō points out Japaneseness of the film's setting in general as well as discussing powerful and realistic recreation of sensations in the film. More recently, Studio Ghibli began to publish a series of books entitled *Jiburi no kyōkasho* (*Textbooks of Ghibli*), starting in 2013. Each volume is dedicated to one of Miyazaki or Takahata films after *Nausicaa* and some other major films created by the studio such as *Whisper of the Heart* and *Karigurashi no Arietti* (*Arietty*, Hiromasa Yonebayashi, 2010). Each volume usually contains a chapter on production history of the film, proposal for the film and/or an essay by the director, interviews with the director and/or Toshio Suzuki and other key staff members, and a section in which academics, creators and critics offer comments on the film.

68 Miyazaki, *Turning Point*, pp.188–9.
69 Hayao Miyazaki, 'Doitsu berurin eigasai intabyū: kaigai no kisha ga Miyazaki kantoku ni tou "mononokehime" e no 44 no shitsumon' [An Interview at Germany's Berlin Film Festival: 44 Questions about *Princess Mononoke* to Miyazaki from Foreign Reporters], *Roman Album Animage Special: Miyazaki Hayao to An'no Hideaki* [*Roman Album Animage Special: Hayao Miyazaki and Hideaki Anno*], 1997, p. 48.
70 Miyazaki, *Turning Point*, pp. 79–93.
71 Hayao Miyazaki, 'Miyazaki Hayao kantoku intai kaiken' [Hayao Miyazaki Retirement Interview], *Neppū: Sutajio jiburi no kōkishin* [*The Hot Wind: Curiosity of Studio Ghibli*] (October 2013), p. 67.

Chapter 2

DEER GODS, NATIVISM AND HISTORY: MYTHICAL AND ARCHAEOLOGICAL LAYERS IN *PRINCESS MONONOKE*

Eija Niskanen

In *Mononokehime* (*Princess Mononoke*, 1997) Hayao Miyazaki depicts the main character, Prince Ashitaka, as a son of the Emishi nation, one of Japan's vanished native tribes, who inhabited West-Northern Japan before the Eastern-Southern Yamato nation took control, starting in the area that is now the basis for modern Japan before claiming the entire country. Emishi, similar to the other native tribes of Northern Japan are often seen as non-civilized barbarians as opposed to the Yamato race.[1] Though *Princess Mononoke* is set in the Muromachi period (1333–1573), when the Yamato society had conquered all the Northern tribes, the strong Emishi village of *Princess Mononoke* recalls Japan's pre-historic times. In the film's settings and details one can find numerous examples of Miyazaki's interest in anthropology, archaeology, Shintō and nativism. It also features multiple layers of historical, archaeological and mythical references. I argue in this chapter that Miyazaki uses these to discuss the building of what we know as Japan, and to discuss the complicated issue of human-nature relationships.

Studio Ghibli films are often noted for their ecological messages: Jonathan Clements and Helen MacCarthy note how *Princess Mononoke* 'is the ultimate prequel to Studio Ghibli's ecological concerns in films such as *Nausicaa* and *Pom poko*,'[2] and for the Studio Ghibli co-produced *The Red Turtle* by Michaël Dudok de Wit (2016) the *Guardian* reviewer says: 'Dudok de Wit has conjured a story that combines Ghibli's familiar ecological themes – with a narrative attuned to European sensibilities.'[3] They are also praised for the way in which definitions of 'good' and 'evil' are discussed with great nuance, adding to the multilayered interpretation of the films. For example, Susan Napier writes: 'Many consider Studio Ghibli's major offerings to the society to be precisely the lack of a clear-cut vision of "good" versus "evil" ' and notes how her students compare Ghibli worlds to the more clear-cut binaries of Disney films.[4] In the following, I look at these ecological issues in the light of Miyazaki's interest in Japan's history, archaeology and notions of the origin of the nation. As primary sources I use the film *Princess Mononoke* itself, as well as the writings and interviews in which Miyazaki discusses these issues. In the film these issues are tied around the easily recognizable ecological theme, and they add to its layered complexity. *Princess Mononoke*'s brilliance as an animated feature lies exactly in these layers of message: it can be seen as an exciting and skilfully animated (and composed, as Joe Hisaishi's score adds to the enjoyment of the film) historical/fantasy adventure, but the layers Miyazaki and his staff have crafted allow for multiple viewings of the film, and attract different interpretations of the film.

As my approach to the film is based on film and animation studies, I do not claim to be a specialist on the archaeology or religions in Japan, but rely on experts in these fields to highlight aspects of the film. Miyazaki is himself a keen historian with huge interest in anything relating to the history and ecology of Japan and does not rely on exact scientific information in his films, but claims to use them 'for the fun of mixing different elements', as he has said in interview.[5] My final intention is to show how *Princess Mononoke* complicates the issues of ecology, nature, society and the history of Japan. I argue that while doing so *Princess Mononoke* deconstructs myths from Japanese history and about its cultural homogeneity, especially critiquing how these myths are depicted in popular culture, such as period drama (*jidaigeki*) films.

The Emishi Nation

Ashitaka and his tribe are established in the film as Emishi, the Northern tribe of Japan's main island, Honshū, who resisted the Yamato Emperor during the subjugation campaign by the Nara-based Imperial court between 744 and 811, but even after that suppression effort a large part of the Emishi's land was still not under the Imperial control.[6] The subjugation process, besides periodic warfare, included settlement of Yamato posts in the Northern region, resettlement of Yamato people in the area and the recruitment of some Emishi leaders to serve the court. Occasionally, though, the Emishi, although smaller in numbers, were successful in conducting a type of guerrilla warfare against the army formations of the Yamato. As a consequence of these mixed tactics of acquiescence and resistance, the last tribes of Emishi did survive for a considerable length of a time, some tribes by co-operating with the Yamato rulers, some by maintaining a half-distanced independence far away from the emerging centre of Yamato power.[7] In some scholarly interpretations of Japanese history, the current native Ainu tribes, tribes that inhabit northern regions of Japan in Hokkaido, are claimed to be a continuance of, or at least liminally related to the Emishi. As this suggests, individual Emishi villages existed for centuries in semi-independence and local rulers, such as the Abe and Fujiwara, emerged.[8]

Princess Mononoke, placed in the Muromachi period happens well after the subjugation wars in a period when the Emishi had been integrated into the Yamato; but, at least in Miyazaki's imagination, remote independent Emishi villages remained.

These tribes were seen as both culturally and physically distinct from the Yamato, who came to dominate Japan. The Emishi were referred to as 'hairy people' or 'barbarians.'[9] In classic writings and Imperial orders, interestingly, Emishi were often described with animal-like qualities: 'In ascending mountains they are like flying birds: in going through the grass they are like fleet quadrupeds' (quoting *Nihon Shoki*).[10] This may help to explain the way Ashitaka's journey to the *Shishigami*'s forest is depicted in *Princess Mononoke*, wherein Ashitaka and his steed Yakul tend to move more swiftly and smoothly through the natural environment than those around them. Friday quotes an Imperial Edict from 780: 'These [Emishi] are like wild-hearted wolf cubs', underlining the Emishi as a people seen as part of nature, rather than of the Yamato race.[11] Miyazaki's blending of historical tropes can be seen in this quotation. It is notable that the character described closest to animals is San, the girl raised by the wolves, although she is not Emishi. Miyazaki uses this blending to create areas of overlap between the worlds of his central protagonists, Ashitaka and San, suggesting sympathetic, overlapping historical origins for the two characters.

Miyazaki's attention to the Emishi nation also goes beyond characterization. *Princess Mononoke* opens with the villagers realizing that something odd is going on: the birds and animals of the surrounding wood have quieted. A wild boar is approaching the village. Prince Ashitaka, the main character of the film, rushes to the village tower and studies the scenery with a village elder. The tower, constructed of lengths of wood that support a series of platforms, enables the two characters to see out over the dense forest landscape surrounding the village (Figure 2.1). The tower is significant because it is reminiscent of the tower from a Jōmon period (14,000–300 BC) settlement at the Sannaimaruyama Iseki archaeological site in Aomori, Northern Japan, which has been rebuilt on the remains of the original tower (see Figure 2.2). The Sannaimaruyama archaeological site, important in the later study of Jōmon people and culture from between 12,000 and 2,300 years ago, was discovered by accident in 1992, when a baseball field was planned to be built on the site. It has become both an important archaeological excavation site, as well as a well-known tourist attraction.[12] There is no exact knowledge about what the original tower looked like, due to the age of the site and the limited archaeological remains, but the reconstruction was based on archaeologists' and anthropologists' assessments about how the tower would most likely have looked.[13]

Miyazaki, a keen amateur researcher of Japan's history and archaeology, has visited the Sannaimaruyama Iseki archaeological site himself, and animators from Studio Ghibli also made sketches for the Emishi village backgrounds

Figure 2.1 The Emishi tower in *Princess Mononoke*.

Figure 2.2 The rebuilt tower at Sannaimaruyama Iseki archaeological site, Aomori. Photo by Eija Niskanen, reproduced with permission.

based on Aomori prefecture's Shirakami-Sanchi mountain. Miyazaki has related how he used the birthplaces of Studio Ghibli staff to draw different parts of the film: the evergreen broadleaf forest of the *Shishigami* was drawn by a background artist from Kyushu, while the North-Eastern beech woods were drawn by an artist from Akita. Miyazaki also claims that: 'We also went to Yakushima and Shirakami-sanchi for location scouting.'[14] These disparate locations, the former a small island off the southern tip of Kyūshū and the latter a northern region of Japan's main island, Honshū, illustrate the geographical expanses involved in the pre-production research undertaken for *Princess Mononoke*'s natural world. In interviews, Miyazaki has several times pointed to the existence of broadleaf evergreen forests that existed in ancient Japan,[15] which were reimagined within *Princess Mononoke* in the form of the forest through which Ashitaka and Yakul travel, and where they and the wolf team shelter. This research was not unusual: all Studio Ghibli films are based on thorough location research and sketching of real locations. However, the final backgrounds of Miyazaki's films, perhaps with the exception of *Kaze tachinu* (*The Wind Rises*, 2013), are not exact copies of particular recognizable locations, but a mixture of different, often geographically dispersed ones.

In the opening sequence, the theme of the ecological order in disruption is established. It affects a distant Emishi village, half-way across the main island Honshū. The wood is acting weirdly. A cursed boar god is seen. Ashitaka shoots his arrow at Nago, the wild boar god, and kills him. While in battle, Nago lethally poisons Ashitaka's arm. The female village oracle – one of Miyazaki's wise old women characters – tells Ashitaka that he is doomed to die unless he finds a cure in the East. She also announces that Ashitaka's curse will make him an outsider to the village, and his people, from now on. As this suggests, Miyazaki does not depict the village in a wholesomely cute light, but establishes Ashitaka right away as an outsider to all the parties of the film, including his own village. Ashitaka cuts his topknot, a visual ritual to show his outcast status, and leaves on a quest to break his curse with his elk Yakul.

In this early sequence, Miyazaki shows how the Emishi culture differed from his vision of the main Yamato culture. The Emishi sustained themselves more by hunting and fishing than the Yamato, who depended primarily on rice farming. Each Emishi tribe lived in their self-governed village (*mura*) making strategic alliances with neighbour villages only during times of unrest.[16] Miyazaki's version of the Emishi tribe is therefore visually and culturally distinctive even within *Princess Mononoke*'s fantasy world. For example, the Emishi characters' clothing is embroidered in a style reminiscent of the Ainu folk costumes, with big, bold and brightly coloured embroidery (see Figures 2.3 and 2.4). In fact, several theories based on both linguistic and archaeological studies have suggested at least a link, if not a direct continuance between the Emishi and the contemporary Ainu of Hokkaido. Also, studies on possible biological differences

Figure 2.3 Emishi Oracle in *Princess Mononoke*.

Figure 2.4 Photo and Ainu clothing model by Miyuki Kaizawa, used by permission of Mamoru Kaizawa/Nibutani Craft Cooperative Association.

between the Yamato and Emishi have been conducted (Matsumura and Dodo, for example, have produced a study on the Tohoku region dental data).[17] On the other hand, the word '*emishi*' refers to the concept of outbound, meaning outsider to the Yamato culture or the Imperial rule. By the latter definition the

Emishi were not necessarily ethnically different from the Yamato, but rather rebel outsiders to the Imperial rule.[18]

As there are no archaeological records of Emishi clothing, Miyazaki used his imagination:

> I thought their clothing must be like those worn by the minority tribes in Bhutan or Yunnan. They wore a kind of kimono . . . I had trouble figuring out what to do with the main character. Putting a topknot on him would suck me into the period dramas of the past. So, taking advantage of the lack of historical references, I made it a Chinese-style topknot.[19]

The mixture in clothing highlights the way Ghibli animators tend to use different cultural and regional references in their films, which can be seen, for example, in the town design of *Majo no takkyūbin* (*Kiki's Delivery Service*, Hayao Miyazaki, 1989), which is a mixture of several European towns. Miyazaki drew on details from Dublin, San Francisco, Paris, Stockholm and, most of all, the Swedish town of Visby. 'The European audience can see [the locations are] all mixed up.' Miyazaki has said in an interview. 'But most Japanese thought it was just a town in Europe. I deceived them beautifully.'[20] That poetic vagueness extends to the period in which *Kiki's Delivery Service* is set: 'I was imagining how the world would have been in the 1950s if the war had never happened. You know: the world that wasn't.'[21] Within *Princess Mononoke*, this technique of cultural and regional mixing also demonstrates Miyazaki's interest in tribal, aboriginal and native cultures from around the world, and his way of creating animated worlds that freely mix elements from different regions and even different historical time periods.

This can be assessed from different angles. Animation, as pictorial art, has always been suitable for the creation of imagined worlds. Simplified but distinctive clothing for characters or character groups helps the creation of the animation, by aiding the audience in recognizing and differentiating the characters. Here, the question of cultural appropriation naturally rises: to what ends is this imaginative freedom in mixing both features of Ainu traditions and other Asian cultural traditions used? In *Princess Mononoke*'s case, I argue that, based on Miyazaki's conscious efforts to show history in a different light, Miyazaki aims not only for a colourful design, but also for a certain deconstruction of what is 'historical' Japan. In interviews during *Princess Mononoke*'s release, he frequently talks about Akira Kurosawa's *Seven Samurai*, which he claims to admire, but, which he claims has formed a model for all subsequent historical depictions in Japanese films.[22] To avoid the common samurai imagery, instead having Ashitaka ride a horse, like Emishi warriors skilfully did, he put Ashitaka on an elk.[23] Further, in the pre-planning notes for *Princess Mononoke* from 1995, Miyazaki states that he wants to break out of the conventions of how period dramas depict history: 'Recent research in history, ethnography, and archaeology shows that our country has a far richer and more diverse past than is generally portrayed.'[24] He therefore further breaks from *Seven Samurai*'s period drama model by replacing the castles with thick forests, the poor peasants and samurai with iron workers and Emishi and the rigid social ceremonies with fluidity and mobility in social positions, especially for women.

The inclusion of the tower in the opening sequence, and the references to Emishi bring into *Princess Mononoke* an interesting subtext in relation to nationalistic discourse, especially in relation to the *Nihonjinron*, theories about Japaneseness. This concept refers to mostly Japan-based post-war theories and writings, ranging from the academic to the popular, about how to interpret Japan and Japanese culture and society. The *Nihonjinron* ranges through different fields from archaeology to biology, language theories and cultural behaviour codes. Common to these theories are the concepts of the uniqueness of Japanese culture, as compared to other cultures and especially to the West, and the homogeneity of the Japanese nation.[25] In *Nihonjinron* the concepts of nationality, ethnicity and culture are consequently often used synonymously.[26]

These ideas are incorporated and critiqued by Miyazaki in *Princess Mononoke*. He clearly highlights that Ashitaka is of a different tribe to the characters around the Tataraba village: when he reaches the Western lands, the people in the town's market square immediately see him as an outsider. Ashitaka also refuses to give his exact tribe or village name to the Easterners and, although the reasons for his obfuscation are not clearly explained in the film, they might be related to the historical fact of the Emishi keeping themselves isolated from, and thereby outside of, the Imperial Yamato rule. Ashitaka is welcomed at the Tataraba village, but is also cast as a neutral go-between (a role usually given to girl characters in Ghibli animation), negotiating with the human and animal god factions in *Princess Mononoke*. At the same time, Ashitaka has been cast out from his village, due to the poisoned wound in his arm, making him all the more isolated and othered within *Princess Mononoke*'s narrative.

In an interview Miyazaki has, in his half-joking style, expressed how he relates to the Emishi people. 'I am a Kantō [the area around Tokyo] person, and we all have Emishi blood in us here', and he has said that 'My face is the face of a Jōmon period person.'[27] The Kantō area, prior to the Tokugawa rule of 1600–1868 that led the establishment of a capital city at Edo (modern day Tokyo), was seen as a remote area, far away from the capital area and refined culture centred around Kyoto and Nara. Consequently, with this statement Miyazaki relates himself to the tribal other, as opposed to the mainstream Yamato culture. Moreover, he counters the *Nihonjinron* claim of Japan as a country with one ethnically-based nationality. In essence, Miyazaki rejects the popular view of Emishi and other native tribes as primitive and barbaric, and builds a more nuanced and complex vision of the interaction of the native/other, the Yamato and the relationships to nature around them.

Miyazaki, Politics and Environment

The forest in *Princess Mononoke* is inhabited by mysterious animals. The *Shishigami* (Deer God), the little rattling *kodama* spirits in the trees and the roaming wolves and furious wild boars are in constant battle with the human expansion. This spirit-inhabited nature, familiar from *Tonari no Totoro* (*My Neighbor Totoro*, Hayao Miyazaki, 1988) and *Sen to Chihiro no kamikakushi* (*Spirited Away*, Hayao Miyazaki, 2001), can be easily connected with Shintō. Interestingly though, by embracing the ancient Shintō, the native religion of Japan, and its nature-related gods, or *kami*, Miyazaki could easily fall into the trap of *Nihonjinron* discourse. The imagery of ancient Japan and its closeness to Shintō rituals and nature worship can be seen as siding with the conservative arguments about still-extant aspects of ancient Japan. Miyazaki's opinions reveal a side of his thinking close to some of the writings of *Nihonbunkaron* (theories of Japaneseness culture), for example, his claim that 'Our ethnic character harbors the elemental power of the forest within a precious part of our spirit.'[28] The constant comparison of Japanese culture to the non-defined 'West', which is central to the writings on *Nihonbunkaron*, does occasionally pop up in Miyazaki's opinions as well, for example when he compares the nature concept of Japan to that what he has seen in France, Italy or Spain.[29] But the critical way Miyazaki depicts history, minorities, women, ecological unbalance, and even class differences, complicates this narrative and makes it hard for any political party to use his films for the propagation of nationalistic ideologies.

In *Princess Mononoke* the discussion on primal nature and advancement is negotiated on different levels, particularly those linked to Miyazaki's early socialist ideas. The Tataraba village and its leader, Lady Eboshi, see themselves as advanced in their ability to use nature for production of iron (and guns), and in their will and drive to conquer the wilderness. They wage war on animal gods and wild beasts alike, hunting the *Shishigami* and fighting with the wolf girl San, to whom the title of the film, *Mononokehime*, *Monster* or *Spirit Princess*, refers. Lady Eboshi is shown as ruthless in her position towards nature, but supportive of people oppressed by the wider Yamato society, such as former prostitutes and leprosy sufferers, whom she has hired to work and live in the Iron Town, or *Tataraba*. Their communal joy in iron production and work is a continuation of a theme from other Ghibli films, where processes of work, be it building airplanes, preparing meals, or baths for guests are given heightened narrative significance. Miyazaki and colleague Isao Takahashi have been associated with the earlier, 1960s leftist movement,[30] and they indeed served actively with their colleague and teacher Yasuo Ōtsuka in the Tōei Dōga labour union.[31] These leftist sentiments have since become combined with environmental concerns in Miyazaki's filmmaking. Both Miyazaki and Takahata recall this period in their work and statements. For instance, Miyazaki has said that 'the tragedy of human beings is that the people [who] try to push forward the most virtuous parts of humanity end up destroying nature,'[32] just like Lady Eboshi does in her advanced, socially conscious Tataraba mine.

Ghibli is, as a reflection of its major themes, often mentioned as the key Japanese animation studio whose films address the problem of global pollution and environmental destruction.[33] In *Nausicaä in the Valley of the Wind* (*Kaze no tani no Naushika*, Hayao Miyazaki, 1984) the main character Nausicaä studies botany, investigating the poisonous plants that are ruining the world. In *Spirited Away* Chihiro gives a bath to *Kawa no Kami* (The River God), whose body consists of things thrown into the river – hence aforementioned references to Ghibli as the studio that protects nature. In *Princess Mononoke*, the studio delivers a multilayered depiction of the human-animal-nature discussion, with no easy answers delivered.

Critics have pointed to the influences from environmentalist authors such as James Lovelock and his Gaia theory on Miyazaki.[34] Gaia is seen as a complex interacting system, a single organism, where all living things have a regulatory effect on how the Earth's environment promotes life. The juxtaposition of the destruction of nature, though with good intentions, with the power of nature to heal itself is something Miyazaki has often returned to in his political ideals since his Tōei Dōga labour movement days,[35] and in his turn towards activities related to conservation. These include: cleaning of the riverside and planting trees in Tokorozawa where he lives;[36] the creation of a 'Totoro wood' in Tokorozawa; a preservation campaign for Yakushima Island, which served as model for the deep woods of *Princess Mononoke*; and, Miyazaki's outspoken opposition to nuclear power after the 2011 Fukushima nuclear accident (see e.g. the documentary *The Kingdom of Dreams and Madness*, Mami Sunada, 2013, where Miyazaki joins an anti-nuclear demonstration). Similar kinds of discourse can be seen in Takahata's film *Heisei tanuki gassen Ponpoko* (*Pompoko*, 1994), which, according to Takahata, is, on one level, a depiction of the messy history of the Japanese student movement of 1960s and 1970s, but on another is a pro-environmental film about the self-destructive denuding of Japan's natural environment in favour of suburbanization.

The characters of *Princess Mononoke* can also be charted in terms of their relationships to nature. Lady Eboshi is the extreme on one end, hostile to nature and proud of the technological advancement in the Tataraba community; whereas, the title character, Princess Mononoke, alias San, has been raised by nature in the form of wolf goddess Moro, with almost no contact with humans. San completely rejects the human society, but then develops a bond with Ashitaka. San is even further distanced from the Yamato culture – shown as an invading samurai force allied to the Tataraba village in the film – than the native other, Ashitaka. This can be seen in her costuming, which was designed after an earlier period of Jōmon art. Ashitaka, on his part, moves between the Yamato and the forest worlds, after having been exiled from his own Emishi village. In these ways, Miyazaki draws the political and historical lines of *Princess Mononoke*'s conflict through a complex refraction of Shintō animism (the forest gods), native peoples and cultures (Ashitaka and the Emishi), pre-modern Japanese history (San), the encroaching modernizing force of the Yamato nation and contemporary Japanese ways of addressing issues like the environment and Japanese national identity.

Native and Nature Religion in Princess Mononoke

As noted above, Miyazaki's representations of the natural world are frequently inhabited by animal-like spirits, who come into contact with humans. Totoro is a helpful, father-like figure for the little girls of *My Neighbor Totoro*, perhaps only a figment of their imaginations. In *Princess Mononoke* Miyazaki moves from the near-suburban village of *My Neighbor Totoro* to a total wilderness, where the nature is not controlled, but in constant chaos and evolution. This version of nature needs to be negotiated with. This is similar to the ancient local beliefs, which came to be called Shintō.

Katharine Buljan and Carole Cusack claim that *Princess Mononoke* is more related to western Pagan ideas than to Japan's native religions, as neither the hero Ashitaka nor the heroine San carry any symbols (sword, mirror and jewel) related to Sun Goddess Amaterasu. These symbols, as well as the Amaterasu goddess, are directly associated with Japan's Imperial family, which claims to trace its lineage all the way back to Amaterasu as the creator of Japan. Hence, Buljan and Cusack miss the point that Miyazaki has created an alternative and multicultural ancient Japan, where Ashitaka and San live outside of the established rule, as do others. By placing Ashitaka and San in a more fluid relationship to Shintō and other forms of animistic religious practices, Miyazaki gives them more freedom to act. But, in this instance, notably the protagonists are both marginalized outsiders: an Emishi youngster and a girl raised by wolves.[37]

Buljan and Cusack also miss the importance of what might be called ecological Shintō to Miyazaki's work. Arne Kalland mentions Miyazaki in his writings on the recently emerged Shintō environmentalist paradigm and its re-imagining of sacred forests (*chinju no mori*). *Chinju no mori* is a central concept related to Shintō and its shrines. The practice of defining big, old trees at Shintō shrines as sacred and marking them with rope or paper cuttings derives from the ancient beliefs in animism. Shintō, an animistic belief system rather than a religion, has been continually and deliberately adapted into different models for ideological reasons in Japan, from its use to prove the Yamato claims to the Japanese throne, through to the Emperor worship of World War II.[38] Recently, at least since the 1990s, ecological thinking has been connected to Shintō. Kalland argues that the Shintō protection of sacred trees and groves around shrines has protected these areas from post-War and more recent rede-velopment plans. This has meant that conscious ecological thinking has been increasingly connected to this school of Shintō in Japan.[39] Aike P. Rots, writing on the Shintō environmentalist paradigm, notes its many uses as a handy contemporary tool of the Shintō association (Jinja Honcho) to make Shintō attractive in contemporary society to priest 'fighters', who have tried to keep construction projects and nuclear power plants away from the shrine grounds. In amongst these activities, local conservation projects have been developed around the shrines.[40]

Kalland contends, however, that nature in Japanese culture is an abstract ideal, a collection of symbols. Kalland further states that practicality has usually taken precedence over high ideals. Only those Japanese who were engaged in occupations which were close to nature, such as fishermen, tended to be interested in its protection.[41] Miyazaki studies the same problematic relationship through *Princess Mononoke*. The Tataraba village is closely engaged with managing and conquering nature, but the film does not suggest an easy way out of the dilemma: both Ashitaka and San's future roles are left open in the end, and the Tataraba is due to be rebuilt. For Miyazaki, humans have to accept their role as consumers of nature, to their advantage, but at the same time they have to accept the unpredictability of nature.[42]

Shintō is a religion with has a close relation between nature, deities (*kami*), and human beings.[43] In a sense, Shintō could be called a negotiation between humans and nature. Shintō scholar Minoru Sonoda points out that in some of the earliest Japanese texts the word *mori*, which translates as 'forest' in modern Japanese, could be used as a synonym of *yashiro*, the ancient word for *kami* shrine.[44] Aspects of nature and the natural world were perceived as *kami*, and religion served to turn the powers of these *kami* into conditions favourable for agricultural production.[45] 'Harm done or accreted pollution can be neutralized by means of ritual purification. The latter, in particular, is a key dimension of the relationship between the Japanese and nature, which warrants "cultivation" and exploitation of the environment on the one hand, yet which on the other emphasizes the need to rectify imbalances between nature, humans, and deities.'[46] After getting wounded and poisoned by the wild board attack in the opening of the film, Ashitaka has to go through this ritual purification, but the attack was caused in the first place through the too-intense human interaction with the nature, in the form of Tataraba village.

Lucy Wright points out the similarities in Miyazaki's vision of the communion between humanity and nature and the Shintō belief system.[47] Shintōism is based on people's interaction with the *kami* of the natural world, in order to be able to live in interaction with nature. In Ghibli films it falls often to a young female character, herself a young girl or woman in the transitory state between childhood and adult life, to negotiate the way between different conflicting groups and between humans and nature. In *Princess Mononoke*, however, this go-between is Ashitaka, and the main female characters, Lady Eboshi and San, are posited as polar opposites to each other. It is this negotiation and interaction which interests Miyazaki, and here is his closest connection to Shintō, with its contemporary ecological twist. In this sense, as Miyazaki has pointed out, the often mentioned image of Studio Ghibli as the nature preservation studio, is misleading. 'Ghibli came to be labelled as a studio that makes films that are kind to nature, which made me feel uncomfortable . . . If we discuss environmental issues or issues of nature without mentioning the irrationality, cruelty, and brutality of life itself, it becomes a shallow and insipid exercise.'[48] For Miyazaki, the interaction between humans and nature is a complicated one, and has been so since the dawn of the mankind.[49] It is revealing that Miyazaki has chosen San to be a wolf-girl, as wolves had completely disappeared from Japan by 1905.[50] There are legends about how wolves have raised infants, and generally wolves were seen a more positive light than in Europe, and are directly related to nature.[51] San, as a wolf-girl, hence carries the attributes of nature directly.

Miyazaki has also talked about a place where an intense feeling of religious purity is possible, like at the forest lake in *Princess Mononoke*.[52] Miyazaki can therefore be seen to be interested in the primitive, Shintōist, pre-historic connection between humans and nature.[53] At the same time, the audience of *Princess Mononoke* is rewarded with intense scenes that connect beautiful natural imagery with magic. These scenes include the one where Ashitaka sees the *Shishigami* for the first time, far away amongst the trees; and again towards the end of the film, when the *Shishigami* walks on the healing water (a scene which, for western audiences, might bring to mind Christian mythology). The hand-painted backgrounds with lush greens, the *kodama* wood spirits and Joe Hisaishi's music generate spectacle for the amazement and wonder of the viewer. All Miyazaki films include these extreme, almost religiously beautiful scenes: the appearance of Totoro in the rain at the bus stop, the sliding of the train over the sea in *Spirited Away*. Consequently, this extreme beauty, when connected to the primal, non-cultured and raw vision of both nature and human interaction in *Princess Mononoke* has created a classical masterpiece of animation and filmmaking.

Conclusion

In *Princess Mononoke*, Miyazaki has dwelt on a ground he had not stepped on before. *Princess Mononoke*, under all its beauty and adventure, provides a serious deconstruction of its topics: of what the Japanese are as a nation; of how a bricolage of historical and mythological depictions can be used to distance audiences from their potential assumptions about character types; and, of how to think about human-nature relations. As Susan Napier has pointed out, *Princess Mononoke* also defies our expectations of what a *jidaigeki*, or historical period film, is supposed to be. There are few samurai, no geisha, no peasants, no cultured court life.[54] The film sidesteps these genre archetypes, presenting different agents of history and mythology: those of the non-Yamato, of early industrialism, of pre-history and animistic beliefs. Nature, now not depicted as cultured gardens, or the typical seasonal clichés of cherry flowers and autumn leaves, is made wild and unpredictable and deep as human imagining in *Princess Mononoke*. Through his approach to Japanese history, welded to nativism and fantastical gods like the *Shishigami*, Miyazaki deconstructs the national myths of Japan, and challenged contemporary Japanese to rethink their relationship with the natural world. Framed through ecological Shintōism, *Princess Mononoke* also portends future problems, as only those outside the current societal structures, like Ashitaka and San, are seen to have answers to the ongoing environmental problems facing Japan.

Notes

1 Miyazaki quoted in: Ryo Saitani, 'Mori to ningen' [Miyazaki's Interview: The Forest and the Human-being], *Princess Mononoke o yomutoku*. Comic Box, 2 (August 1997), pp. 72–81.
2 Jonathan Clements and Helen McCarthy, *The Anime Encyclopedia*, 2nd edn (Berkeley, CA: Stone Bridge Press, 2011), p. 433.
3 Mark Kermode, 'The Red Turtle Review – Rapturous Minimalism from Studio Ghibli', *The Guardian*, 28 May 2017.
4 Susan J. Napier, 'The World of Anime Fandom in America' in Frenchy Lunning (ed.), *Mechademia: Emerging Worlds of Anime and Manga* (Minneapolis, MN: University of Minnesota Press, 2006), p. 60.
5 Eija Niskanen, 'Kalalapsi, joka halusi olla ihminen' [The Little Fish, who wanted to become Human], *Helsingin Sanomat*, 19 September 2009. http://www.hs.fi/kulttuuri/art-2000004680111.html (accessed 15 April 2017).
6 Karl F. Friday, 'Pushing beyond the Pale: The Yamato Conquest of the Emishi and Northern Japan', *Journal of Japanese Studies*, vol. 23, no. 1 (1997), pp. 1–24.
7 Friday, 'Pushing beyond the Pale', pp. 1–24.
8 Friday, 'Pushing beyond the Pale', pp. 1–24.
9 Miyazaki in Saitani, 'Miyazaki's Interview'.
10 Friday, 'Pushing beyond the Pale'.
11 Friday, 'Pushing beyond the Pale', p. 11.
12 Tomoko Shibuya, 'Excavation Sheds Light on Jomon Life', *Japan Times*, 10 November–16 November, vol. 37, no. 45 (1997), p. 15.
13 Saitani, 'Miyazaki's Interview', pp. 74–81.
14 Hayao Miyazaki, *Starting Point 1979–1996*, trans. Beth Cary and Frederik L. Schodt (San Francisco, CA: VIZ Media, 2009 [1996]), p. 47.
15 Miyazaki, *Starting Point*, pp. 36 and 60.
16 Friday, 'Pushing beyond the Pale'.
17 Hirofumi Matsumura and Yukio Dodo, 'Dental Characteristics of Tohoku Residents in Japan: Implications for Biological Affinity with Ancient Emishi', *Anthropological Science*, vol. 117, no. 2 (2009), pp. 95–105.
18 Friday, 'Pushing beyond the Pale'.
19 Miyazaki, *Starting Point*, p. 49.
20 Kazna Ng, 'Miyazaki on Creating Kiki's Delivery Service', Vimeo.com. https://vimeo.com/45200524 (accessed 20 June 2017).

21   Ryan Gilbey, '*Kiki's Delivery Service*: Japanese Classic Returns in Time for
     Christmas', *Guardian*, 28 November 2016. https://www.theguardian.com/stage/
     2016/nov/28/kikis-delivery-service-japanese-classic-christmas-show-southwark-
     playouse-london (accessed 17 April 2017).

22   Miyazaki, *Starting Point*, pp. 48 and 97.

23   *Mononokehime Pamfuletto* 1997.

24   Hayao Miyazaki, *Shuppatsu ten [Starting Point]* (Tokyo: Tokuma shoten, 1996),
     pp. 272–4.

25   Peter Dale, *The Myth of Japanese Uniqueness* (London: Routledge, 1986).

26   Yoshio Sugimoto, 'Making Sense of *Nihonjinron*', *Thesis Eleven*, vol. 57, no. 1
     (1999), pp. 81–96.

27   Saitani, 'Miyazaki's Interview', p. 77.

28   Hayao Miyazaki, *Turning Point 1997–2008*, trans. Beth Cary and Frederik L.
     Schodt (San Francisco, CA: VIZ Media 2014 [2009]), p. 36.

29   Miyazaki, *Starting Point*, p.51.

30   Mamoru Oshii has discussed this generational shift in animators in their relation
     to the 1960s leftist movement, and counts himself belonging to the post-1968
     generation.

31   Tze-Yue G. Hu, *Frames of Anime: Culture and Image-Building* (Hong Kong: Hong
     Kong University Press, 2010), pp. 139–40.

32   Miyazaki, *Turning Point*, p. 84.

33   James Clarke, 'Ecology and Animation: Animation Gone Wild: *Bambi* vs
     Princess Mononoke', *Imagine*, no.31 (May 2010), pp. 36–9; Susan J. Napier,
     Anime from Akira to Howl's Moving Castle (New York: Palgrave Macmillan,
     2005), pp. 231–48; Michelle J. Smith and Elizabeth Parsons, 'Animating Child
     Activism: Environmentalism and Class Politics in Ghibli's *Princess Mononoke*
     (1997) and Fox's *Fern Gully* (1992)', *Continuum: Journal of Media and Cultural
     Studies*, no.26 (1 February 2012), pp. 25–37.

34   Elena Usai, '*L'epoca delle donne: Miyazaki e le principesse selvagge*', *Lundici*, no.87
     (October 2015). http://www.lundici.it/2015/10/lepoca-delle-donne-miyazaki-e-le-
     principesse-selvagge/ (accessed 17 April 2017).

35   Hu, *Frames of Anime*.

36   Miyazaki, *Turning Point*, pp. 137 and 140.

37   Katherine Buljan and Carole M. Cusack, *Anime, Religion and Spirituality Profane
     and Sacred Worlds in Contemporary Japan* (Sydney: Equinox, 2015), p. 134.

38   Aike P. Rots, 'Sacred Forests, Sacred Nation: The Shinto Environmentalist
     Paradigm and the Rediscovery of "Chinju no Mori"', *Japanese Journal of Religious
     Studies*, vol. 42, no. 2 (2015), pp. 205–33.

39   Arne Kalland, 'Culture in Japanese Nature' in Ole Bruun and Arne Kalland (eds),
     Asian Perception of Nature: A Critical Approach (London: Curzon Press, 1995), pp.
     218–33.

40   Rots, 'Sacred Forests, Sacred Nation'.

41   Kalland, 'Culture in Japanese Nature', pp. 218–33.

42   Saitani, 'Miyazaki's Interview', pp. 76–7.

43   Rosemarie Bernard, 'Shintō and Ecology: Practice and Orientations to Nature',
     Forum on Religion and Ecology at Yale, 1998. http://fore.yale.edu/religion/Shintō/
     (accessed 15 April 2017).

44 Minoru Sonoda, 'Shintō and the Natural Environment' in John Breen and Mark
    Teeuwen (eds), *Shintō in History: Ways of the Kami* (Richmond: Curzon Press,
    2000), pp. 32–46.
45 Thomson Gale, 'Ecology and Religion: Ecology and Shintō', *Encyclopedia of
    Religion*, 2005. http://www.encyclopedia.com/environment/encyclopedias-
    almanacs-transcripts-and-maps/ecology-and-religion-ecology-and-Shintō
    (accessed 15 April 2017).
46 Bernard, 'Shintō and Ecology'.
47 Lucy Wright, 'Forest Spirits, Giant Insects and World Trees: The Nature Vision of
    Hayao Miyazaki', *Journal of Religion and Popular Culture*, vol. 10, no. 1 (Summer
    2005). http://www.jurn.org/ejournal/art10-miyazaki.html (accessed 17 June 2017),
    pp. 219–34.
48 Hayao Miyazaki, '*Mori to ningen*' [The Forest and the Human-Being],
    Mononokehime o yomitoku [*Reading Princess Mononoke*], Comic Box, 2 (August
    1997), pp. 74–81.
49 Saitani, 'Miyazaki's Interview'.
50 John Knight, 'On the Extinction of the Japanese Wolf', *Asian Folklore Studies*, vol.
    56, no. 1 (1997), pp. 129–59.
51 Knight, 'On the Extinction of the Japanese Wolf', pp. 129–59.
52 Miyazaki, *Turning Point*, p. 88.
53 Saitani, 'Miyazaki's Interview', s.77.
54 Susan J. Napier, *Anime from Akira to Princess Mononoke: Experiencing
    Contemporary Japanese Animation* (New York: Palgrave Macmillan, 2001), p. 233.

Chapter 3

TO 'SEE WITH EYES UNCLOUDED BY HATE': *PRINCESS MONONOKE* AND THE QUEST FOR ENVIRONMENTAL BALANCE

Tracey Daniels-Lerberg and Matthew Lerberg

In Hayao Miyazaki's classic anime film, *Princess Mononoke*, Jiko bō (Jigo in the US version), who often serves as a comedic foil, voices one of the film's pivotal questions: 'Just whose side is he on anyway?' Jiko bō opens the interrogation into the uncertain motivation of the young Emishi prince Ashitaka, who despite the film's title, is the primary protagonist and serves as the 'mediator'[1] in an epic contest between the people of the Iron Town (Tataraba), who represent the dangers of industrialization, and the Forest Spirit, who serves as the supernatural arbiter of life and death. As Melanie Chan argues, 'the representation of the depletion of natural resources during the production of iron' serves as a pivot point in the film.[2] Iron Town is nestled in a beautifully lush forest that was cultivated and cared for as much as modern day gardens. The film 'couples unspoiled pre-industrial forest settings with scenes of technological invention as it builds toward a violent, unpredictable climax' that resists resolution precisely because Ashitaka's allegiances are tenuous and complex.[3] His positioning in what appears to be a sharply divided battle seems unsteady, shifting and even dissatisfying at moments in the film. The uneasiness related to Ashitaka's positioning emerges from the film's 'emotional' rather than 'rational' exploration of the relationship between the 'human and non-human realm'.[4] Ashitaka helps both sides of the epic battle: the forest gods, spirits and San, who are determined to protect the forest from the voracious and destructive consumption of humans, but he also protects those humans – the citizens of Iron Town – from certain annihilation.

Ashitaka's desire to resolve the dispute without taking sides disrupts traditional narratives of environmental conflict, and leads to uncertainty that may be dissatisfying for some viewers. But the question also resonates with Jiko bō, who is himself a monk and a mercenary, and Lady Eboshi, who is responsible for ruthless environmental destruction even as she offers meaningful employment to a group of prostitutes and sanctuary to lepers, raising inevitable questions about the indeterminacy of strictly drawn affiliations, and simplistic notions of good and bad. *Princess Mononoke* resists even a rudimentary engagement with the Western binaries that proliferate in many American-made animated films that take up the environment. As Donna Haraway argues, 'All these dualisms', especially those that seem to retain a measure of symbolic power in Western culture, 'escape philosophical confinement or religious ritual to find themselves built into weapons, states, economies, taxonomies'.[5] *Princess Mononoke* refuses to traffic in these dualisms, thereby stripping them of their power and embracing the unpredictable outcomes that emerge in the uncertainty that remains. Despite its sharp resistance to Western binaries, the film became a critical success in the United States after Miramax released the English language version in 1999. The obscurity of precisely drawn and stable allegiances in *Princess Mononoke* underscores a larger environmental issue in the film: sides cease to exist as environmental upheaval threatens all living beings, even those responsible for initiating environmental catastrophe.

The film further complicates the borders between the two warring groups as they are united against the corruption of boar gods into 'demons', or *tatarigami* (cursed gods), whose bodies are consumed by black squirming tendrils fuelled by hatred. The demon is a contagion, takes possession of other living creatures, and passes through other bodies. No side is safe from the physical possession of the demon, nor the psychological crisis wrought by demonic possession. Bodies become liminal sites of sociocultural exchange, where individual identities no longer make claims to discreet positions as environmental calamity spreads both within and across bodies, illustrating the futility of demarcating borders between pastoral/industrial (modern), human/non-human, and civilization/nature.

Through Ashitaka's reticence to choose sides, *Princess Mononoke* embraces an environmental logic that refuses sides, and instead recognizes that actions and thoughts bleed through, and moreover that hate and retaliation only lead to further degradation. Although set in the late Muromachi period of Japanese history and released 20 years ago, the film remains salient, especially in an age when the battle in and for the environment continues to impose borders over balance. Haraway warns of 'an appropriationist logic of domination built into the nature/culture binarism'.[6] In *Princess Mononoke*, bodies become liminal sites of sociocultural exchange, where individual identities no longer make claims to discreet positions as environmental calamity spreads both within and across bodies, similar to material feminist theories such as Stacy Alaimo's transcorporeality.[7] Reading *Princess Mononoke* through material feminist and post-human environmental theories illustrates the futility of demarcating borders between industrial/pastoral, human/non-human, culture/nature, spirituality/physicality and even good/evil.

Industrial/Pastoral

Modern environmental discourse often circulates around debates over the lasting repercussions of environmental catastrophe: real, potential and imagined. These debates, particularly among American citizens, are too-often presented along firmly drawn lines that place the present problem against a past state of imagined stasis, and humans against humans, humans against other animals, private rights against public interests, corporations against individuals, communities, or the government. This has been especially true in the United States, where the very foundation of capitalism rested on the exploitation of natural resources, whether through logging and mining in the early industrial period, or current oil and natural gas extraction. The most recent battle in the United States, the Dakota Access Pipeline (DAPL), a 1,172-mile-long stretch of pipe that will move crude oil through North Dakota, South Dakota, Iowa and Illinois, and under Lake Oahe, highlights the problems with rigid boundaries as they are deployed in discourses about the environment, and as tribal rights are pitted against national interests, Native lands and people against farmers, corporate profits against environmental rights.[8] Members of the Standing Rock Sioux opposed the pipeline, citing the potential environmental hazard and fearing that a leak might contaminate their drinking water.[9] After months of protests, and clashes between protestors and the police, construction on the pipeline was halted in December 2016 as former President Barack Obama requested a review.[10] The halt, however, was temporary. The Governor of North Dakota ordered protestors to evacuate their camps and construction on the project resumed in March 2017 following the urging of President Donald Trump.[11] The following month, in April 2017, DAPL crews spilled 84 gallons of crude oil, according to the Associated Press. The spill, though minor and cleaned quickly, reignited fears among the members of the Standing Rock Sioux and fuelled a 4-day march in Washington, DC.[12] The ongoing dispute highlights the complex and competing desires that surround environmental disputes. Much of the rhetoric surrounding environmental discourse promotes the ideal of taking a stand, of taking sides, and in doing so deploys the language of heated battle rather than peaceful negotiation that might lead to lasting change. *Princess Mononoke* appeals to the impulses that give rise to these binary strongholds. But, despite the pastoral yearnings that seem to give rise to the narrative, *Princess Mononoke* avoids the sentimental trap of pure nostalgia often associated with what Lawrence Buell identifies with the romantic pastoral, and instead exposes the problematic western fable in which taking sides as it pertains to environmental disaster might lead to a satisfactory resolution.[13]

The opening scenes of *Princess Mononoke* are punctuated by this romantic pastoral longing as the animation skims across a dark, cloud-covered mountain range that gives way to lush, green meadows. The film signals a romantic desire for a return to the pastoral as the visual field of the film arches down and back to 'ancient times' marked by land that 'lay covered in forests' presumably yet undisturbed by human interventions. The narrator, voiced by Keith David in the English translation of the film released in the United States two years after the 1997 Japanese release, invokes the language of the pastoral as he recalls a time 'long past' when both 'man and beast lived in harmony'. The opening scenes create 'a picture of essential changelessness, which human activity scarcely disturbs'.[14] While Greg Garrard's remarks respond to the opening lines of Rachel Carson's *Silent Spring*,[15] which begins with 'There was once a town in the heart of America where all life seemed to live in harmony with its surroundings . . . then a strange blight crept over the area and everything began to change', Miyazaki's film closely echoes the groundbreaking text. And, like *Silent Spring*, *Princess Mononoke* marks a passage of time that disrupts the pastoral for, as the setting changes, the narrator signals a distant future in which the 'great forests were destroyed'.

The ruptured pastoral moment is highlighted as Ashitaka rushes back through the lush grasses, naturally bounded by dense forests, to his remote village. Something foreign lurks in the forest, and brings the Emishi people under attack. In order to protect them, Ashitaka bounds deftly up a large, but crudely built watch tower. As he arrives, an elder statesman sits in the tower, surveilling the surrounding forest for signs of invasion, suggesting that the Emishi people keep careful guard over their small pastoral setting, and perhaps serves as a sign that they have suffered past attacks. In the act of constructing the tower, the Emishi people demonstrate a desire to retain the pastoral, to create a temporal and geographic zone impenetrable by outside forces (see Chapter 2 for more on the Emishi).

At the same time, however, the tower stands as a very human geographic touchstone to the vulnerability of the pastoral, and even perhaps as a testament to its false claims and desires. The monument articulates an ancient recognition that the pastoral was always and already invaded, for the tower stands in stark contrast to the idealized setting that surrounds it: built in the middle of a meadow just outside of the village, it penetrates the landscape without any pretence to being in harmony with it. Further, the tower monumentalizes the pastoral as always and already vulnerable to further invasions, thus discounting any claims to a pastoral site of harmonious interactions, untouched and changeless. Instead, the film practices a 'complex pastoral' that refuses the hallmark romantic poetics that seem obsessed with recalling and maintaining strict boundaries between culture and nature, past and present.[16] Rather, the film is suggestive of an eternal environmental imperative from which the human cannot be extricated.

The attack on the village is precipitated not by competing villagers or an aggressive war party determined to take over control of the land, but rather by an environmental catastrophe far removed from the Emishi village – in another once-pastoral setting. Ashitaka reluctantly kills the intruder, a cursed, hate-filled boar god, but in doing so their two bodies become entangled and ensnared with one another and Ashitaka is infected with the contagion that plagues the boar god in its final moments. Ashitaka saves his village, at least momentarily, but he is ultimately contaminated and forever marked by the encounter. The marking is not merely psychical, but is also material as the scar on Ashitaka's arm not only persists, but grows. The bodily exchange shows that, as Donna Haraway argues, there

> is no border where evolution ends and history begins, where genes stop and environment takes up, where culture rules and nature submits, or vice versa. Instead there are turtles upon turtles of naturecultures all the way down. Every being that matters is a congeries of its formative histories – all of them – even as any genome worth the salt to precipitate it is a convention of all the infectious events cobbled together into the provisional, permanently emerging things Westerners call individuals, but the Melanesians, perhaps more presciently, call individuals.[17]

As Ashitaka's body is marked by the encounter, so too are the inextricably intertwined trajectories of nature and culture in Miyazaki's film. Ashitaka 'lives in tune with nature but remains fully human' even after the encounter that sees him forced from his village and catapulted into a larger battle that repeatedly demands that he take sides.[18]

Princess Mononoke takes the pre-modern historical moment as its central concern, locating the 'blight' that Carson's opening chapter to *Silent Spring*, 'A Fable for Tomorrow',[19] identified in America in the twentieth century much further back in time. Set in the Muromachi period (1336–1573), Miyazaki certainly uses the historic to account for the lasting material degradation of particular Japanese lands, and all those living upon them. But the film also engages in the 'aggressive reinvention' of Japanese history that both invokes a particular time and place,[20] even as it works to dislodge any claim to temporal or geographic specificity. For instance, Tucker's exhaustive analysis of *Princess Mononoke* in terms of Japanese 'history, legends and ideology' succeeds in demonstrating the intertextuality of the film with 'various narratives of Japanese history' that appeal to a Japanese audience.[21] But such a rendering does not account for the film's success among English-speaking audiences who have little or no connection to the historic and cultural references in the film. And as Kamijimi notes,[22] the specificity of the setting may be irrelevant to a deeper understanding of the film,[23] which evokes a sense of the timelessness of environmental vulnerability and exploitation that is revealed in the pastoral fable.

Furthermore, unlike many pastoral fables, the film brings into focus rather than obscures the 'realities of labour and hardship' that have always existed,[24] even in supposedly idyllic pastoral settings. The main site of conflict in the film, Iron Town, is populated by hard-working former prostitutes whose bodily labour is exploited in the service of extracting precious minerals from beneath the soil's surface. They are a jovial group of women, who laugh frequently, and seem genuinely grateful to be working for Lady Eboshi. Additionally, a colony of bandaged lepers is made useful as they create ever more accurate weapons to protect the mining operation. These are the castaways, those who live on the fringes of society, and whose labours have historically been exploited. Yet, as figures of exploitation, their presence has traditionally been erased from the historical record. Their foregrounding as vital to the mining operation marks a shift from the unblemished purity of the romantic pastoral. And the film makes clear that Lady Eboshi, the leader of Iron Town, has 'saved' the women from an even more deplorable existence; and, although she might be seen as the repugnant villain in a traditional narrative of environmental justice, she demonstrates a true affection for the disease-stricken peasants who would otherwise be abused or shunned. Lady Eboshi's characterization highlights one of the unique and fascinating features of *Princes Mononoke*, its ambiguity (for more see Chapter 6). The film transcends the historic and geographic boundaries of its own production, and provides viewers with 'unsettling counterpoints' that do not fit neatly into historical fiction or pastoral fantasy.[25]

So even as Susan Napier argues that the historical inversions in the film instigated a national dialogue and created an opportunity for national reform in Japan,[26] *Princess Mononoke* also anticipates non-Japanese viewers and the present, connecting the past of the film to 'our modern social context' in ways that are both unsettling and problematic.[27] The film transcends cultural, geographic and temporal specificity. Miyazaki's film thus argues against the desire to embrace neatly contained cultural, temporal, regional and biological boundaries. *Princess Mononoke* instead engages with the uncertainty of slippages across and within boundaries as it takes up the universality of human-orchestrated ecological damage whose history began 'long ago', thus undermining a sharp division between the pastoral and modern. Consequently, the film speaks to Haraway's desire to 'build ongoing stories rather than histories that end'.[28] *Princess Mononoke* is not a tale about endings, but about beginnings; about future possibilities that we might create if we forge a new relationship to the environment, to the past, and to other living things. As Haraway argues, in considering 'ongoing stories' she seeks to redefine kinships that are 'about keeping the lineages going, even while defamiliarizing their members and turning lines into webs, trees into esplanades, and pedigrees into affinity groups'.[29]

Princess Mononoke works to establish affinity groups along non-traditional trajectories without valorizing the past, or suppressing its tangled histories, but rather moves battle lines into webs of relations. When, during one of the most contested battle scenes in the film Jiko bō asks 'Just whose side is he on anyway?' in reference to Ashitaka's desire to protect both San and the people of Iron Town, it is meant to reflect back on the viewer not as an ironic or comic interlude, but as a serious contemplation of the fault lines that destabilize the film's contested boundaries. Ashitaka refuses sides, preferring instead to rehearse a posture that embraces even the most unlikely web of relations. In the end, Ashitaka does not return to his village, for there is no return to the pastoral, and it cannot provide a defence against the advancement of technology. Instead of making claims to an unattainable past, the film's ending embraces the idea of moving beyond a return, a movement away from nostalgia, but also a refusal to simply accept the history that has been inscribed to us. Ashitaka's middling stance that remains unwavering throughout the film reflects an impassioned hope that in refusing sides we might reanimate a comingled history.

Human/Non-Human

The ambiguity of Ashitaka's allegiance not only reveals a comingled history, but also intertwined relationships between human and non-human animals. The complicated intersections between the human and non-human character further muddies the film's murky portrayal of the allegiances and environmental issues. Rather than portray the human and non-human animals as distinctly separate, Miyazaki blurs the line between them through the connections between San and Moro, Ashitaka and Yakkuru, and Ashitaka and Nago. In all three cases, separating human from non-human becomes an exercise of ambiguity and nuance, rather than clearly demarcated lines that cleave any affinity between them.

San, the human 'daughter' of wolf goddess Moro, proclaims herself as wolf, denying her human ancestry despite biological evidence otherwise. Yet, her defiance demonstrates the ongoing ambiguity in the film as she embraces her adoptive family, creating what Deleuze and Guattari term a rhizomatic block of becoming. San's desire to establish her difference from her biological roots and embrace her cross-species affinity aligns with Deleuze and Guattari's abhorrence for rigid categories that restrict possibility. They state, 'any point of a rhizome can be connected to anything other, and must be.'[30] In this instance, human and non-human are connected and *must be*. The latter point becomes a reoccurring theme in the film as Miyazaki works tirelessly to unsettle any certainty based on clearly demarcated positions. Moreover, just as Miyazaki blends factual and fictive history, thereby illustrating the connectivity of materiality and myth, his refusal to sever the human from non-human or history from myth further illustrates the rhizomatic nature of *Princess Mononoke* as the various 'lines always tie back to one another. That is why one can never posit a dualism or a dichotomy, even in the rudimentary form of the good and the bad.'[31] The film exhibits a similar resistance to dualism, including whether characters are rudimentarily good or bad, by promoting uncertainty.

The abundant uncertainty in *Princess Mononoke* also results from the rhizomatic connections that bleed across, through and amongst the various characters and plot lines. Human and non-human characters are intimately intertwined, just as 'a rhizome has no beginning or end; it is always in the middle, between things, interbeing, *intermezzo*'.[32] That is, the alliances between San and the wolf clan follow Deleuze and Guattari's argument against arboreal structures. San, abandoned by her parents, forms a new alliance, one that resists topological designation (she does not descend from Moro in the evolutionary sense), thereby obfuscating her status as either human or non-human. Rather she is entangled in associations, not detached by designations. Deleuze and Guattari argue a similar point stating, 'the tree is filiation, but the rhizome is alliance, uniquely alliance. The tree imposes the verb "to be," but the fabric of the rhizome is the conjunction, "and . . . and . . . and." '[33] San's alliance with the wolf clan, therefore, stems from linking (*and*) rather than defining (*to be*). She becomes part of the pack, an assemblage of human, non-human, history and myth.

Thus, by denying her humanness San embraces her role as a member of a pack, a multiplicity. Deleuze and Guattari make this distinction, coincidentally using wolves as their example, when they state, 'you can't be one wolf, you're always eight or nine, six or seven. Not six or seven wolves all by yourself all at once, but one wolf among others, with five or six others'.[34] Their larger point signals the importance of being *among* and relates to their intentionally challenging concept 'becoming-animal' (in this case, wolf), which 'always involves a pack, a band, a population, a peopling, in short, a multiplicity'.[35] *Princess Mononoke* extends this concept further, as there are numerous packs throughout the film: human, non-human and interspecies. The common thread amongst these multiplicities is that in each exists 'an exceptional individual, and it is with that individual that an alliance must be made in order to become-animal. There may be no such thing as a lone wolf, but there is a leader of the pack'.[36] Yet, as with the ambiguity found in the other themes in *Princess Mononoke*, the identity of the anomalous remains indeterminate, which is appropriate considering Deleuze and Guattari's distaste for singular or fixed identity categories. In the wolf clan, Moro seems the obvious choice. She is, after all, a larger than life forest god whose wisdom guides the clan. Moro deserves consideration as anomalous, being the leader of the pack and as a mythic being who speaks. This places her outside the rules of 'animal' and 'natural' as she has supernatural abilities and has adopted and raised a human child. However, Moro is part of the forest and remains connected to the human and non-human characters in the film.

However, Deleuze and Guattari define the anomalous as 'that which is outside rules or goes against the rules'.[37] In this respect, San emerges as an anomalous figure. San is not the leader of the pack (although this distinction changes by the end of the film); however, San is positioned outside rules of human/ non-human in *Princess Mononoke* (as conceived via dualistic thinking) and she frequently goes against the rules. While Lady Eboshi, whose alliances are always with other humans as she follows the industrial motto 'rules of progress', follows a familiar trajectory, one that is comfortably stable. But San's alliances, which unfurl the desire for human primacy, challenge the very notion of rules based on the particular notions of the 'place' of the 'the human'. Yet, San's refusal to embrace her human biology bolsters her entrenched position. Unlike

Ashitaka, her allegiance remains with the forest and its inhabitants because she views herself as other-than-human, as a wolf.

San's disavowal of her ancestry paradoxically resists and reinforces the rhizome. She is in an alliance of human and non-human, and yet resists being designated as human. Also, her alliance potentially engenders what Donna Haraway terms the 'philosophy of the sublime' because one of the members of the alliance must be 'an exceptional individual'.[38] While Haraway appreciates much of Deleuze and Guattari's work with alliances, affinities and multiplicities, she criticizes their reliance on the exceptional because it leads to their disdain for the ordinary – the mud, the earthly – and an 'absence of curiosity about or respect for and with actual animals'.[39] Although Miyazaki includes these 'exceptional' non-human animals (gods) who possibly overshadow the ordinary animals in the film, according to Susan McHugh, he also includes a companion-species relation through the 'cross-species relating' of Ashitaka and his red elk steed, Yakkuru (Yakul in English).[40] McHugh argues 'Yakkuru subtly and consistently grounds an alternative sense of agency that proceeds from a commitment to cross-species sociality'.[41] This commitment also grounds an alternative sense of historically knotted connections across species as *Princess Mononoke* reveals the storied relationship between the Emishi people and the red elk. The relationship between these two species is, as Haraway argues, 'a knot of species coshaping one another in layers of reciprocating complexity all the way down'.[42] Ashitaka and Yakul's knot – material, agential and social – includes their 'muddled histories',[43] which for both Ashitaka and Yakul is a blend of factual and fictional histories. For example, McHugh states Yakul 'is consistently referred to as a red elk, referencing the extinct giant Irish elk, a species that (despite its name) once ranged as far as Japan'.[44] Similarly, Ashitaka is a member of the historically marginalized Emishi people.[45] This muddled history, which blends both fact and fiction, illustrates the need for the type of cospecies 'response and respect [that is] possible only in those knots, with actual animals and people looking back at each other, sticky with all their muddled histories'.[46]

Although Ashitaka and Yakul are fictional characters with fictional histories, both represent the importance of difference in co-species alliances. McHugh's description of Yakul echoes Haraway's discussion of companion-species (real humans entangled with actual animals) in her chapter 'Training in the Contact Zone'.[47] McHugh states, 'the elk is universally recognized as smart, not easily spooked yet wary, carefully earning and granting the trust that seems so profoundly lost among as well as between humans and the animal gods'.[48] Similarly, Haraway highlights the intelligence, trust and agency that emerge from 'coperformance' in 'contact zones' between humans and dogs.[49] Yakul and Ashitaka's relationship in the film demonstrates the type of care and respect McHugh identifies through the type of coperformance Haraway argues exists between companion species. Yakul trusts Ashitaka despite being in situations that are dangerous and the animal exhibits an awareness and throughout the film he exhibits an intelligence that matches the human characters. The relationship between the two emerges from their companion status in Miyazaki's proposed co-evolution between the Emishi and the red elk.

The presence of both a companion-species alliance and the rhizomatic alliance further reinforces Miyazaki's refusal to 'choose sides'. Similarly Ashitaka's unsettling refusal to align himself solely with San or Lady Eboshi mirrors the difficulty of neatly separating humans from non-human animals in the film. As Ashitaka and San are a part of, not apart from, their animal mess mates or their human mess mates. Similar to the film these alliances, per Deleuze and Guattari and Haraway, insist 'on difference'.[50] The collision of differences in the film ensures that ambiguity-as-difference leaks between and among the various characters, settings and plot points. This seepage is more than just the cross-species relationship that McHugh rightly highlights between Ashitaka and Yakul. The line between human and non-human animals also comes under assault from the trans-species contagion, the curse physically manifesting from Nago's body at the start of the film.

By passing the curse from animal to human, the film evokes another description of Deleuze and Guattari's rhizome. They state:

> Under certain conditions, a virus can connect to germ cells and transmit itself as the cellular gene of a complex species; moreover, it can take flight, move into the cells of an entirely different species, but not without bringing with it the 'genetic information' from the first host . . . We form a rhizome with our viruses, or rather our viruses cause us to form a rhizome with other animals.[51]

Although this example of the rhizome is another of Deleuze and Guattari's metaphors and the curse in the film is supernatural, passing both contagion and genetic material through and across bodies demonstrates a primary reason for Ashitaka's reluctance to 'choose a side'. This curse, devouring his body from inside out, does not differentiate between human and non-human animals. In fact, as a larger environmental concern it illustrates the interconnectivity and fragility of both 'sides', thereby eroding the very idea of sides in the grander scheme.

Culture/Nature

As Miyazaki complicates fictive and factual history and the line between human and non-human animals, he obscures the line between nature and culture. That is, the supposed stark divide between nature and culture, represented most starkly through the positions of the two female protagonists – Lady Eboshi and San – and in the markedly contrasting landscapes of Iron Town and the *Shishigami*'s forest, unravels as the narrative progresses. Miyazaki thoughtfully interjects intricate portrayals of the fraught relationships between nature and culture, thereby avoiding what Stacy Alaimo addresses as the 'rather shabby theoretical and rhetorical treatment of "matter" and the "environment" in the late twentieth and early twenty-first centuries'.[52] Under the leadership of Lady Eboshi, the inhabitants of Iron Town decimate the forest, leaving a markedly scarred and diminished eco-system evident from the juxtaposition of the town (fortress) and the distant forest. The absence of trees in the landscape in proximity to Iron Town demonstrates the impoverished view of nature Stacy Alaimo highlights. She notes that, generally, 'the *environment* has been drained of its blood, its lively creatures, its interactions and relations – in short, all that is recognizable as "nature" – in order that it become a mere empty space, an "uncontested ground," for human "development."'[53]

Yet, the complicated relationships between the various agents in *Princess Mononoke* (human and non-human) – on the periphery of Iron Town, inside its walls and in the remaining forest – disallow for the type of depleted view of nature that circulates in the late twentieth and early twenty-first century theory and rhetoric about which Alaimo argues. More specifically, the non-human agents (including the liminal characters of San and Ashitaka) ensure the environment remains *contested ground*. Indeed it becomes a bastion of active and lively space for numerous constituents, thereby aligning the non-human agents with Alaimo's idea of a more active nature, where non-human agents surprise and resist human dominion. In this manner, Miyazaki's film places the various characters in contact zones that, as Alaimo argues, could generate 'potent ethical and political possibilities [emerging] from the literal contact zone between human corporality and more-than-human nature'.[54] The film contains many moments where the characters' violent conflicts reveal complex ethical questions because of the ambiguity created from the complicated characters. While Lady Eboshi is a complicated character, her primary concern remains firmly grounded in anthropocentrism – the non-human animals hamper her progress and threaten the well-being of her workers. Her position erects a seemingly clear divide between culture (Iron Town) and nature (the forest and its inhabitants); however, the film complicates such easily divisible positions through the environmental consequences of both Iron Town's lead industry and the forest creatures' acts of resistance.

For instance, the interspecies contagion transferred from Nago to Ashitaka not only demonstrates the difficulty of severing human and non-human animals, but it also provides a potent example of 'imagining human corporality as trans-corporality, in which the human is always intermeshed with the more-than-human world', and 'underlies the extent to which the substance of the human is ultimately inseparable from the "environment."'[55] The lead bullet that pierced Nago's hide festers inside of him, poisoning his mind and body. Nago's subsequent transformation to the wormy/snake-like 'demon' portrays a sickness that writhes both within and outside his body. He is wounded, both physically and mentally. As Sean Cubitt argues, Nago's affliction stems from a 'technological wound – the bullet – [that] denatures even a god, and leaves him ravening for revenge on the humans who introduced the technological into his natural world'.[56] While Cubitt's analysis focuses on how animals are drawn (by hand, gestural, versus CGI, technological), his identification of the conflict between technology (culture) and the natural fits with the overarching environmental concerns *Princess Mononoke* addresses. Moreover, the introduction of the 'technological into [Nago's] natural world' illustrates the 'trans' of Alaimo's theoretical model. Nago's quickly degenerating body and mind, stemming from the poison coursing through his body and fuelling his rage, becomes a contact zone as well. His body acts unpredictably, the black worms exuding from his flesh, reaching out across distances to infect others. Having contracted the curse, Ashitaka's body becomes unruly via this supernatural agent. This exchange, a passing of environmental contagion from Nago to Ashitaka, illustrates Alaimo's trans-corporality, which means:

> thinking across bodies may catalyze the recognition that the environment, which is too often imagined as inert, empty space or as a resource for human use, is, in fact, a world of fleshy beings with their own needs, claims, and actions. By emphasizing the movement across bodies, trans-corporality reveals the interchanges and interconnections between the various bodily natures. By underscoring that *trans* indicates movement across different sites, trans-corporality also opens up a mobile space that acknowledges the often unpredictable and unwanted actions of human bodies, nonhuman creatures, ecological systems, chemical agents, and other actors.[57]

Imaging Nago and Ashitaka's shared contagion as an example of transcorporeality underscores the difficulty of drawing distinct lines between humans/non-humans and culture/nature. The contagion spreads across boundaries, infecting and transforming bodies and places.

Ashitaka's curse (illness) is also unpredictable. His body is a contact zone wherein he attempts to resist the unwanted advances of the curse. Despite his agency, the infection spreads and he must physically and mentally resist the supernatural curse that attempts to influence his actions. The unpredictable and unwanted actions of his affliction are best illustrated when he meets Lady Eboshi in Iron Town. Her disregard for the forest and its inhabitants alarms Ashitaka. As she chides Ashitaka, 'his infected right arm, which magically links him to the spirit realm, inadvertently writhes and goes to draw his sword; he grips his uncontrollable wrist with his left hand, physically enacting his split attitude toward the ancient and civilized worlds'.[58] While this scene certainly highlights a split – the curse wants him to kill Lady Eboshi, while he resists – the 'split' is more complicated as the writhing black infection grows in size and power through hate. Ashitaka is, more precisely, connected to the curse both physically and emotionally. His hate fuels it, providing it sustenance to exert 'its' will, which in this scene is to kill Lady Eboshi. Ashitaka admits he would kill Lady Eboshi if he thought her death would remove his curse. However, he resists not only because killing her will not lift his curse, but also because, as Lady Eboshi notes, he would need to kill all humans to rid himself of the curse.

This revelation underscores why Ashitaka's allegiance confuses the various characters. He realizes the end game will result in the death of one or both of the sides, thereby reinforcing the very binary thinking he attempts to resist. His dual allegiance serves as his means to undermine dualistic thinking. This is even more evident as he places himself literally between Lady Eboshi and San as they attempt to kill one another. His place, between the two both literally and figuratively places him between the two sides. His actions are equally equitable as, rather than help one over the other he subdues both, rather violently, and returns them to their respective places (Lady Eboshi to her patrons and San to the wolves). As MJ Smith and E Parsons argue, 'Ashitaka occupies a position between culture (the people and occupants of Iron Town) and nature (the forest) . . . *Princess Mononoke* depicts the dividing line between these binaries as not only as able to be transgressed but as fluid and, in doing so, dissolves difference.'[59]

Although Ashitaka travels between nature and culture (both literally and figuratively), the dividing line between the binaries culture/nature is less fluid than Smith and Parsons suggest. Fluidity, according to Nancy Tuana, 'too likely promote[s] a notion of open possibilities and [overlooks] sites of resistance and opposition.'[60] For example, Ashitaka's movements between Iron Town and the forest result in boisterous threats by both humans and non-humans, and even in his being shot and later mauled. Therefore, while occupying a place between nature and culture, Ashitaka's movements between these sites creates even more unpredictability and unwanted actions between the numerous human and non-human agents. Therefore, these contact zones, where histories, humans, non-humans, cultures and natures collide, engender the type of swirling, messy mix of unpredictable agencies Alaimo suggests are necessary for a more robust vision of the environment. This vision opens a space where nature and culture co-exist, overlap and co-constitute one another, just as with the bullet-induced contagion that spreads through Ashitaka's body and the hate that spreads between Iron Town and the forest gods. The underlying result of this more intricate version of the environment echoes in *Princess Mononoke*'s conclusion, as for both sides uncertainty lingers.

Ashitaka's determination to 'not take sides', thereby resisting binary categories, reflects how scholars interpret the film. For example, Michelle J. Smith and Elizabeth Parsons argue that

the closure of *Princess Mononoke* offers no such universal solution, nor is there a complete restoration of order or triumph for San, as the adult world of industry that is represented by Lady Eboshi has not been eliminated. Furthermore, while the forest spirit's head is cut off and then replaced, his fall to earth implies that his physically manifest form has now dissipated and his power will only now exist in the natural cycles of growth and regeneration.[61]

Miyazaki's refusal to neatly conclude the film by offering a universal or satisfactory solution highlights Ashitaka's predicament throughout *Princess Mononoke* – through interspecies contagion and interspecies relationships he resides in both nature and culture as they cannot be easily demarcated in such messy contact zones. Moreover, by blending factual and fictive histories, sides dissipate as locating them temporally is as difficult as locating them spatially.

Smith and Parsons identify the loss of the 'supernatural' at the conclusion of the film as significant because future environmental degradation will be subject to natural cycles, not the accelerated supernatural growth and regeneration resulting from the forest spirit's fall.[62] The loss of the forest spirit and subsequent claims by both Lady Eboshi and Ashitaka that they will rebuild Iron Town, along with San's refusal to forgive, leads Cubitt to argue that '*Mononoke* doesn't promise a final truce but an undeterminable repetition. The only alternatives would be either the victory of the forest and the end of humans, or the victory of progress: either no time at all or a linear time of destruction.'[63] The lack of an equitable truce certainly occludes a satisfying resolution, and the desire to rebuild Iron Town certainly could lead to a repetition of environmental destruction because Iron Town will require natural resources to manufacture lead weapons. Yet, Cubitt's either/or alternative reinforces the very oppositional position Ashitaka resists. In this respect, to see with 'eyes unclouded with hate' requires, as Donna Haraway argues, 'to practice saying "none of the above." There can be an elsewhere, not as a utopian fantasy or relativist escape, but an elsewhere born out of the hard (and sometimes joyful) work of getting on together in a kin group that includes cyborgs and goddesses working for earthly survival'.[64]

The final moments of the film may provide such an option. Through the majority of the film, as Ursula Heise argues, 'the nature and intentions of the *Shishigami*, the elusive spirit of the forest who appears in a deer-like shape by day and in a gelatinous humanoid shape by night, are not understood by either animals or humans'.[65] However, the end of the film Kōroku, one of the Iron Town inhabitants, states 'I didn't know the forest spirit made the flowers grow'. His environmental revelation is one of wonder. Prior to this moment the inhabitants of Iron Town viewed the forest gods, including the *Shishigami*, as adversaries whose actions bring only destruction and death, rather than growth and beauty. The epiphany indicates some semblance of environmental awareness and growth, even if it is rudimentary. Lady Eboshi has a similar realization as she states with much surprise, 'amazing the wolves and the crazy little wolf girl helped saved us all . . . we're going to start all over again. This time we will build a better town'. Although start again indicates a potential repetition, as Cubbit suggests, Lady Eboshi's surprise that her adversaries saved her alongside her statement about 'a better town' implies a potential change in her approach.

Also, the combination of the bright, lush landscape and the harmonious score signify a change for the better.

However, if Lady Eboshi eventually strays, returning to her adversarial view of nature, Ashitaka remains behind to remind all who will listen that the great forest spirit is 'life itself, he's not dead . . . he's here right now trying to tell us something, that it's time for both of us [Ashitaka and San] to live'. What Ashitaka gleans from the return of the green mountainside and abatement of violence reflects Nathalie op de Beeck's statement that 'in Miyazaki's *animé*, as in the actual world, nature is not distant but coexists within civilization (and vice versa). Humans and wild animals have no choice but to share their territory; the boundaries overlap and bleed into one another. Nature and civilization are interdependent'.[66] Recognizing the interdependence between humans and non-humans dispels the confusion of Ashitaka's loyalty. The supposed sides are interconnected, as is his commitment to the inhabitants of Iron Town and the forest. As Haraway argues they are 'together in situated histories, situated naturecultures, in which all the actors become who they are in the dance of relating, not from scratch, not ex nihilo, but full of the patterns of their sometimes-joined, sometimes-separate heritages both before and lateral to this encounter'.[67] To see with eyes unclouded by hate acknowledges the liberatory possibilities that emerge when we cease to choose sides, but instead choose to embrace the inevitable relations that connect us even to the others whom we might try to resist.

Notes

1 Christine Hoff Kraemer, 'Between Worlds: Liminality and Self-Sacrifice in *Princess Mononoke*', *Journal of Religion and Film*, vol. 8, no. 2 (2004), Article 1. http://digitalcommons.unomaha.edu/jrf/vol8/iss2/1/ (accessed 15 April 2017), p. 2.

2 Melanie Chan, 'Environmentalism and the Animated Landscape in *Nausicaä of the Valley of the Wind* (1984) and *Princess Mononoke* (1997)' in Chris Pallant (ed.), *Animated Landscapes: History, Form and Function* (New York: Bloomsbury, 2015), p. 99.

3 Nathalie op de Beeck, 'Anima and Animé: Environmental Perspectives and New Frontiers in *Princess Mononoke* and *Spirited Away*' in Mark I. West (ed.), *The Japanification of Children's Popular Culture: From Godzilla to Miyazaki* (Lanham: Scarecrow Press, 2009), p. 267.

4 Chan, 'Environmentalism and the Animated Landscape', p. 93.

5 Donna Haraway, *The Haraway Reader* (New York: Routledge, 2004), p. 2.

6 Donna Haraway, *Primate Visions: Gender, Race, and Nature in the World of Modern Science* (New York and London: Routledge, 1989), p. 13.

7 Stacy Alaimo, *Bodily Natures* (Bloomington, IN: Indiana University Press, 2010).

8 Chas Danner, 'Standing Rock Protesters Declare Victory after Construction of Dakota Access Oil Pipeline Suspended', *Daily Intelligencer*, 4 December 2016. http://nymag.com/daily/intelligencer/2016/12/report-construction-of-dakota-access-pipeline-halted.html (accessed 16 June 2016); Rebecca Hersher,

'Protesters Leave Dakota Access Pipeline Area; Some Stay and Are Arrested', *National Public Radio* (NPR), 22 February 2017. http://www.npr.org/sections/thetwo-way/2017/02/22/516448749/protesters-leave-dakota-access-pipeline-area-some-stay-and-are-arrested (accessed 16 June 2017); William Yardley, 'Construction to Resume on Dakota Access Pipeline'. *Los Angeles Times*, 9 February 2017. http://www.latimes.com/politics/washington/la-na-essential-washington-updates-construction-resumes-on-dakota-access-1486673813-htmlstory.html (accessed 17 June 2017).

9   'Dakota Pipeline: What's Behind the Controversy?', *BBC News* [online], 7 February 2017. http://www.bbc.co.uk/news/world-us-canada-37863955 (accessed 21 June 2017).

10 Danner, 'Standing Rock Protesters Declare Victory'.

11 Hersher, 'Protesters Leave Dakota Access Pipeline Area'; Yardley, 'Construction to Resume on Dakota Access Pipeline'.

12 ICMN Staff, 'Dakota Access Pipeline Springs a Leak', *Indian Country Today*, 16 May 2017. https://indiancountrymedianetwork.com/news/environment/dakota-access-pipeline-leak/ (accessed 21 June 2017).

13 Lawrence Buell, *The Environmental Imagination: Thoreau, Nature Writing, and the Formation of American Culture* (Cambridge, MA: Harvard University Press, 1996).

14 Greg Garrard, *Ecocriticism* (New York: Routledge, 2012), p. 1.

15 Rachel Carson, *Silent Spring* (Boston, MA: Houghton Mifflin, 1962).

16 Buell, *The Environmental Imagination*, p. 15.

17 Haraway, *The Haraway Reader*, p. 2.

18 Hoff Kraemer, 'Between Worlds', p. 2.

19 Carson, *Silent Spring*, p. 2.

20 John A. Tucker, 'Anime and Historical Inversion in Miyazaki Hayao's *Princess Mononoke*', *Japan Studies Review*, vol. 7, no. 1 (2003), p. 68.

21 Ibid.

22 Kamijimi quoted in Yoshiko Okuyama, *Japanese Mythology in Film: A Semiotic Approach to Reading Japanese Film and Anime* (Lanham: Lexington Books, 2015).

23 Kamijimi quoted in Okuyama, *Japanese Mythology in Film*, p. 118.

24 Garrard, *Ecocriticism*, p. 40.

25 Beeck, 'Anima and Animé', p. 269.

26 Susan J. Napier, *Anime from Akira to Princess Mononoke: Experiencing Contemporary Japanese Animation* (New York: Palgrave Macmillan, 2001).

27 Hoff Kraemer, 'Between Worlds', p. 2.

28 Haraway, *The Haraway Reader*, p. 1.

29 Ibid.

30 Gilles Deleuze and Félix Guattari, *A Thousand Plateaus: Capitalism and Schizophrenia*, trans. Brian Massumi (Minneapolis, MN: University of Minnesota Press, 1987), p.7.

31 Ibid.

32 Deleuze and Guattari, *A Thousand Plateaus*, p. 25.

33 Ibid.

34 Deleuze and Guattari, *A Thousand Plateaus*, p. 29.

35 Deleuze and Guattari, *A Thousand Plateaus*, p. 239.

36 Deleuze and Guattari, *A Thousand Plateaus*, p. 243.

37 Deleuze and Guattari, *A Thousand Plateaus*, p. 243–4.

38 Donna Haraway, *When Species Meet* (Minneapolis, MN: University of Minnesota Press, 2008), p. 28.
39 Haraway, *When Species Meet*, p. 27.
40 Susan McHugh, 'Animal Gods in Extinction Stories: *Power* and *Princess Mononoke*' in Jeanne Dubino, Ziba Rishidian and Andrew Smyth (eds), *Representing the Modern Animal in Culture*, Kindle edn (Gordonsville: Palgrave Macmillan, 2014), p. 215.
41 Ibid.
42 Haraway, *When Species Meet*, p. 42.
43 Ibid.
44 McHugh, 'Animal Gods in Extinction Stories', p. 215.
45 Susan J. Napier, 'Confronting Master Narratives: History as Vision in Miyazaki Hayao's Cinema of De-assurance', *East Asian Cultures Critique*, vol. 9, no. 2 (2001), p. 478.
46 Haraway, *When Species Meet*, p. 42.
47 McHugh, 'Animal Gods in Extinction Stories'.
48 McHugh, 'Animal Gods in Extinction Stories', p. 215.
49 Haraway, *When Species Meet*, p. 229.
50 Napier, 'Confronting Master Narratives', p. 486.
51 Deleuze and Guattari, *A Thousand Plateaus*, p. 10.
52 Stacy Alaimo, *Bodily Natures* (Bloomington, IN: Indiana University Press, 2010), p. 1.
53 Alaimo, *Bodily Natures*, p. 1–2.
54 Alaimo, *Bodily Natures*, p. 2.
55 Alaimo, *Bodily Natures*, p. 2.
56 Sean Cubbit, *Eco Media* (Amsterdam: Rodopi, 2005), p. 34.
57 Alaimo, *Bodily Natures*, p, 2.
58 Beeck, 'Anima and Animé', p. 273.
59 Michelle J. Smith and Elizabeth Parsons, 'Animating Child Activism: Environmentalism and Class Politics in Ghibli's *Princess Mononoke* (1997) and Fox's *Fern Gully* (1992)'. *Continuum: Journal of Media and Cultural Studies,* vol. 1, no.26 (1 February 2012), p. 34.
60 Nancy Tuana, 'Viscous Porosity: Witnessing Katrina' in Stacy Alaimo and Susan Heckman (eds), *Material Feminisms* (Bloomington, IN: Indiana University Press, 2008), p. 194.
61 Smith and Parsons, 'Animating Child Activism', p. 32.
62 Smith and Parsons, 'Animating Child Activism'.
63 Cubbit, *Eco Media*, p. 35.
64 Haraway, *The Haraway Reader*, p. 3.
65 Ursula Heise, 'Plasmatic Nature: Environmentalism and Animated Film', *Public Culture*, vol. 26, no. 2 (2014), p. 309.
66 Beeck, 'Anima and Animé', p. 271.
67 Haraway, *The Haraway Reader*, p. 25.

Part 2

PRINCESS MONONOKE'S FEMALE
CHARACTERS: ANIMATION INFLUENCES,
FEMINISM AND CULTURAL LIMINALITY

Chapter 4

SPIRIT PRINCESS AND SNOW QUEEN: THE SOVIET ROOTS OF *PRINCESS MONONOKE*

Julia Alekseyeva

The Ghibli Museum in Mitaka includes a wall of Hayao Miyazaki's myriad inspirations, within which hangs a framed portrait of a cartoon owl. Although given no explanation for its appearance in the museum, the owl derives from Yuri Norstein's 1975 film *Yozhik v Tumane* (*Hedgehog in the Fog*), a Soviet animation. Miyazaki was greatly inspired by Norstein, and Soviet animation generally. Indeed, Miyazaki writes that Lev Atamanov's 1957 film *Snezhnaya Koroleva* (*The Snow Queen*) – one of the most popular Soviet animated films worldwide[1] – was immensely influential in his decision to continue pursuing animation. As Miyazaki states:

> I started working as a new animator for Toei Animation in 1963, but I frankly didn't enjoy my job at all. I felt ill at ease every day – I couldn't understand the works we were producing, or even the proposals we were working on . . . Had I not one day seen *Snedronningen*[2] (*The Snow Queen*) during a film screening hosted by the company labor union, I honestly doubt that I would have continued working as an animator.[3]

So important was the Soviet film for the budding animator that it became the impetus for his continued presence in the field of animation. Without the *The Snow Queen,* it is doubtful that works as profound as *Sen to Chihiro no kami-kakushi* (*Spirited Away*, 2001), *Kaze no tani no Naushika* (*Nausicaä of the Valley of the* Wind, 1984) or *Tenkū no shiro Lapyuta* (*Castle in the Sky*, 1986) would have been created. For Miyazaki, Atamanov's film, which highlights strong female characters, empathetic social relations and environmentalism, is capable of great emotional depth as well as brilliant technical prowess. Although all of Miyazaki's animated films are indebted to Soviet animation, such as the highly praised *The Snow Queen*, no film makes this connection clearer than the deeply affecting *Mononokehime* (*Princess Mononoke*, 1997).

Indeed, the two films are so similar that *Princess Mononoke* can be interpreted as an homage to the Soviet film. And, as we will see, *The Snow Queen* also influenced other films by Ghibli, notably the short masterpiece *House Hunting* (*Yadosagashi*, Hayao Miyazaki, 2006), to which we will later return. To unearth the Soviet roots of *Princess Mononoke*, I will first analyse the similarities between the two films, then discuss the reception of *The Snow Queen* in Japan in the 1960s; finally, I will analyse the aspects of the Soviet film which Miyazaki found most groundbreaking. As we will see, the Japanese animator praised the Soviet work's ambitious quasi-realist – but fundamentally aesthetic – style; he used this style to create distance between his own animation aesthetic and that of Disney productions. In other words, Miyazaki was struck by the singular animating style of Atamanov's animation, as well as the emotional response produced by these selfsame animation techniques. However, before delving into these characteristics, we must examine *The Snow Queen* – a film beloved by many generations of school-children in the former USSR – which is still rarely discussed and largely unknown elsewhere.

Between Snow Queen *and* Princess Mononoke: *A Comparative Analysis*

Even a cursory look at Atamanov's *The Snow Queen*, derived loosely from the Hans Christian Andersen story of the same name, reveals many similarities to *Princess Mononoke*. Unlike the rather violent and adult-themed *Princess Mononoke*, however, *The Snow Queen* is primarily meant for children, as witnessed by a grandfather-like troll character who narrates the film's tale and invokes children to be respectful, brave and obedient, lest they 'sleep without dreams'. However, this character is only a framing device, and does not appear very often. An extensive look at the plot and stylistic components of *The Snow Queen* will reveal much in common with Miyazaki's *oeuvre*, and *Mononoke* especially.

In the narrative of *The Snow Queen*, a girl (Gerda) and boy (Kay) are best friends and love one another. One day during a snowstorm, Kay's grandmother tells the children a story about the Snow Queen, and Kay jests that he would defeat her by melting her on a stove. In revenge, the Snow Queen appears and makes a splinter of glass fall into Kay's eye and heart, causing him to scorn love, beauty and friendship. A few days later, the Snow Queen appears again; Kay ties his sled to the back of her enchanted chariot and she whisks Kay away in a rush of snow and wind. When the weather warms, Gerda sets out on an epic quest to find Kay, encountering a great many people – a sorceress, a prince and princess, robbers, a Lapland woman, a Finnish woman – and numerous animals, who guide her along her odyssey. Finally, she arrives at the Snow Queen's palace and finds Kay, who cries when he sees her – so much so that the splinter of glass falls out, and the Snow Queen is defeated. Helped by all those who helped Gerda earlier, the two children are brought back to their town.

Although this story is less complex than the narrative of *Princess Mononoke*, there are a great many similarities between the two. For one, neither film shies away from depictions of death: even in the Soviet film, obviously meant for younger children than *Mononoke*, the Snow Queen's frost kills a dove while she protects her three chicks; though subtle, the limp, broken body of the dove is terrifying for all ages. It entails a far more brutal and realistic portrayal of death than any film in Disney's repertoire, where the deaths of characters are usually alluded to off-frame.[4] As Jack Zipes notes, Walt Disney changed the narrative of *Snow White and the Seven Dwarfs* (1937) from the original Grimm's fairy tale by omitting the death of the mother.[5] By changing a classical fairy tale, Disney was able to confirm a traditional or socially conservative world view.[6] Miyazaki and Atamanov, however, avoid such indirect and conventional depictions. In *Princess Mononoke*, animals are shown dying, and humans are shown maimed and with torn limbs. The result avoids grotesque violence in the manner of Takashi Miike or Quentin Tarantino, but is nonetheless rather terrifying in its direct portrayal of bodily harm. In addition, even *The Snow Queen*, which was created for young children, depicts violent drunkenness when the bandits celebrate their bounty after having robbed Gerda. Similarly, *Princess Mononoke* never shirks from portraying injury or disease, such as the lepers (though wrapped in cloth) working for Lady Eboshi. Injury to the body of either human or animal is never ignored after the fact, but has extremely realistic consequences: for Ashitaka, the demonic poison on his arm will seep into his bones until death. *Mononoke* represents what Susan Napier has termed a 'cinema of "deassurance"' due to its 'disturbing' nature and rather ambiguous ending: San and Ashitaka part ways, agreeing to visit one another occasionally.[7] Thus, although neither film follows a firm model of 'realism' with regard to form, their depth is predicated on a commitment to emotional and affective realism.

Even more of a similarity between the two films, however, is the liminal space between magical/supernatural beings and humanity occupied by Gerda, San, and Ashitaka. In *Princess Mononoke*, San is raised by wolf gods, and is capable of communing in a more direct way with nature. She alone is privy to the speech of animals that others cannot understand. Indeed, her name – *Mononokehime* – means 'spirit princess', exemplifying an otherworldly quality. In addition, Ashitaka, by virtue of his cursed arm, becomes capable of great feats of strength. Although he does not understand the speech of animals as clearly as San, he is able to accurately guess their intentions. Both protagonists inhabit unique ontological states, becoming 'neither human nor animal' – a phrase used to describe both San and Ashitaka by the townsfolk in *Mononoke*. Likewise, in *The Snow Queen* Gerda is able to quietly ask nature and animals to do her bidding. She talks with animals – beings as disparate as swallows, goats, crows, doves and reindeer – in the same voice and manner as human beings, and these animals are able to respond in kind. All animals in *The Snow Queen* unanimously aid Gerda in her quest; indeed, she has sway over nature as well. Early in her journey, she places a pair of new red shoes into the river as an offering; the river eventually takes her shoes and guides her along. Gerda appears to have seemingly innate knowledge of the secret codes of non-human forms of life, all of which then come to her aid without any pomp or circumstance.

This character – a child (often a girl) occupying a liminal space between nature-god and human being – recurs in many films directed by Miyazaki, including *Princess Mononoke*, *Nausicaä of the Valley of the Wind*, *Majo no takkyūbin* (*Kiki's Delivery Service*, 1989) and *Castle in the Sky*. For example, as Napier reminds us, Nausicaä has an extraordinary, almost telepathic, ability to commune with animals and insects,[8] and is seen as having virtually godlike powers.[9] Many more characters in Miyazaki's oeuvre, if not quite magical in and of themselves, are capable of witnessing supernatural elements in nature – aspects of the world that adults are no longer capable of experiencing. For instance, in *Tonari no Totoro* (*My Neighbor Totoro*, 1988), Totoro, 'King of the Forest', reveals himself to the young girls Mei and Satsuki, but not their father. These Ghibli characters are all children, who arrive at such circumstances entirely through intuition – much like Gerda knowing to offer her most precious belonging, her new red shoes, as a gift to the river. Importantly, Miyazaki takes his emphasis on the experience of children from Soviet animation, which, in contrast to most Disney films, highlights child protagonists who are, notably, still *childlike*.

For both Miyazaki and many Soviet directors, this emphasis on children can be interpreted as a distinctly political act. As Anna Fishzon writes, on Soviet post-war animation:

> Children were especially apt symbols of generational rebellion against both capitalism and the socialist state because, childhood, as delimited in the twentieth century, signifies a queer temporality, a period of delay, and a world apart from adult concerns. In their supposed flower-picking innocence and through play with siblings, friends, and animals, real and figural children can offer adults the possibility of a life outside the normative family and law-enforcing state.[10]

The seemingly innocent play of children, and the emphasis on children in animated film, thus signifies a political rebellion against authoritarian figures. Children's 'time' also signified what Fishzon terms a 'queer temporality . . . a world apart from adult concerns'. Children in Soviet animation thus served to subvert the monotonous, normative pacing of the status quo, thus introducing 'a period of delay'. Children's spaces were thus created as a space of freedom, critical of both sides of the Iron Curtain in the 1950s and 1960s. Similarly, Susan Napier argues that *shōjo*, or young female, characters in Japanese anime and manga often subvert or problematize dominant patriarchal roles – thus crafting images of female resistance.[11] As we will see, this rebellion against both capitalism and Stalinism inherent to representations of children was well acknowledged by Japanese film critics in their analyses of Soviet films.

Miyazaki had similar thoughts to the Soviet directors and purposely filled his oeuvre with famous depictions of children acting their age, engaging in quotidian activities normally forgotten by force of habit. Although *Princess Mononoke* includes some of the oldest protagonists in the Ghibli repertoire, it is worth noting that both Ashitaka and San are still teenagers, and the youngest characters portrayed in the film. Other characters, especially the women ironworkers flirting with Ashitaka, often comment on his youth and small stature compared to other members of their community. Thus, although *Princess Mononoke* does not appear to fit the mould of a Soviet film with child protagonists, it does link its two youngest characters with 'a life outside the normative family and law-enforcing state'. Their 'supposed . . . innocence' masks a deeply revolutionary core.

In addition, the young people in Miyazaki's films maintain an intuition generally lost as one grows older. This intuition often manifests as an acceptance and understanding of supernatural or superstitious landscapes. As Dani Cavallaro notes, in Miyazaki's films children have a fundamental capacity to grasp the world intuitively; this intuition allows them to accept as normal a world involving occurrences and situations that most adults would deem quite preposterous and therefore unacceptable.[12] This is true for Miyazaki's more supernatural characters (Kiki, Sheeta, Nausicaä or San) as well as his human beings (Mei, Satsuki, or Chihiro). Similarly, in *The Snow Queen*, Gerda's intuition allows her to perform quasi-supernatural feats. However, a characters' ontological liminality, evident in both *The Snow Queen* and many of Miyazaki's heroines, extends beyond what most children would even deem acceptable. Indeed, as one middle school girl wrote to Miyazaki: 'I can't believe that those kinds of girls really exist.'[13] The more supernaturally-inclined girls in Miyazaki and Atamanov – Gerda, San, or Kiki – embody a quasi-Utopian ideal for a more direct communion with nature. Gerda is thus able to gift her shoes to the river not simply because she is a child, but because she is extraordinary. San is able to fight and run like a wolf not only because of her young age but because she is, after all, a wolf princess. Gerda and San therefore embody a knowledge that surpasses the capacity of most humans, including children; after all, not every child would give their favourite shoes to the river and have the river heed her beck and call.

Gerda's act of gifting her shoes to the river appears to have been very influential for Miyazaki, for it recurs almost completely in another film written, produced and directed by the animator: the short film *House Hunting*, created for the Saturn Theater of the Ghibli Museum. This 12-minute film, exclusive to the museum, is notable for being entirely worldless, except for the sounds of nature. These sounds, aside from being auditory, physically follow the protagonist by means of enormous on-screen Japanese onomatopoeia; thus, the film is both semi-silent and deeply textual, as the audience both hears and reads the sounds expressed on screen.

More notable than even this creative formal framework is the protagonist, a preteen girl named Fuki. The girl sets out to find a camping spot by packing an enormous rucksack full of clothes, cookware and utensils as well as freshly-picked apples. Thus perfectly prepared, Fuki begins her hiking journey in the Japanese wilderness, unafraid of the many dangers that might befall her. But before crossing any natural boundary or attempting to use nature's bounty, she places an apple in front of the creature as an offering – be it grass, tree, river, or mysterious insect. With the same ease and unexplained magic as Gerda offering her shoes to the river, Fuki's apple offering allows her to traverse the boundary between human and natural worlds. The offering even allows her to find an abandoned old house in the woods, now entirely inhabited by insects. Fuki draws a circle around her with chalk and places food as an offering for the insects, and then sleeps within the circle, entirely unperturbed by the creatures around her. Whereas most humans would sleep in terror, or attempt to vanquish the scores of creeping and crawling insects around them, Fuki trusts in the power of her offering to keep her safe.

Cavallaro argues that the action of Fuki in *House Hunting* 'seeks to speak to children in their own language, by invoking rules which grown-ups would probably consider preposterous, but young spectators are capable of recognizing without effort'.[14] However, I claim that the preteen Fuki and the child Gerda are nonetheless remarkable: both are idealizations of a human existence whose pure intentions and respect to other living beings allow them to occupy a liminal space between the human and the supernatural. Children might play similar games, but Gerda and Fuki actualize this animistic relationship between nature and humanity. In her spunk, fortitude and bravery, Fuki is nothing other than a Gerda set in a contemporary Japanese landscape; just as Gerda journeys in bare feet and no clothing, confident the peaceful earth will come to her aid, so does Fuki trust the insects, grass, trees and river to take her apple offering and help her in her journey. Likewise, Fuki's complete trust in the natural, and her canny knowledge of rituals unknown to other humans, mirrors San's ability to request help from divine beings: after Ashitaka is mortally wounded, San places the dying Ashitaka beside a small island frequented by the *Shishigami*, who is solely capable of saving the human's life.

Indeed, there is no malevolence in the wild world of *House Hunting*, just as there are no truly malevolent characters in either *Princess Mononoke* or *The Snow Queen*. In *The Snow Queen*, even the eponymous queen treats Kay with a great deal of affection and tenderness, kissing him on his cheeks. The boy has free reign of her palace and she appears as a stunningly beautiful mother-figure. More importantly, all the characters who come across Gerda on her journey appear not evil but temporarily misguided. Similiarly, in *Princess Mononoke*, even Lady Eboshi, threatening to kill San, inspires respect for her industriousness, and admiration for the aid she gives the women working for her. Likewise, her tender care of lepers, whom she employs as gunsmiths, inspires reverence. As Napier notes, Eboshi is an odd amalgamation of the nurturing and the ferocious.[15] In addition, the Boar-*tatarigami* (cursed god), Nago, furiously destructive, is also treated with kindness and respect; even Ashitaka, cursed to die by its demonic venom, fully empathizes with the root of its trauma.

Other moments in *The Snow Queen* similarly avoid meanspirited characters: when Gerda meets the sorceress, who attempts to make Gerda forget her past in the style of Homer's famous Lotus-Eaters, the old woman comes across not as a malevolent witch but a kindly grandmother, doting on the young girl with care and attention. When Gerda encounters an extremely spoiled young prince and princess, the two pompous royals are at first alarmed at her presence, but then immediately offer to help – even giving Gerda a chariot, two guards and warm furs for the journey. Finally, even the little robber girl (Figure 4.1), who steals these newly-procured riches immediately after, is no malicious figure: although originally she appears to treat Gerda as another one of her many wild pets, kept squirreled away in her bandits' den, the girl melts upon listening to Gerda's tale. Indeed, this girl aids Gerda more than any other, giving her a reindeer knowledgeable about the path to the Snow Queen. The robber girl appears to have a crisis of conscience upon seeing the reindeer and Gerda ride off into the woods, bursting into tears and immediately releasing all of the wild animals she previously caged.

Figure 4.1 The robber girl of *Snezhnaya Koroleva* (*The Snow Queen*).

This robber girl is, in fact, quite similar to another famous warrior-girl in animation history: San, or Princess Mononoke (Figure 4.2). Indeed, with their short, dark hair in disarray, stern expressions, and dark eyes, Atamanov's robber girl and Miyazaki's wild princess look eerily identical.

They also have similar personalities: both are strong, ferocious and stubborn; raised in the wilderness, both girls follow a code vastly different from the rest of humanity. Both girls wield short daggers and are extremely agile, evoking an animal of prey: when Gerda is first robbed, the robber girl jumps maniacally onto the back of her bandit mother, biting her ear until she lets Gerda go. Similarly, San, as a wolf princess, acts like a wolf cub, biting Ashitaka's arm as he tries to separate her from Lady Eboshi. She is shown to be a ruthless figure of virtually unrelenting violence.[16] In addition, both characters have nearly identical temperaments: they are both fearless and tend to isolation, but have an inner tenderness they share with very few. Both Miyazaki and Atamanov's animated films therefore highlight, and elevate, the more base and animalistic of human temperaments. Their positive portrayals of earthy girl characters explicitly presents the grittier and more primordial aspects of human existence. Indeed, these primal sensibilities represent yet another liminality: between earth and human, as well as human and divine. While in the Judeo-Christian tradition humans occupy a space between the natural and the divine – Adam, for instance, was created to oversee a subservient natural world – Miyazaki subverts this by fusing the animal with the divine.

It is therefore no accident that both Atamanov and Miyazaki's antagonists appear entirely distanced from this animalistic nature. Another eerie similarity exists between the aesthetic depictions of Lady Eboshi (Figure 4.3) and the eponymous Snow Queen (Figure 4.4): both are tall and thin, exemplifying a

Figure 4.2 San, warrior and eponymous *Princess Mononoke*.

certain standard of Western beauty as well as modernity. The Snow Queen is often described as ravishingly beautiful; Kay asks his grandmother, 'Is she pretty?' and his grandmother responds: 'You can't even imagine how beautiful she is' (*trudno sebe predstavit' kak ona khorosha*). Similarly, Lady Eboshi is often drawn from a low angle, exaggerating her height (she is at least a foot taller than Ashitaka) and cold, striking features. Both characters have the same slight, closed-lipped smiles, deep voices and imperious characterization. Importantly, in both films, these are the only women who wear traditional makeup: the

Figure 4.3 Lady Eboshi in *Princess Mononoke*.

Figure 4.4 The Snow Queen in *The Snow Queen*.

Snow Queen with heavily painted eyes and eyelashes, and Lady Eboshi with her characteristic red lipstick. As such, both films mark makeup as a signifier for more normative – and therefore oppressive – modes of human existence.[17] Interestingly, the only other characters with any trace of makeup are San, with red war paint on her cheeks, and the robber girl, whose dark eyeshadow bestows a more fearsome expression, and gives her a similarly war-paint-like quality (see Figures 4.1 and 4.2).

It is worth noting here that Miyazaki folded yet another aspect of the *Snow Queen* into his filmmaking practice: the predominance of female characters. Although Miyazaki is often praised for using girls as his most common protagonist, and generally includes many strong women, *The Snow Queen* exceeds even the late-twentieth century feminism of Miyazaki: every character with any measure of agency is a woman, and every character lacking agency (whether by servitude, age, or glass splinter bestowed by the Snow Queen) is a man. In so doing, the *Snow Queen* subverts many of the stereotypes of women in cinema: no longer damsels in distress, in this Soviet film, women are rulers of every kingdom. They exclusively impart knowledge, whether a kindly grandmother or wise woman from the Lapland regions, and are leaders in any circumstance. In addition, not only is it a *girl* who rescues a boy in *The Snow Queen*, but every character with power, whether villain(ness), hero(ine), or helper, happens to be a woman. Even the crow which leads Gerda to the palace

Figure 4.5 The reindeer who carries Gerda in *The Snow Queen*.

Figure 4.6 Yakul, Ashitaka's red elk steed in *Princess Mononoke*.

where she meets the spoiled prince and princess is a *female* crow, with privileged access to the palace grounds that her betrothed, a male crow, lacks.

The one exception to this predominance of women in *The Snow Queen* is the male reindeer (Figure 4.5), who carries Gerda on his back to the far corners of the Arctic. Importantly, this reindeer yet again prefigures Ashitaka's faithful steed, the red elk Yakul in *Princess Mononoke* (Figure 4.6). Both reindeer and elk are portrayed in a very similar fashion: loyal, hard-working and wise, they figure centrally in both tales and directly result in the film's most cathartic moments. In *Princess Mononoke,* Yakul, though incapable of speech, becomes one of the film's protagonists, while the reindeer in *The Snow Queen,* a deep-voiced adult man, carries her through torturous snowstorms to the very best of his abilities, before collapsing in a heap directly before the Snow Queen's ice palace. Both filmmakers are evidently enamoured with these animals, and take great pains to animate extensive scenes of the protagonist riding them through scenic wilderness.

The Snow Queen *in the Japanese 1960s*

Having analysed the thematic similarities between the two films, it is now important to trace their histories, especially within a Japanese context. *The Snow Queen* remains one of the most beloved works of Soviet animation, and has won many awards since its creation. Few scholars of Soviet animation, however, acknowledge the film's immediate warm reception in Japan, screened on television in the 1960s and distributed through a number of outlets, such as union organizers with Soviet ties. Miyazaki, for instance, first saw the film in about 1963, while he was involved in the union at Toei Dōga.[18]

In May 1960, however, *The Snow Queen* appeared to make quite a splash in even the most elite of Japanese film journals; indeed, the long-running journal *Eiga Hyouron*, or *Film Criticism*, devoted fourteen pages to a discussion of the work: an extraordinary number, as most articles are only a page or two long. The article, written by Takuya Mori, an animation critic, appears near an article on the launch of the Nouvelle Vague with Godard's film *À bout de souffle* (*Breathless*, 1960) released in Japan two months prior; in the succeeding months, the publication delved into the burgeoning works of the political avant-garde in Japan, including Nagisa Oshima, Shōhei Imamura and Susumu Hani; it became one of the first publications to name the new film movement *Nihon Nuberu Bagu*, or Japanese New Wave. It was very rare at this time for *Film Criticism* to delve into what is usually considered pop culture, and especially rare for this journal to devote such a large percentage of its pages to its analysis. Indeed, it was rather rare for this elite publication to delve into the study any animated works, making this lengthy exposition on Soviet animation especially remarkable.

The article itself, titled 'The Genealogy of Soviet Animated Films: Focus on the Masterpiece *The Snow Queen*', attempts an outline of Soviet animation in its recent history. The writer often describes his less-than-ideal circumstances when watching these brilliant films; more often than not, he must watch them on a black and white television in his home. Nonetheless, Mori finds the films profoundly affective and effective on a formal level, and sees them launching a new era of superior animation. Interestingly, although Mori's article provides a general plot summary and formal analysis of many Soviet films, he weaves the (carefully detailed) plot of *The Snow Queen* between his synopses in a quasi-experimental mode indebted to avant-gardist writers such as Kōbō Abe or Kenzaburō Ōe. With this portrayal, *The Snow Queen* is meant to be a paragon of Soviet filmmaking and exemplifies many of the traits he describes. He concludes his analysis as follows:

> *The Snow Queen.* I will daringly call it a gem – one that was first entrenched in Walt Disney, but then melted, and from which a new, single crystal was extracted. This is no longer something borrowed from America. It lacks comedic gags, and even a sense of rhythm, but this is no drawback, for gags and rhythm are not necessary to produce physiological pleasure . . . In the clear air of our neighbour to the North, the climate is harsh. But it is exactly the theme of this story that is able to melt snow with a single-minded love . . . and this because she [Russia] yearns for Spring.[19]

Mori thus uses the metaphor of a glass splinter in Kay's eye, and instead turns this splinter into a gem: a new genre or art form crafted by Japan's 'neighbour to the North'. He views *The Snow Queen* as a film which is able to use techniques borrowed from Disney, within whom the film is 'first entrenched', but then is able to 'melt' them – just as Gerda's love caused the Snow Queen to dissipate into thin air, and just as Kay's tears are able to dislodge the glass splinter. An example of this might be the level of aesthetic detail: both the *Snow Queen* and works such as *Snow White and the Seven Dwarfs* (David Hand et.al., 1937) use a combination of painterly backgrounds and flat planes in the foreground, but Atamanov simplified the faces of characters, removing shadows to reflect a more potent emotional tone. In addition, some characters in *The Snow Queen*, such as the sorceress's soldiers, are drawn in a toy-like fashion (Figure 4.7).

The result is a combination of a variety of different animating styles that nonetheless weaves seamlessly into a coherent whole, and creates a sense of liveliness. The product – 'a gem', 'a new, single crystal' – thus becomes a form of children's animation 'no longer . . . borrowed from America'. Mori tends towards a politicized reading of the film, awkwardly viewing the film as a strangely literal metaphor for Khruschev's Thaw – the Soviet Union's attempt to escape the 'harsh climate' of Stalinism. This perspective was rather common for the period, as the Soviet animation studio Soyuzmultfilm was perceived to be a 'safe haven' for dissenting messages, or at the very least, newly emerging countercultures.[20] Nonetheless, Mori's argument resounds on a formal level. After all, even the aspects of *The Snow Queen* that appear Disney-like – the use of a fairy-tale genre, or talking animals, for instance – are seen in new light, and avoid the trappings of a milquetoast moralistic tale.

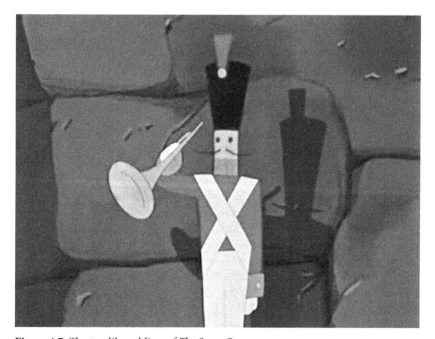

Figure 4.7 The toy-like soldiers of *The Snow Queen*.

Interestingly, Miyazaki would make similar formal claims about *The Snow Queen* in his own interviews decades later. It is also no surprise that he, like Mori, admires the work for its lack of comedic 'gags'. Although I disagree with Mori's claim that the film lacks 'rhythm', this might specifically be a comedic rhythm – and indeed Atamanov's film is no comedy. Or, it might refer to the strange ending of *The Snow Queen*: the battle between Gerda and the Snow Queen lasts all of two seconds, and the Queen does not even fight. Instead, the Queen's image simply melts into the air and her ice castle slowly dissipates. There is no cathartic confrontation between opposing forces. This strangely fast-paced ending, which disregards the consistent rhythm of the film's earlier moments, was also noted by Miyazaki, who commented: 'why do the final scenes of cartoon movies always have to be so ridiculous? This was true with *Snedronningen* (*The Snow Queen*); its ending was that film's greatest flaw'.[21]

Of course, this criticism does not cause Miyazaki to disregard the film; after all, as the Japanese director continues to claim, '*The Snow Queen* is my destiny and my favorite film'.[22] Instead, Miyazaki was inspired by the work's interaction with, but inevitable distance from, Disney animation: as Mori noted, the film, though initially 'entrenched' in Disney, instead melted every Disney-like aspect away to create a new, alternative animating style. *The Snow Queen* would thus be a particularly inspiring film for an animator like Miyazaki, whose views of contemporary Disney films ranged from ambivalent to outright negative: Miyazaki famously lectured that Disney animation went downhill after the *Silly Symphonies* in the 1930s, even before the creation of *Snow White and the Seven Dwarfs*.[23] Remarkably, in one 1988 lecture, he even announced: 'I must say that I hate Disney's works.'[24] Mori also writes of the 'downturn' of Disney's animation in the early 1960s, observing that the rejection of Disney led to a reaction against Disney-like animating techniques in Japan contemporaneously.[25]

Evidently, the response to Disney in the USSR at this period was similarly unfavourable. David MacFadyen notes that Disney was 'occasionally rejected in Russia with great volume and vigour', and that Disney's animals were dubbed 'too naturalistic'.[26] Soviet animators similarly denounced Disney's rotoscope technique (*éclair* in Russian) of simply drawing on top of live footage for a photographically accurate representation of reality. As MacFadyen writes, directors attempting this rotoscopic realism during this period 'would nonetheless be loudly criticized because [it] reduced reality to external elements of actuality, slavishly emulated photography, and thus lost all fairy tale imaginativeness (*skazochnost*')'.[27] Instead, Soviet animators attempted to find an aesthetic style somehow *more real* than the photographic representation of nature.[28]

Lev Atamanov, creator of *The Snow Queen*, shared this desire to retain the *skazchnost'* of animation. Although he was not against rotoscopic animation *per se*,[29] and even used it on occasion – notably, for the figure of the Snow Queen herself[30] – he maintained that the technique should not be used when attempting verisimilitude. For this reason, the figure of the Snow Queen appears more physically detached and ethereal; contrary to Disney's use of the rotoscopic technique, Atamanov's usage creates an otherworldly element. By contrast, the more abstracted faces and cartoon-like gestures of Gerda, Kay, or the robber girl fit more cohesively into the film's diegetic space. Thus, Atamanov is able to avoid naturalism even while using a technique grounded in supposedly "natural" human movements.

Atamanov claimed that such hyper-realistic techniques, as utilized by Disney, should generally be avoided. He writes:

> Animation is characterized by wide generalization, careful selection and, most importantly, grotesque exaggeration. Therein lies its power, its genuine realism. By breaking the laws of art, we inevitably slip into tired verisimilitude, which we often attempt to pass off as realism, even though it has nothing to do with either the truth of art or the truth of life.[31]

Thus, for Atamanov, a rotoscopic technique, if used towards 'naturalistic' ends, breaks fundamental rules of animation: 'wide generalization, careful selection, and . . . grotesque exaggeration'. In other words, animation is rooted in abstraction and *artfulness*. This, according to Atamanov, is where its 'power' and 'genuine realism' lies. At the opposing end is a 'tired verisimilitude' favoured by Disney, although this attempt at a photographic depiction of nature is opposed to both the 'truth of art' and the 'truth of life'. Otherwise put, art is most 'real' when it does not hide its inherently aesthetic nature.

To support his point, Atamanov evokes the art of ballet. He states: 'Attempts were made to bring ballet closer to realism. Instead of dancing, the dancers began simply walking. Did that add realism? Quite the contrary: it is precisely this faithfulness that looked particularly fake on stage.'[32] Thus, like ballet, animation only looks most 'real' when it does not aim to be 'closer to realism'. After all, ballet, stripped of its aesthetically oriented positions and sequences is not ballet, but simple walking. Paradoxically, the less 'artistry' is used in a performance such as ballet, the more 'particularly fake' it appears on stage. Fittingly, Miyazaki also evoked ballet in his analysis of *The Snow Queen*: he writes that animation is more suited to the dramatic arts of traditional theatre, in which gestures are exaggerated, rather than the subtle art of film acting. For this reason, *The Snow Queen*, he claims, 'depends on movements like those in a girls' ballet'.[33] Both Miyazaki and Atamanov, then, equate ballet and animation with artworks that retain their sense of 'realness' and 'truthfulness' through a reliance on aesthetic technique, rather than a slavish imitation of reality.

Mihaela Mihailova writes that a term widely used by Atamanov during this period – *uslovnost'* – is representative of this tendency towards 'artistry' and away from photographic naturalism. Although the word is usually translated as 'conventionality' in English, this translation lacks the nuance that accompanies usage of the term in the context of artistic production. In fact, *uslvnost'* might mean that which makes art *artistic*. Mihailova writes:

> In the context of the discourse around traditional animation in Russia, *uslovnost'* appears to refer to the cartoon's capacity to single out given aspects of a character or background and amplify, exaggerate, and otherwise play with them in a manner that breaks away from the particulars of physical reality while still preserving the essence of what makes said background or character believable to an audience. *Uslovnost'* is not about adherence to reality, but rather selective dissociation from it.[34]

Thus, *uslovnost'* refers to a 'selective dissociation' from naturalistic representation. It is, in other words, the inherent property of animation that separates it from reality, singling out 'given aspects of a character or background', and playing with this to amplify or exaggerate certain traits. Nonetheless, because of the nature of the cartoon – and the audience's understanding that this not an objective depiction of reality – the exaggerations still appear believable. Soviet animators, then, rather than strive continuously to attain a Holy Grail of photographic representation *à la* Disney, understood the artfulness or *uslovnost'* inherent in animation as a medium.

Unsurprisingly, Miyazaki would share this ideology, claiming that Disney's attempt to imitate shows contempt for the viewer. He writes: 'The barrier to both the entry and exit of Disney films is too low and too wide. To me, they show nothing but contempt for the audience.'[35] For Miyazaki – and, one could imagine, for Soviet animators such as Atamanov – respect for the audience entailed a certain level of artistry. Although *The Snow Queen* is not, by any means, an abstract or avant-garde animation, it still retained a very profound sense of *uslovnost'* and artistry. As Mori claims, it used aspects of Disney's technique to create a new animation style – much like Miyazaki would several decades later.

The first characteristic of *The Snow Queen* that Miyazaki appreciated is thus formal: an emphasis on artfulness and *uslovnost'*.[36] However, Miyazaki also greatly admired the affective response produced directly by the film through its formal techniques. He writes:

> *Snedroningen* is proof of how much love can be invested in the act of making drawings move, and how much the movement of drawings can be sublimi- nated into the process of acting. It proves that when it comes to depicting simple yet strong, powerful, piercing emotions in an earnest and pure fash- ion, animation can fully hold its own with the best of what other media genres can offer, moving us powerfully.[37]

What struck Miyazaki, then, was animation's ability to 'move us powerfully' simply by the 'act of making drawings move'. For instance, it does not come as a surprise to anyone when a live-action melodrama is able to produce a strong emotional response in the viewer. However, a screening of *The Snow Queen*, an entirely aesthetically-created production, can entail a similarly strong – and even more powerful – effect (and affect)[38] than a Hollywood melodrama. And even more so, the animation could depict 'simple yet strong, powerful, piercing emotions in an earnest and pure fashion' – far purer and far more earnest, then, than standard box office fare. Miyazaki noted the painstaking care and love involved in the process of animation, and the emotional effect in the viewer that could be produced by this kind of labour. Given that Miyazaki saw this film in the early 1960s, it should come as no surprise that he was amazed by the artistry involved; at this moment in history, due to the demands of television programming, Japanese animation was in a rather rudimentary state, and was generally characterized by repeated frames and little movement. Seeing the tricks and subtleties of animation depicted in *The Snow Queen* – for instance, the snow swirling endlessly in the distance, or waves crashing dramatically before the ice palace – Miyazaki's emotional response is quite understandable. For this reason, Miyazaki's films such as *Princess Mononoke* evoke the same painstaking care he witnessed in *The Snow Queen*, knowing the auratic nature of this labour-intensive animating style would yield a particularly strong affective response in the viewer.

Eric S. Jenkins writes that this type of emotional or affective response to animation is inherent in the medium itself, forming a *punctum* similar to what Roland Barthes saw in photographs, as described in *Camera Lucida*.[39] Jenkins writes:

> The *punctum* sparks a dual animation, an affect and an affection, moving in both directions between image and observer. The image animates viewers by punctuating the spatiotemporal coordinates of their perceptual mode, and the viewer animates images by embarking on adventures into the past or future or into questions of ontology or metaphysics, to name just a few.[40]

In other words, animation is capable of dehabituating the viewer from her standard modes of perceiving the world. Animation opens up new worlds, creating a space for freedom, and challenging the notions of 'reality' to which we have become accustomed. In such a way, animation can move us powerfully, allowing us to 'embark on adventures into the past or future' and creating a space where one's ontological condition and metaphysical state can be questioned and challenged. By working against the grain of our habitual formulations and sense of reality, a more aesthetically inclined or formally experimental animation might be even more capable than the *punctum* of photography or documentary film to create 'an affect and an affection' in the viewer.

If one combines this formulation with Miyazaki's response to *The Snow Queen*, we find that this *punctum* in animation, combined with what Miyazaki called the 'simple . . . yet powerful' narrative conveyed, creates exactly the kind of artistic work to which Miyazaki aspires. Obviously overworked and

pessimistic about the state of Japanese animation in the 1960s, the animator saw in Atamanov's work a *punctum* capable of rupturing spatiotemporal
modes in the viewer. *The Snow Queen* would inspire Miyazaki to create similar
films, where the obvious care that went into the film's creation – coupled with
a 'pure' and 'earnest' narrative – could arouse a similar viewing experience.

Princess Mononoke is one of many examples of Miyazaki's films which meet
this formidable challenge. Many films in his oeuvre, as well as the works of
Ghibli, generally follow these same formulations: for one, they put a great deal
of attention and care into the animation's artistry, which produces a deeply
emotive response in the viewer; in addition, they emphasize the conventions
of artistry (*uslovnost'*) in their formal techniques, taking precautions to retain
an aesthetic that keeps photographic realism at an admirable distance. I claim,
nonetheless, that *Princess Mononoke* not only meets these two characteristics
found in *The Snow Queen*, but also serves as a heartfelt homage to the beloved
Soviet film. As we have seen, the characters of *The Snow Queen* – whether
Gerda, the robber girl, or the Snow Queen herself – are reinterpreted, or rein-
carnated, into figures in *Princess Mononoke*. The quest of the protagonist, jour-
neying on an elk-like creature, is likewise similar, and both Gerda and Ashitaka
transform into quasi-supernatural creatures, capable of superhuman feats of
strength, persuasion, or understanding. Just as the wise, steadfast reindeer serving Gerda transformed into Ashitaka's loyal red elk Yakul, so too did Miyazaki
integrate the many features of the Soviet film and Danish folk tale into a wholly
Japanese context. Miyazaki's film is therefore transnational, indebted not only
to Japanese history and his own characteristic worldview, but to this Soviet animation and others, which he so deeply admired. Though *Princess Mononoke* is
a film profoundly tied to its Japanese context, its historical roots are markedly,
and proudly, Soviet.

Notes

1 '*Kakie Sovetskie multfilmi ochen' populyarni za rubezhom?*' [Which Soviet
   Animations Are Very Popular Abroad?], *Kino-Expert*. http://kino-expert.info/
   articles/kakie-sovetskie-multfilmi-ochen-populyarni-za-rubezhom.html (accessed
   14 September 2016).
2 Given the ambiguity of the translation, it is unclear whether Miyazaki used the
   Japanese title *Yuki no Joou* when referring to the *Snow Queen*, or *Snedronningen*,
   the Danish title of the original Hans Christian Anderson story.
3 Hayao Miyazaki, *Starting Point 1979–1996*, trans. Beth Cary and Frederik L.
   Schodt (San Francisco, CA: VIZ Media, 2009 [1996]), pp. 70–1.
4 For example, in the mother's death in *Bambi* (1942), arguably the most famous
   death in pre-Disney Renaissance animation, a gunshot is heard, but the death is
   never shown.
5 Jack Zipes, *Fairy Tale as Myth/Myth as Fairy Tale*, Kindle edn.
   (Lexington: University of Kentucky Press, 2013), p. 87.

6   Zipes, *Fairy Tale as Myth*, p. 9.
7   Susan J. Napier, 'Confronting Master Narratives: History as Vision in Miyazaki Hayao's Cinema of De-assurance', *East Asian Cultures Critique*, vol. 9, no. 2 (2001), p. 180.
8   Susan J. Napier, 'Vampires, Psychic Girls, Flying Women and Sailor Scouts: Four Faces of the Young Female in Japanese Popular Culture' in Dolores P. Martinez (ed.), *The Worlds of Japanese Popular Culture: Gender, Shifting Boundaries and Global Cultures* (Cambridge: Cambridge University Press, 1998), p. 101.
9   Napier, 'Vampires, Psychic Girls, Flying Women and Sailor Scouts', p. 102.
10 Anna Fishzon, 'The Fog of Stagnation: Explorations of Time and Affect in Late Soviet Animation', *Cahiers du monde russe*, vol. 56, no. 2 (2006). http://www.cairn.info.ezp-prod1.hul.harvard.edu/revue-cahiers-du-monde-russe-2015-2-page-571.htm#pa65 (accessed 14 September 2016), p. 65.
11 Napier, 'Vampires, Psychic Girls, Flying Women and Sailor Scouts', p. 91.
12 Dani Cavallaro, *Hayao Miyazaki's World Picture* (Jefferson, NC: McFarland, 2015), p. 29.
13 Miyazaki quoted in Susan J. Napier, *Anime from Akira to Howl's Moving Castle* (New York: Palgrave Macmillan, 2005), p. 151.
14 Cavallaro, *Hayao Miyazaki's World Picture*, p. 113.
15 Susan J. Napier, *Anime from Akira to Princess Mononoke: Experiencing Contemporary Japanese Animation* (New York: Palgrave Macmillan, 2001), p. 183.
16 Napier, *Anime from Akira to Princess Mononoke*, p. 182.
17 Although the question of Miyazaki's or Atamanov's feminism is not discussed in this article, it is worth noting that the equivalence between makeup and normativity can be deeply criticized from a feminist perspective. Depicting the most 'painted' characters as the most villainous – even if these characters are still admired otherwise – corresponds with an early feminism which is quite outdated in the contemporary landscape.
18 Miyazaki, *Starting Point*, p. 71.
19 Takuya Mori, 'Sovieto manga eiga no keifu: Shuusaku "Yuki no Joou" o chūshin ni' [The Genealogy of Soviet Animated Films: Focus on the Masterpiece *The Snow Queen*], *Eiga Hyouron* [*Film Criticism*], vol. 17, no. 5 (1960), p. 95.
20 Fishzon, 'The Fog of Stagnation', p. 1.
21 Miyazaki, *Starting Point*, p. 118.
22 Terumi Kayano, 'The World of Spirituality: *Princess Mononoke* Interpreted through Shinto' (MA dissertation submitted to the Hawaii Pacific University, 2009), p. 26.
23 Miyazaki, *Starting Point*, p. 124.
24 Miyazaki, *Starting Point*, p. 72.
25 Mori, 'The Genealogy of Soviet Animated Films', p. 93.
26 David MacFadyen, *Yellow Crocodiles and Blue Oranges: Russian Animated Film since World War II* (Montreal: McGill-Queen's University Press, 2005), p. 36.
27 MacFadyen, *Yellow Crocodiles and Blue Oranges*, p. 76.
28 MacFadyen, *Yellow Crocodiles and Blue Oranges*, p. 36–7, my emphasis.
29 Misha Mihailova, 'Animating Global Realities in the Digital Age' (PhD thesis submitted to Yale University, 2017).
30 'Snezhnaya Koroleva 55: Kholod' i krasota' [Snow Queen 55: Cold and Beauty], *Animator: Site ob animatsii v rossii i ne tolko* [*Site on Russian Animation, Etc*], 7

December 2012. http://www.animator.ru/?p=show_news&nid=1501 (accessed 14 September 2016).

31 Mihailova, 'Animating Global Realities in the Digital Age'.

32 Mihailova, 'Animating Global Realities in the Digital Age'.

33 Miyazaki, *Starting Point*, p. 75.

34 Mihailova, 'Animating Global Realities in the Digital Age'.

35 Miyazaki, *Starting Point*, p. 72.

36 No perfect Japanese translation of *uslovnost'* exists, but the term *kanrei* (慣例) perhaps comes closest in its dual meaning of custom and practice. However, it does not include the subtle sense that Mihailova describes.

37 Miyazaki, *Starting Point*, p. 71.

38 Although Brian Massumi, working from Gilles Deleuze's *Thousand Plateaus*, famously set apart affect, feeling and emotion as three separate entities and experiences, because the same nuance does not exist in Japanese, and because Miyazaki's article was reprinted in English translation, I will not distinguish them here. However, given Miyazaki's other statements on cinema, I would posit that he means *affect* rather than feeling, as an affect is 'always prior to and/or outside of consciousness'. Eric Shouse, 'Feeling, Emotion, Affect', *M/C Journal: A Journal of Media and Culture*, vol. 8 (6 December 2005). http://journal.media-culture.org.au/0512/03-shouse.php (accessed 15 September 2016).

39 Roland Barthes, *Camera Lucida: Reflections on Photography*, trans. Richard Howard (London: Cape, 1982).

40 Eric S. Jenkins, 'Another *Punctum*: Animation, Affect, and Ideology', *Critical Inquiry*, vol. 39, no. 3 (2013), p. 580.

Chapter 5

TEENAGE WILDLIFE: *PRINCESS MONONOKE* AND HAYAO MIYAZAKI'S THEORY OF THE FEMININE

Helen McCarthy

Hayao Miyazaki's[1] film *Mononokehime* (*Princess Mononoke*) was released in 1997. Its release brought to an end one of the most productive and creatively fulfilling cycles in the history of animation. From the time he embarked on the creation of his manga *Kaze no tani no Naushika* (*Nausicaä of the Valley of Winds*) in 1983, Miyazaki had been laying the groundwork to create a protagonist who could fight evil without demonizing its proponents (for more on *Princess* Mononoke's antagonist, see Chapter 6).

He wanted to do this to open up the story and give it more possibilities, to ensure that the leading character would linger in the minds of the audience as someone who could cope with whatever life had in store. Promoting the movie in 1984 he told *Young* magazine 'Nausicaä is not a protagonist who defeats an opponent, but a protagonist who understands, or accepts. She is someone who lives in a different dimension. That kind of character should be female rather than male.'[2] In an interview with Ryū Murakami several years later, Miyazaki said, 'If it's a story like, "Everything will be fine once we defeat him," it's better to have a male as a lead. But, if we try to make an adventure story with a male lead, we have no choice other than doing Indiana Jones. With a Nazi, or someone else who is a villain.'[3]

This is an interesting viewpoint from a man who had experienced war as a small child and had grown up in a country in the process of being invaded, culturally as well as physically, by the society that would go on to create Indiana Jones.

The young Osamu Tezuka observed the American invasion of Japan in his first published manga, *Maa-chan no nikkichou* (*Maa-chan's Diary*) in 1946. The 5-year-old protagonist's view of the invaders was that they were infinitely cooler and more intriguing than his Japanese father. Miyazaki, who turned 5 years old in the year of Tezuka's debut, seems to have taken away a different impression, one that Tezuka also articulated in later manga such as *MW* (1976–78), where the American military colonists are sometimes depicted as bombastic,

arrogant villains. Miyazaki uses the term Nazi as shorthand for a villain, much
as it is used in the Indiana Jones films, where the hero makes two clearly equivalent statements: that he hates snakes, and that he hates Nazis. In Miyazaki's
eyes, dehumanizing the villain is an inevitable consequence of idolizing the
male hero, and of identifying conflicts as best resolved by defeat rather than
negotiation.

Miyazaki first set out to make audiences accept the possibility, then the primacy, of the young female hero – a girl as capable in action and intellect as any
male, but with the ability to embrace and promote reconciliation and coexis-
tence. Having created a market for a different kind of heroine, he could map
her qualities onto a hero no longer forced to wear a white hat or shoot without
asking questions. Movie by movie, he forged his sacrificial warrior-prince –
Ashitaka – from a succession of glorious girls, conditioning his audiences to
accept tolerance, openness and willingness to live and let live in a heroic male
by demonstrating how these qualities did not hamper heroism in a female. But
throughout the process he did not waver from his starting point – that women
inhabit a different dimension.

Princess Mononoke can be summarized in many ways – as Tarzan starring
Jane, as boy meets girl with a twist, as the clash of rural life and industrialization, or as a new riff on the mediaeval story that Miyazaki loved, the tale of a
clever princess who loved insects.[4] This princess would not fuss over fashion,
or follow the extreme makeup codes of Heian Japan. Instead, she wandered
the fields studying and marvelling at the insect world. Our age reads this
ancient fable as a story of a young girl refusing to let her individuality be
compromised by the fashions of her day.[5] For Miyazaki, the boy from a well-
to-do middle-class home educated at an elite university, the rebellion at the
heart of the story must have seemed like pure and heroic self-determination.
The era for which it was written, however, may have seen the tale as a satire
on those who are fashionably eccentric, who deliberately break the social
norms, or even as a cautionary tale suggesting that those who stray too far
outside their society's boundaries may lose the chance of love and acceptance inside them.

I argue in this chapter that Miyazaki's women and girls are all wonderfully
observed creations – alive, convincing, sometimes enchanting and sometimes
repellent; but they are all viewed through the director's masculine lens and their
utility is determined from an entirely masculine perspective. Several Japanese
and foreign DVD releases of *Nausicaa* include a featurette entitled 'The Birth of
Studio Ghibli' in which Toshio Suzuki, Miyazaki's producer, fixer and friend for
over 30 years, says, 'Miyazaki is a feminist, actually. He has this conviction that
to be successful, companies have to make it possible for their female employees
to succeed too. You can see this attitude in *Princess Mononoke*. All [the] characters working the bellows in the iron works are women. Then there's *Porco
Rosso*. Porco's plane is rebuilt entirely by women.' But, this view of feminism is
at one and the same time profoundly patriarchal and profoundly socialist. Its

women succeed in, and on the terms of, a world defined, designed and managed by men. It is undoubtedly better for the women of the Tataraba iron works in *Princess Mononoke* to be paid a fair wage than to be sex slaves; but is it better for them to be cogs in the industrial machine than to live a more hazardous but more self-determined life like San?

Miyazaki obviously thinks so; he never made another female character like her. At the high point of a career spent creating and taming his heroines, using them as the matrix from which he could forge his perfect hero, Miyazaki chose to mate that hero with an untameable nature spirit. Then, rather than going on to experiment even further with this original and daring character, he suggested the incompatibility of any such relationship with male self-determination and dignity in his 2008 movie *Gake no ue no Ponyo* (*Ponyo*). San is not only the culmination of a line of characters that transformed the animation world's view of the heroine's function, but also a truly revolutionary character type. In her absolute rejection of conventional life, even for the sake of love, she is the only truly free and independent protagonist in the Miyazaki canon, and one of far too few in the whole of film.

San does not fit in. She does not want to and she does not try to. In Japan, where the nail that sticks up must be hammered down (*deru kugi wa utateru*), and in the patriarchal socialism of the Miyazaki movie, this is revolutionary. Miyazaki's female characters are creatures of magic and power,[6] irresistible, but dangerous unless that power is tamed and contained within defined social structures. Men who love such creatures can only safely do so if the women are willing to give up their magic and accept conformity as the price of love. Women who start life with such powers in Miyazaki's films must surrender them or risk exclusion from the conventional happiness of love, marriage and social acceptance. Only in old age can women reclaim some of their abandoned powers, and even then the risks are extreme.

Miyazaki also sets San in a context that brings her into contact, and conflict, with females as remarkable as she is – the wolf goddess Moro and the revolutionary Eboshi. Both are important aspects of the Miyazaki female archetype, and Eboshi appears closest of all his female characters to the political sympathies and conflicted relationship with ecology expressed in his work, in interviews, in his published conversations with novelist Ernest Callenbach and his association with Welsh-Japanese environmentalist CW Nicol,[7] whose novel *Tree* he illustrated.[8] In August 1993, Miyazaki told *Animēju* (*Animage*) magazine that 'there has never been a work of art which didn't somehow reflect its own time. *Nausicaä* comes from the new world view regarding nature which came about in the 1970s'.[9] Speaking at San Diego Comic-Con in 2009 Miyazaki also said:

I don't think we're born with a natural tendency to protect the environment. I think it's something we learn if we're educated and brought up to have the manners to care for the world. At some stage in our lives, the greed factor

became stronger, and that has led us to the horrible situation we're in now.
A change is necessary, and I believe my films convey that.

And, in considering San, and how the purity and ferocity of her self-
determination differentiates her from Moro and Eboshi, Miyazaki led me to
consider the very different treatment of his heroic young females and the older
women in his works. For an auteur often lauded as a feminist, Miyazaki is neither kind nor flattering to many of his female creations.

Starting Points

All scholars of Miyazaki should, in my opinion, read Maureen Murdock's book
The Heroine's Journey.[10] This fascinating text sets out a mythic archetype modelled on the Hero's Journey from Joseph Campbell's *The Hero with a Thousand
Faces*,[11] but with the important difference that Murdock specifically highlights
the advantages and strengths gained by incorporating both masculine and feminine principles within a character. So, in a sense, she is charting Miyazaki's quest
since he set out to make *Nausicaa*. Two older sources will also prove valuable in
the analysis of San. Miyazaki himself has commented on how the work of British
novelists including Rosemary Sutcliff influenced his thinking while he was
working on *Tenkū no Shiro Lapyuta* (*Castle in the Sky*, 1984). Sutcliff's *The Mark
of the Horse Lord* could,[12] with only minor historical and technological varia-
tions, be mapped onto the world of *Princess Mononoke*. Sutcliff's hero-kings,
whose ultimate purpose is to sacrifice themselves for the life of the tribe, are here
represented by an outsider, carried irrevocably far from home by circumstance,
who falls in love with a wild creature determined to defend her heart and soul at
any cost. Sutcliff, one of the most pragmatic of romantic writers, does not give
her young lovers the happy ending that Miyazaki conjures for San and Ashitaka,
but she foreshadows the course of their true love with remarkable accuracy.

I would be intrigued to know if Miyazaki has ever read the second of my
sources, a strangely bewitching book by the British poet and novelist Robert
Graves: *The White Goddess: a Historical Grammar of Poetic Myth*.[13] Graves
advances the view, based purely on literary and poetic evidence, that ancient
worship of three deified aspects of womanhood – the Maiden, embodying
youth, potential and sexual energy, the Mother, embodying maturity, fruit-
fulness and nurturing, and the Crone, embodying age, wisdom, and reflection - influences writers down the millennia. A Gravesian reading of *Princess
Mononoke* has many rewards. Certainly one can view San as the Maiden aspect
of Graves' Goddess, with Eboshi and Moro almost interchangeable in the roles
of the Mother and the Crone, their archetypal qualities ideally fitted to Graves'
romantic warping of mythology, poetry and dream. Many other Miyazaki
female characters fall into one or more Gravesian archetypes. It is particularly
interesting, when considering *Princess Mononoke*, to read Graves' comments in

The White Goddess on Sir James George Frazer's seminal anthropological work *The Golden Bough*: 'What he was saying-not-saying was that Christian legend, dogma and ritual are the refinement of a great body of primitive and even barbarous beliefs, and that almost the only original element in Christianity is the personality of Jesus.'[14] Replace Jesus with Ashitaka, Christianity with Shintō, and this comment could fairly be applied to Miyazaki's film.

But the most detailed and rewarding source of revelation on Miyazaki's inspiration and intent in creating his remarkable female characters and their supporting cast is his own back catalogue. As well as creating the perfect hero, Miyazaki's movies have also been essays in editing and revising the perfect heroine. By comparing the females of *Princess Mononoke* to the females who preceded and followed them in the Miyazaki canon, we can better understand the deliberate intent, and perhaps grasp a little of the unconscious artistry, of one of the greatest filmmakers of his generation.

Miyazaki is often presented as a film-maker with strong feminist sympathies, but this is a very simplistic reading of an artist whose portrayal of womanhood is less than universally supportive. He presents some very positive role models for young women, but his view of the life options of older women is less favourable. In an interview in *The Guardian* in 2011, I pointed out that there are strong reactionary elements to Miyazaki's work: 'Not anti-feminist but not in line with feminist thinking. In a lot of his work, he's saying that men and women have established functions in the social order. While you're a child, anything is possible but when grown-up women step outside their roles, they tend to have a tough time in his movies.'[15] I believe that by examining the way female characters other than the heroine are portrayed in Miyazaki's work, we can arrive at a more nuanced understanding of his artistic relationship with the feminine principle.

The Once and Future Princess

Looking at *Nausicaä of the Valley of the Wind* and *Princess Mononoke*, the gulf of 13 years between the two movies can be measured in terms of the growth of the hero. Asbel of Pejite is a conventionally brave and conventionally minded Prince, unable to save the girl with whom he has built a friendship from being used as a political bargaining chip by his own troops. Nausicaä is saved and enabled to fulfil her messianic destiny by Asbel's mother and a handful of women, working in secret. In comparison, in *Princess Mononoke*, Ashitaka not only offers up his own life to save San after she has shown him nothing but hostility, but works alongside the common women of Tataraba as an equal and views the forest gods and beasts as living beings with the same capacity to reason and choose as humans.

When we look at the women of both movies, and their role in the story, it is almost as if we are looking at the same movie. In a Gravesian reading older women of both stories are simultaneously the Mother, the nurturing and cherishing force, and the Crone, in her form as death goddess. The Miyazakian, collectivist reading teaches them that their survival depends instead on the relationships they have built – on their feminine magic, not their masculine functionality.

Nausicaä and San, the Maiden-avatars, are still unchanged, still standing at the gates of womanhood but now able – from their observations of the women around them as well as their own experience – to foresee the cost of the passage. This is particularly relevant to San, who was literally raised by wolves. Abandoned as an infant, she has no experience of human socialization and therefore no learned norms of feminine behaviour. Early in her journey Nausicaä remembers how, in her childhood, her father overrode her mother's pleas to force her to give up a baby Ohmu she wanted to save; she remembers how she had to hide the pioneering scientific work that helped her to save her people. She accepts the need for a woman's life to differ from a girl's, and from a man's, because she accepts the ways of her people. San can never find such acceptance. Her people are a wolf goddess and her subordinate sons. Her mother converses on equal terms with the forces of nature. How is she to fit into a society where women are grateful for factory work as a way out of prostitution?

We can also observe Nausicaä's realization dawning on 9-year-old Satsuki throughout *Tonari no Totoro* (*My Neighbor Totoro*, Hayao Miyazaki, 1988). Satsuki is no princess or goddess, just an ordinary girl, not especially pretty or clever, a loving and beloved daughter and older sister. As she realizes that her mother might not come home from the hospital, Miyazaki delicately observes her growing terror that doors she has not even opened may be locked forever, that her fate may be to take her mother's place 15 years before she is ready, without choice or discussion. Housework, basic schooling and the care of a feisty little girl will leave her no time for adventures or magic. Satsuki's delight when Totoro invites her to fly with him and her little sister is beautiful, but also pathetic. San has never known such fears as Satsuki's, despite the hints in the text that at least some of the forest gods share the human view of her as an oddity. Her wolf mother has given her access to the enchanted forest as a birthright. Older than Satsuki, with enough strength and daring to fight for her freedom, San has no intention of being civilized. She can deal with being female but she has no intention of accepting her society's version of womanhood.

If Miyazaki were to make a sequel to *Nausicaä of the Valley of Winds* showing a grown-up Nausicaä, as Osamu Tezuka made a manga about the grown-up, married princess who had been the cross-dressing, swashbuckling hero of *hon no kishi* (*Princess Knight*, anime television show 1967–68) we could speculate that it might look like *Majo no takkyūbin* (*Kiki's Delivery Service*, Hayao ...aki, 1989) in medieval clothes. Nausicaä would be Koriki, Kiki's mother, ...d to a devoted husband and carrying on with her work in the service of ...ommunity, worrying that her teenage daughter is too young to set out ... adventures but waving her off with a smile anyway.

San would never fit that comfortable scenario, the happily-ever-after of conventional romance. With no memory of her human family except rejection, she is determined never to rejoin the race that killed her loving and supportive adoptive wolf mother. She tells Ashitaka she loves him but she can't live among humans. Where an ordinary hero would tell her she must choose between him and her own ideals, Ashitaka suggests they live apart and meet in their own private space between the deep forests and the human world. His wild love will remain wild, and her own person, because he is a truly revolutionary hero – he does not need to transform her from a free spirit to a domestic goddess to secure his own happiness. His happiness consists in loving her and being loved by her exactly as she is. Their children, male and female, will be free to choose to roam at their mother's side or settle at their father's, heirs alike to the wild lands and the warm hearth. What kind of stories could be made from such a breed of heroes?

Modern Love

Sadly, Miyazaki is yet to expand on his creation of a relationship of absolute trust and respect between equals. In all his later movies, the clear expectation is that adult freedom of choice will be sacrificed to conventional social roles for the sake of social stability, and that Maidens who pass through the gates of womanhood, rather than those of death, will become the guardians of hearth and home. They will trade their magic for the ability to bear children to men who may not stay with them for long. Those who choose another way will, like Kushana and Eboshi, be damaged and perhaps even broken by that choice. Their only safety and protection is in the domestic social milieu, the moving castle of heart, home and community.

The one exception, and the character most like San in all his works, is found in his 2008 movie *Ponyo*. Heroine Ponyo's mother Gran Mamare is a goddess of mercy and a sea goddess, mighty and beautiful. She is most emphatically not a domesticated deity. Her children, all daughters, are brooded like a sea-horse's eggs by her comically fretful husband, the sea wizard Fujimoto. Unlike Kiki's father in *Kiki's Delivery Service*, who lives in a close-knit and accepting community with his magical spouse and beloved child, Fujimoto wanders the seas alone except for his thousands of tiny daughters, cursed with the self-appointed task of gathering magic from the sea to try to protect the world from human pollution. The balance of power in this relationship is all on the feminine side. A control freak married to an uncontrollable force of nature, Fujimoto seems perpetually unhappy and ineffectual. His lack of focus on his work and inability to control his daughters leads directly to the release of sea magic and the endangering of human and animal life on a huge scale.

By contrast, the film's other separated couple, Sōsuke's parents, have a more conventional power balance. Keisuke stays away from home frequently. Despite

Lisa's protests, he leaves her with the whole burden of running their home and looking after their son, using work as an excuse. And to reinforce the rightness of the existing order, Miyazaki takes great care to show that Lisa, who might at first seem to deserve all our sympathy, is far from perfect. In one of the film's largest plot holes, this devoted mother is shown abandoning her 5-year-old son and his friend to the mercy of an oncoming storm of epic proportions while she drives to work to check on something that could be covered by other staff whom she knows are on duty there. This shocking dereliction of common sense and maternal duty takes a pop at working women, calls Lisa's previously unassailable parenting credentials into doubt and creates the previously non-existent opportunity for Miyazaki to segue into one of the most breathtaking set-pieces of the movie, and set up one of its most tear-jerking moments. As plot holes go, the writer-director certainly gets maximum value out of this one.

The strong implication, drawn from the direct juxtaposition of these two sets of parents and situations in *Ponyo*, is that a family where the man and the woman both have authority and agency, but where his views and needs prevail while she makes it work, is a happy one, with well-adjusted children. By contrast, a family where the man has less authority and agency than the woman is a dysfunctional one with children who defy their fathers.

It is scarcely a surprising world-view for a patriarchal socialist of Miyazaki's age. Perhaps this is why he has yet to take San forward into the future where she and Ashitaka inhabit different worlds but share their private universe of true and equal love; perhaps he is simply unable or unwilling to construct the world in which this love could survive to maturity. And yet he has already recognized the possibility of a relationship in which both parties are different but manifestly equal. In the relationship of Kiki's parents, her father a man with a job so ordinary it is never mentioned, her mother a woman happy to use her skill at healing in a small community; we see two people at ease with their roles and their marriage in a happy circle of friends. The marriage of Professor Kusakabe and his sick wife in *My Neighbor Totoro* is never presented as anything but equally loving and equally supportive. And the marriage of Ma Dola and her deceased spouse from *Castle in the Sky* seems, from the clues in the film, to have been a very happy one.

This Woman's Work

In the movies after *Princess Mononoke* the representation of women and their relationships seems to take several steps backwards. The women of *Spirited Away* form a Gravesian trinity with a gaping hole at its heart. The three Goddesses have no purpose, no aim and no drive. Chihiro, the Maiden, is a pre-teen slacker, spoiled and reluctant to take responsibility for anything, but her parents are all the excuse she needs. Shallow, greedy and venal, her mother is no Mother Goddess but a freeloader content to follow her husband's lead in pigging out on illicit food. And the Crone, the witch and bath-house owner, Yubāba, is as selfish and spoiled as Chihiro's parents, a Mother grown into the worst possible habits of domineering self-absorption. The Maiden is saved and enabled to grow to her full stature by the intervention of two outside forces: an amnesiac river god with whom she has a forgotten childhood romance that fits better into a Rumiko Takahashi manga than a Hayao Miyazaki movie, and the grandmotherly assistance of Yubāba's sister Zeniba, a witch whose work has taken her 'the right way', into a quiet, supportive and non-domineering life in a fairy tale forest cottage. Unlike San, Chihiro does not feel strongly about anything in her life until everything, even her name, is taken away from her and she is left as Sen, a servant surviving on the whim of a capricious employer. Unlike Kiki, Sen never expected to have to take responsibility for herself as part of her preparation for adult life. Miyazaki said he was commenting on a modern generation of children when he created the movie, trying to encourage them to find their own initiative and courage.[16] But in order to do so, he had to take his central character away from all her established relationships and re-orient her in a community where she could learn the skills that the twenty-first-century nuclear family and education system had so signally failed to give her.

That community has interesting echoes of the community in *Princess Mononoke*. The customers who must be pampered and pandered to, and from whom all gold flows, are as capricious and alien as the Emperor and his nobles in ancient Japan;[17] the men and beasts who work in the bath-house are as venal and worldly as the priest Jiko bō and the men of Tataraba. Some of the women, too, are venal and all are tough, but they provide Sen with friendship, guidance and support. I do not share the fan theory that *Spirited Away* is an allegory of prostitution;[18] the bath-house/whore-house analogy is not signalled in the film and does not map comfortably on to it. But there is an interesting res-onance in the fact that of the two groups of working girls, the women of the Tataraba forges and the women of the magical bath-house, at least one explic-itly includes, and embraces, ex-whores.

In these two movies it seems that Miyazaki is interested in the role of romance, not simply in the lives of his heroines, but in the life of the commu-nity: how love shapes girls into women, and in so doing shapes women into supportive and useful community members. This theme continues in 2008's *Haoru no ugoku shiro* (*Howl's Moving Castle*, Hayao Miyazaki), considered by writers including myself, as Miyazaki's love letter to his wife of more than half a century, Akemi Ōta.[19] Ōta, herself a gifted animator, gave up work after the cou-ple's second son Gorō was born and devoted herself to their children and home.

When we consider what we know of Miyazaki's family life, it seems that many of his movies have sketched it out for us already. In Kiki's happy childhood with two engaged and supportive parents he showed us the ideal of Japanese family life. In Professor Kusakabe's slipshod but devoted parenting in *My Neighbor Totoro* we see how most fathers probably see themselves. In *Princess Mononoke* we have a world in which parents abandon, sell or enslave their children to the harsh world beyond the home, and in *Spirited Away* a world in which greedy and selfish parents have to be rescued by their children. *Howl's Moving Castle* shows us a highly romantic portrait of a sensible Maiden becoming a Mother to a capricious, gifted, irresistible wizard and an adopted nuclear family cobbled together from the debris of his previous life – an apprentice wizard, a burnt-out Crone, an asthmatic dog and a loveably dangerous fire spirit. Nothing in Sophie's new life is entirely hers except her wizard, and for his love she sacrifices all she was and all she might have become. The novel, by British writer Diana Wynne Jones,[20] presents Sophie as a powerful sorceress in her own right; but, this element is abandoned in the movie. In Miyazaki's adaptation, Howl's recognition of this sacrifice, and the implied happily-ever-after in the final shot of them lurching into the sunset in his castle, is her reward. San would, I believe, consider this a ridiculously unequal exchange.

In *The White Goddess*, Graves presents the Goddess as the force of nature – both life and death, like the *Shishigami* (Deer God) in *Princess Mononoke*. Ashitaka has one moment of 'mansplaining' in the movie when he tells San, who has been living with the God in his forest from infancy, that the God has not died because he is both life and death. In Gravesian myth all of nature is both life and death; although individuals die, the great forces of life and death are in constant interplay. Ashitaka too is a Gravesian archetype, a sacrificial King in the mould of Frazer's theories in *The Golden Bough*. The work of the Goddess is to kill him so that he can be reborn and the cycle of nature can continue. San is perfectly willing to do her job, but a musket ball hits Ashitaka first, and as he nears death he tells San that she must live. This forces a shift in San's Goddess-hood, transforming her from Maiden to Mother. Of course, given that her role model for mothering is a wolf goddess, she is not the softest of maternal figures, but despite her distaste for all humans she takes Ashitaka into the mystic womb of the forest and ensures he survives until the God can give him a further chance at life. Having achieved the astonishing feat of freeing him for his rebirth, there seems no good reason why she would want to spend the rest of her life serving him. Sophie's choice of a domestic life with her beloved is not for San.

Venus as a Boy

A fascinating contrast between Maiden and Mother and a clear bridge between the two are presented in *Kurenai no buta* (*Porco Rosso*, Hayao Miyazaki, 1993) by young heroine Fio Piccolo and beautiful businesswoman and singer Gina. Gina has married and buried three pilots. Her heart still belongs to her childhood love but she is pragmatic and he is pig-headed. He refuses to look for a way they could be together; she maintains her independence and refuses to beg, despite indulging in fantasy bets with herself in private. Perhaps their relationship is what San and Ashitaka's might have been in a more conventional movie than *Princess Mononoke*. If we notice the tiny red seaplane docked at Gina's island in the final frames of the film, we can carry the love story of Marco and Gina forward; but what could happen for them? No more a pirate, will Marco be able to settle into civilian life? Will Gina be able to share the island that has been hers alone for so long? Will they, like San and Ashitaka, agree to live apart and meet in Gina's secret garden? Even there, the equilibrium of nature is shattered; it is her garden, not a space in which both are absolutely equal as children of nature.

Fio is pure energy and charm, 17 years old and precociously talented. Her sweetness and courage win her many admirers, most of them much older men. The only time we see her with a boy her own age, he is ferrying supplies out to a flying boat on a lake, a teenager employed in the family store – hardly serious competition for the glamour and dash of flying aces two or three times her age. She and Gina maintain a subtle romantic tension across *Porco Rosso*, their complementary roles as contemporary love goddesses never allowed to spill into crude rivalry, but both able to manipulate the men in their circles without even trying.

Fio's tomboy characteristics are a major part of her appeal, both to us watching the movie and her fellow characters within it. We never see her in girls' clothing, while Gina is always presented as an elegant and stylish woman. Again, neither way of being female is presented as better than the other – they are simply both aspects of the romantic heroine. In fact, Fio comes closest of all Miyazaki's girl heroines to emulating San. In her voice-over at the end of the movie, she tells us that she and Gina remain close friends, and there is a hint that Gina has finally won the stubborn heart of her childhood love, but no suggestion of a man in Fio's life. She has taken over the family aircraft company, she sees old friends whenever she can, she takes every summer off to spend with Gina at her hotel; from all the information we have, she has a full, rich and happy life on her own terms.

The role of clothing and personal style for the women of *Porco Rosso* and *Princess Mononoke* is an interesting topic. Eboshi's clothing is somewhat masculine, but as chic and as carefully chosen as Gina's wardrobe, and it is far less overtly 'savage' than San's skins and bones (for more details, see Chapters 2 and 6). Fio's tomboy outfits are a protective cover in a world of masculinity, while San's is a flag of defiance. Gina, Fio and Eboshi are all dressing for particular roles in a world in which men hold all the power; San too is dressing to fit her habitat, but her mask and smears of blood show that she is dressing to strike fear into others rather than to fit in with them.

The fickleness and stupidity of men, especially middle-aged men, is highlighted throughout *Porco Rosso*. Hero flying ace Marco Pagott turns himself into a pig on principle. American ace Donald Curtis falls in love every time he sees a pretty face, and out again when the next one comes along. They sky pirates talk a good menace but are helpless against the gang of determined, feisty kindergarten girls they kidnap, and are putty in Fio's hands. The purpose of women, as presented in *Porco Rosso*, appears to be two-fold: to save men from themselves, and to keep the world going in the midst of the obscenity of war. There are echoes of the same theme in *Howl's Moving Castle*. In *Princess Mononoke* Miyazaki returns to this theme, creating slapstick characters such as ox herder Kōroku and classic heavies like Eboshi's lieutenant Gonza, as well as the venal, stupid samurai and the cunning priest Jiko bō. In contrast to the women of the story, their men appear almost as primitive as the apes who haunt the borderland between the deep forest and the Tataraba, hoping to be allowed to consume Ashitaka's flesh, just like the Emperor who wants the *Shishigami*'s blood.

It's a Man's Man's Man's World

Masculinity and femininity in primitive cultures are both mystical and functional. Every culture has its own myths and magic, poorly if at all understood by outsiders, but they also have functions derived from the relative physical strength of the sexes and the inevitable rhythms of childbirth and child-rearing. Only women can bear children and children are essential to the life of the tribe. Men tend to be better adapted to hauling heavy objects, hunting and fighting. *Princess Mononoke* reminds us that these broad-brush categorizations, born of ferocious necessity, have been bent and subverted throughout human history. Eboshi's pragmatic genius turns her leper technicians, a despised outcast group because they are considered unable to make any contribution to the subsistence economy they live in, into an asset – people who can engineer better, lighter weapons so that her women, already tough, devoted and used to hard work, can be taught to shoot. The women are devoted like the lepers because she rescued them from a much worse way of life, and tough because of their physical labour on the steel factory's huge bellows. Within such a close-knit community there are enough people to help out with childminding and food-preparation, so women can become more involved in the masculine functions.

Moro's wolf clan is an interesting variant on the subversion of masculine and feminine roles. In folklore wolves are generally predators, sexual, demonic or simply murderous, and usually male. It is only in modern times, as travel into dark and isolated places has become less dangerous, that the role of wolves as nature spirits, common in Native American cultures, has become more popular. As an alpha female who has subjugated her pack to her adopted human daughter, Moro is a rarity.

The relationships in Miyazaki's *Ponyo* once again show us how the love of women shapes the community. Young hero Sōsuke has an absentee father who takes on extra work on his boat and stays away overnight rather than coming home to dinner with his wife and son. Although Sōsuke is only five, his father's treatment of his mother is already playing through into his own relationship with Ponyo. He is constantly marvelling at her, in the way one marvels at an amazing toy; yet, on the one occasion when she needs him to do something for her – to kiss her and seal the spell that will strip away her magic and make her fully human – he is distracted and forgets. The only way Ponyo can ensure she gives up everything to claim her love is to kiss him herself. Sōsuke, like his father and Ponyo's, is already so caught up in the distractions of the masculine world that his beloved will have to take care of everything else around his frequent absences. Rant as Lisa will, she cannot change this; it is a truth as vast and unfathomable as the ocean. In folklore the conditionality of love and acceptance hangs like a sword of Damocles over women daring to claim any power as their own, even the limited and hearth-bound powers of conventional mating and motherhood. Ponyo's origin story, *The Little Mermaid* by Hans Christian Andersen,[21] is known to most in one of many sanitized versions leading up to the successful Disney movie of 1989. The original story contains terrifying fetishistic rituals of pain and loss, and its transcendent ending begins three centuries of servitude for the heroine during which she could still be condemned as unfit for the human heaven. Whatever you give up, folklore tells us, it will never be enough to tear a man's attention from his toys.

Kaze tachinu (*The Wind Rises*, Hayao Miyazaki, 2013) seals this truth in the cruellest way imaginable. Protagonist Jirō Horikoshi, a heavily fictionalized fig-ure from the history of Japanese aviation, is so devoted to his work as an aircraft designer that he allows his fragile wife, dying of tuberculosis, to spend long days and nights alone as he works. When she finally leaves him so as to die somewhere out of the way and not impede his work, he accepts this – regret-fully, but not so much so as to stop work and go and find her so that she can die in the presence of her adored husband. In Miyazaki's films men must work, and women must accept that. The dream of love for a person might be enough for a woman, but for a man, the dream of love for things he makes or discovers or pursues or drives or owns will trump that every time. Kiki's father, Professor Kusakabe, the devoted husbands and fathers who spend time with their wives and help to raise their children are in the minority in Miyazaki's mythology. Men, it seems, are almost entirely women's fault.

The portrayal of advancing age in Miyazaki's work also breaks down along broad gender archetypes. Older men, like Uncle Pom in *Castle in the Sky*, or the clock winder in *Kiki's Delivery Service*, are often still employed or engaged in the profession to which they have given their lives. Uncle Pom and boiler-house operator Kamaji in *Spirited Away* come from the same mould, still engaged in the work that has given purpose, routine and community to their whole lives. The same focus on work as the thing that glues men into the community spreads further down the generations. The barrel-chested mine engineering boss in *Castle in The Sky*, still strong enough to give the burly sons of pirate queen Dola the street fight of their lives, is not so far removed from the solitary old mystic Pom as might at first appear. Both are wholly committed to their love of the mines, and while Pom's solitary ways have taken him out of the daily life of the community he shares its concerns. Pom also has much in common with Fujimoto, the father of Ponyo, who shuns the society of others to explore the esoteric science of the sea. There are few elders in *Princess Mononoke* except the still vigorous and sprightly Jiko bō, but the lepers fit the same space; people normally marginalized as their productivity declines, given purpose and a place in the community by their specialist skills and years of experience.

Encouraged by her mother Moro, San will have none of this. Her demands are simple and straightforward: stop destroying the forest. When they are not met, or indeed even considered, she reacts like an animal, or a man: she defends her home and her people. Most of the invaders of her home see her as a savage animal to be put down. Only Ashitaka sees the possibility of compromise, and San, whose instinct for reality is better than his, knows that for a beautiful illusion.

In the absence of men, women can also take up community service outside the home provided their primary responsibilities are met. The women of the Piccolo family in *Porco Rocco* haul their babies along while they do a hard day's work in the airplane factory, replacing the men who have left for higher wages to the United States with no noticeable drop in the quality of the family's final product. One is reminded, perhaps deliberately, of Miyazaki's first employers, Tōei Dōga, who hired women for the basic paint and trace tasks of making anime because they were clean, quick, cheap and less inclined to make trouble and demand better treatment than men.[22] The advancement of 17-year-old wunderkind Fio to aircraft design might never have happened if the men of the family had still been around, just as innovative, gifted female animators like Reiko Okuyama and Kazuko Nakamura had to struggle for many years or leave Tōei to gain the recognition and status their work deserved.[23]

In contrast to older men, defined by their former profession, older women are defined by their role in the community. Whether or not they are still active mothers, women portrayed positively have nurturing roles, like Grandmother in *Nausicaä*, Gina in *Porco Rosso* or Gran Mamare and Lisa in *Ponyo*. The Oracle, the wise woman of Ashitaka's Northern tribe, is a spiritual nurturer, a communicator with the gods and nature spirits on behalf of the community. But in their later years, when their children are off their hands and the community no longer needs their service, Miyazaki's women are sometimes permitted to return to the charming self-centredness of childhood.

Here, and only here, the nail that sticks up need not be hammered down. In line with Japanese social practices, old women from the outrageous yet marshmallow-hearted Ma Dola of *Castle in the Sky* to the trio of sweet and tart old biddies in *Ponyo* can – and do – behave exactly as they please and meet with tolerance, if not outright admiration. Zeniba, the sweet old witch in *Spirited Away* who lives in the woods, welcomes Chihiro, her magically transformed nephew and their strange friends with unquestioning acceptance, and never parades her power. She is the sort of little old lady everyone loves, but even the bad-tempered old lady Toki in *Ponyo* is tolerated with great kindness.

Conclusion

There is, of course, a line that must be held. The most Gravesian of Miyazaki's old women, the true Crone goddesses, the Witch of the Waste and Lady Suliman in *Howl's Moving Castle*, the witch Yubāba in *Spirited Away* and hard-boiled Ma Dola in *Castle in The Sky*, are capricious, selfish, and driven entirely by their own needs and desires. All lose in the end, but it is interesting to observe how their loss is modulated in relation to their social and maternal status. The Lady Suliman, as an arm of secular power, remains untouched except in terms of the blow that losing to Howl deals to her pride and prestige. Ma Dola is indulged with a happy ending, because she is a mother with true maternal feelings despite her veneer of toughness, and because she only steals from the wealthy. The Witch of the Waste is given the cruellest and most inevitable of ends at the hands of another woman, Lady Suliman; her magic failed, she is reduced from evil magnificence to a chair by the fire to mumble away her final years, being cared for by the wife of the enemy who has all but forgotten her. Yubāba, in a sense, gets off lightly. Her magical powers remain, her business is unaffected, her relationship with her only child may even have changed for the better. Yet she is still defeated, reinforcing the theme that a woman who stands against her community cannot win. These defanged, tamed Crone Goddesses stir echoes of San's rejection by her own family and community. Outsiders all their lives, now that their powers have deserted them they face a future of tolerance, but without power or agency. As the world outside the forest rejects San and all that she stands for as irrelevant, their worlds have sidelined them.

And yet, with the creation of San, Miyazaki presents us with the possibility that the replaying of the old romantic tropes, the game of male and female jockeying for supremacy, could simply stop; that men might not need women to dance attendance on them and women might not need men to validate them; that both sides could simply agree to live their own lives and make a private space belonging equally and entirely to them both. This is far more revolutionary than the creation of a hero who doesn't need to kill to be heroic. This changes the game of the representation of women in Japanese popular culture.

Or it could. If we let the Maiden, the Mother and the Crone, the goddesses of old, become the millions of magically ordinary people that they really are; if we let women express themselves without reference to men but acknowledge the importance of men in their lives; if we let men accept that they can be loved without being masters of those who love them – then we could forge a whole new universe of glorious stories.

I have no idea why Miyazaki opened the gates of this marvellous possibility in *Princess Mononoke*, and then turned back down the old familiar roads. Perhaps he had too much unfinished business to explore to start a new venture, too many creative roads half-travelled to open up another new one. I also acknowledge that my own reading of the Miyazaki canon has changed over the years, shifting my view of his worlds from wide-eyed amazement at the wonderfully real and effective female characters he created to a more reasoned, and possibly more jaded, awareness of the limitations placed on these characters by their creator. But I would have liked to see him open up the possibilities he had created in San, instead of returning – retreating? – to the familiar world of cloud-castles and children's games.

Notes

1   Throughout this essay I use the family name Miyazaki to refer to Hayao Miyazaki unless otherwise indicated.
2   'Interview with Hayao Miyazaki', *Young Magazine*, 20 February, reprinted in Archives of Studio Ghibli, 1, 1996, p. 54.
3   Ryū Murakami, 'Murakami Ryū in Conversation with Hayao Miyazaki', *Animage*, November 1988, reprinted in *Shuppatsuten* [*Starting Point*] (Tokyo: Tokuma shoten, 1996). <http://www.nausicaa.net/miyazaki/interviews/heroines.html (accessed 17 April 2017).
4   *Mushi Mezuru Himegimi* (*The Princess Who Loved Insects*) is a Heian-era short story by an unnamed author.
5   Hideko J. Taniguchi, 'The Representation of the Child and Childhood in *The Princess Who Loved Insects*', Conference Paper, *22nd Biennial Congress of IRSCL*, University of Worcester, 8–12 August 2015.
6   Susan J. Napier, *Anime from Akira to Howl's Moving Castle* (New York: Palgrave Macmillan, 2005).
7   Earnest Callenbach, *Ecotopia: The Notebooks and Reports of William Weston* (New York: Bantam, 1975).
8   Clive W. Nicol, *Tree*, illustrator Hayao Miyazaki (Tokyo: Tokuma shoten, 1991).
9   Takayuki Karahashi, 'The Whimsy and Wonder of Hayao Miyazaki', trans. Takashi Oshiguchi, *Animerica Magazine*, August 1993, p. 55.
10 Maureen Murdock, *The Heroine's Journey* (Boston, MA: Shambhala, 1990).
11 Joseph Campbell, *The Hero with a Thousand Faces* (New York: Pantheon, 1949).
12 Rosemary Sutcliff, *The Mark of the Horse Lord* (Oxford: Oxford University Press, 1965).
13 Robert Graves, *The White Goddess: A Historical Grammar of Poetic Myth* (London: Faber and Faber, 1948).
14 Graves, *The White Goddess*, p. 242.
15 Steve Rose, 'Studio Ghibli: Leave the Boys Behind', *The Guardian*, 14 July 2011. https://www.theguardian.com/film/2011/jul/14/studio-ghibli-arrietty-heroines (accessed 21 June 2017).
16 Hayao Miyazaki, *Turning Point 1997–2008*, trans. Beth Cary and Frederik L. Schodt (San Francisco, CA: VIZ Media 2014 [2009]).
17 Tom Mes, 'Hayao Miyazaki', *Midnight Eye*, 11–23 December 2001. http://www.midnighteye.com/interviews/hayao-miyazaki/ (accessed 22 December 2016).
18 For full information on the fan theories concerning *Spirited Away*, see: online FanTheories Wiki. http://fantheories.wikia.com/wiki/Spirited_Away; Brammesz.

http://9gag.com/gag/aRgKKq7?ref=fsidebar and MoviePilot. https://moviepilot.com/posts/2297900 (accessed 12 December 2017).

19 Jonathan Clements and Helen McCarthy, *The Anime Encyclopedia*, 2nd edn. (Berkeley, CA: Stone Bridge Press, 2011), p. 289.

20 Diana Wynne Jones, *Howl's Moving Castle* (New York: Harper Collins, 1986).

21 Hans Christian Anderson, *Den Lille Havfrue* [*The Little Mermaid*], trans. H. B. Paull (USA: Hythloday Press, 2014 [1836]).

22 'Trailer', *Hakujaden* [*The White Serpent*], Toei, 1958. https://www.youtube.com/watch?v=cN0i8v9VTWE (accessed 21 June 2017).

23 Ben Ettinger, 'Two Pioneer Women Animators', *Anipages*, 11 November 2006. http://www.pelleas.net/aniTOP/index.php/notable_women_animators (accessed 2 January 2017).

Chapter 6

BEYOND GIRLHOOD IN GHIBLI: MAPPING HEROINE DEVELOPMENT AGAINST THE ADULT WOMAN ANTI-HERO IN *PRINCESS MONONOKE*

Alice Vernon

Many of the films of Studio Ghibli feature a child or young adult protagonist. In most of these cases, the audience is presented with a celebration of girlhood. From *Tonari no Totoro* (*My Neighbor Totoro,* Hayao Miyazaki, 1988) to *Omoide no Mānī* (*When Marnie Was There,* Hiromasa Yonebayashi, 2014), Studio Ghibli has explored the adolescent heroine in stories of fantasy, realism, comedy and drama. In *Mononokehime* (*Princess Mononoke,* Hayao Miyazaki, 1997), the heroine, San, is set against a female antagonist in such way that both personalities are problematized (for more on San's unique position within Ghibli's history see Chapter 5). It is through Hayao Miyazaki's inclusion of Lady Eboshi that the director examines the relationship between the heroine and an adult woman anti-hero. This chapter identifies the parallels between San and Lady Eboshi in terms of their personalities and interactions as well as in comparison with wider cultural contexts, in order to investigate *Princess Mononoke*'s exploration of femininity extending beyond girlhood.

The first part of this chapter analyses Miyazaki's presentation of San and Lady Eboshi in *Princess Mononoke*. From the similarities in their introductory scenes to the possible symbiotic nature of their relationship, this chapter discusses the ways in which Miyazaki demonstrates a spectrum of images of femininity within these two characters. The analysis will show how, through San's behaviour, Miyazaki both adheres to and deviates from constructed images of the girl princess. Regarding Lady Eboshi's character, this chapter focuses in particular on her self-sustaining community within the Tataraba, the iron works, and the various admirable roles she assumes – roles that complicate her identity as the supposed antagonist in the film. Despite her harmful quest to kill the *Shishigami* (Deer God), Miyazaki seems to construct Eboshi as a positive answer to various dark moments in history. Where she fails to take care of nature, she steps in to take care of those who are shunned by the rest of society.

In drawing parallels between the roles and the position of authority and independence occupied by Eboshi and San, this chapter puts forward the idea that Miyazaki is constructing a symbiotic female relationship. Through identification of the careful echoing of Eboshi and San's personalities, the analysis will discuss how *Princess Mononoke* establishes the importance of homosocial relationships during the shift from girl- to adulthood. Following this examination, the chapter compares Eboshi to the adult women featured in the subsequent works of Studio Ghibli.

A precursor to the relationship between San and Eboshi can be seen in Hayao Miyazaki's *Kaze no tani no Naushika* (*Nausicaä of the Valley of the Wind*, 1984, hereafter referred to as *Nausicaä*). Despite being released prior to the formation of Studio Ghibli as a company name, *Nausicaä* is an adaptation of Miyazaki's manga series (1982–94), and thus presents many of the themes that became key to Studio Ghibli's legacy. As adapted from Miyazaki's manga, the film involves a parallel between its protagonist Nausicaä and its villain, Kushana. Kushana's visual similarities to Nausicaä seem based on the idea of Kushana seeing her younger self as she ought to have been. Where, as this chapter argues, Eboshi represents San's adult independence, Kushana is a kind of 'ghost of Nausicaä's future' – she embodies the patriarchal views that Nausicaä rejected. In a society where the father is ruler of his household, Miyazaki emphasizes that it is important for young girls to maintain their own ideals if they do not agree with those forced upon them, using the heroine Nausicaä as his vessel. The dynamic between Kushana and Nausicaä, followed by Eboshi and San, shows a long-standing focus on women's representation in Miyazaki's films.

Whether the connection between San and Lady Eboshi has influenced recent fiction, or whether these women stand alone, their personalities and appearances in Miyazaki's *Princess Mononoke* are important to consider. Not only do they disrupt the distinction between socially constructed gender roles, they also present a spectrum of heroic female behaviours. Both Eboshi and San are ambitious caregivers and warriors who nurse the injured, some human, some not. In addition, San's wolf goddess mother, Moro, demonstrates the ferocity that can be located in maternal instincts. *Princess Mononoke*, therefore, encourages the viewer to expand their understanding of the heroine and the female villain character types.

Woman as Warrior, Nurse and Mother in Princess Mononoke

Released in 1997, *Princess Mononoke* is an historical fiction whose critical themes transcend the Muromachi period (1336–1573) in which it is set. Miyazaki is known for his ecocritical and pacifist approach to his stories (see Chapters 1 and 3), but these themes are made explicit in *Princess Mononoke*. As Kozo, Solomon and Chang explain, his films – particularly *Princess Mononoke* – involve the presentation of 'pseudo-historical environmental conflicts' that enable Miyazaki to 'draw viewers into the difficulties of real environmental problem solving'.[1] In other words, Miyazaki blends new anxieties into historical situations and settings, showing the timelessness of environmental issues as well as enlightening his audience by demonstrating modern problems from a different perspective.

The environmental questions of *Princess Mononoke* are the main and most immediately apparent of Miyazaki's criticisms. But, alongside and intermingling with the struggle between delicate ecosystems and poisonous but seemingly inevitable human development, there is an extensive deconstruction of female gender roles. Where San protects the forest, Lady Eboshi seeks to destroy it, but Miyazaki intentionally complicates the extent to which the women represent the fictional tropes of good and evil. As with his inclusion of environmental criticism, Miyazaki presents a bitter feud between these two female characters in a way that draws attention to some of the past and ongoing challenges faced by Japanese women.

In *Princess Mononoke*, San – a young girl raised by wolf gods in the forest – stands to defend her environment from corruption. With Miyazaki's stance on environmental preservation in mind, the audience might immediately assume that San is the inherently 'good' heroine against the destructive human force embodied in Lady Eboshi. But it is in Lady Eboshi that Miyazaki creates an antagonist *as* heroine. She is the leader of the Tataraba, a secluded island in a lake, which is dedicated to the production of iron and, more damagingly, the development and manufacture of guns. It is from a single ball of Lady Eboshi's iron that the plot of the film emerges; the boar god Nago, after being shot with one of the Tataraba's guns, turns into a ferocious and demonic *tatarigami*. Even before the audience knows her name, Miyazaki introduces Lady Eboshi through the destructive aftermath of her enterprise. By the motif of the iron ball alone, the audience perceives its maker as the villain of the film.

Of the two main female characters, it is Lady Eboshi whom the audience first meets. Keeping with the reputation that Miyazaki has loaded into the simple iron ball, the first image of Lady Eboshi is in her role as a leader. She is an authoritative, commanding figure whose grace and confidence is maintained during the mountain pass scene as she faces San and the wolves. Amid the chaos and fear of her male workers, Eboshi calmly holds her ground and fires a gun – an action that further embeds her association with the enraged *tatarigami* – at Moro, piercing the wolf goddess's flesh with the same iron that killed Nago. The audience's initial impression of Eboshi, then, further pins her to the role of villain. She is the formidable source of conflict in the story, and it is interesting that Miyazaki presents her as so immediately transgressive of the feminine ideal. In writing of Asian representation in Hollywood, Gina Marchetti explains that, in particular reference to Chinese-American cinema, there exists the 'fantasy' whereby 'Asian women are "saved" from the excesses of the Chinese patriarchy by Anglo-American heroes'.[2] By contrast, in just a short introduction, Lady Eboshi is shown to be an adult woman not in need of saving; rather, she is the dominant force among her group of men.

Following this introduction, however, Miyazaki takes pains to problematize Eboshi's character. Ashitaka comes across the wreckage of the mountain pass fight, and he rescues and returns two injured men back to the iron works. It is in the Tataraba that we see a rather different Eboshi to the cold and cunning woman on the mountain pass. She appears surrounded by smiling women, sincerely apologising to one of the wounded men and his wife, calling them both by name. She is both a matriarch and guardian who is as personable as she is formidable. Through Ashitaka's eyes while resting in the Tataraba, the audience sees a thriving and healthy community. Everyone he meets admires their matriarch, particularly the women, who are explained as having been rescued from brothels by Eboshi herself. This stands in contrast to Eboshi's introduction as the root of corruption in the world of the film.

Indeed, Eboshi's character seems to represent, but subsequently dismantles, the Japanese literary trope of 'poison women' stories (*dokufumono*). According to Christine L. Marran, these dangerous figures of feminine transgression were 'nondomestic' and 'sexually available' women, who were presented as a 'sick perversion of femininity and the antithesis of "progress," "evolution," "enlightenment" and "civilization."'[3] Eboshi is, in a literal sense, a 'poison woman' in that her actions lead to the pollution of the environment. However, Miyazaki presents Eboshi against this fictional trope because she has built a successful, self-sustaining civilization within the Tataraba. She also contributes to technological progress in the development and manufacture of guns. On the one hand, Eboshi is a figure of corruption. But on the other hand, she has the strength and independence to single-handedly establish new communities and trigger the progression of the iron industry.

It is interesting, then, that our first impressions of San can be analysed in much the same way. The scene that takes place shortly after the fight on the mountain pass parallels (albeit with a rather savage twist) the multiple sides Miyazaki presents in Eboshi's character. After the fiery conflict with Eboshi, San and the wolves retreat to the forest. Ashitaka, resting by a river, quickly hides as the injured clan emerge on the other side of the water. Moro snarls as San sucks and spits out the poisoned blood from her wound. The discs hanging from her ears delicately glint in the sunlight, which stands in stark contrast to the blood smeared across her face. The presentation of her character blends the fierce with the feminine, never dismissing one in favour of the other.

Later in the film, when Ashitaka is severely wounded and too weak to eat, San chews a piece of dried meat before pressing her mouth to his in order to feed it to him. This 'first kiss', like the red blood smeared across her mouth, is a strange parody of femininity – beneath the superficial contact between San and Ashitaka is a demonstration of primitive survival instincts and of nurturing behaviour that echoes the earlier scene in which San treats Moro's wound. Furthermore, in a later scene Ashitaka gives San his sister's necklace – a blue piece of crystal shaped like a sharp arrowhead. San holds it up and exclaims, 'It's pretty'. Miyazaki again demonstrates a natural blend between the tropes of ordinary girlhood and animalistic warrior, of the feminine and the feral, coexisting quite comfortably within San's personality.

San belongs to what Anne Allison describes as the 'warrior girls' subgenre in Japan.[4] This character trope, perhaps most famously observed in Naoko Takeuchi's *Sailor Moon* manga series (1991–97), depicts the combination of strength and style. The *Sailor Moon* girls are renowned for their sailor-style school uniforms, as well as for the accessories they wear upon transformation into their superhero alter egos. As Tamaki Saitō demonstrates, where these powerful, feminine characters appeal to teenage girls, they are also desired by adult men not just in terms of sexuality but also in response to a 'clothing fetish'.[5] The iconic transformation scenes in this genre, in which the young girl protagonist becomes magically equipped with her superhero outfit, are what Allison calls an 'intricate and intimate display of bodies'.[6] San, in *Princess Mononoke*, is a warrior girl in a more literal sense; as Susan Napier accurately describes, she displays 'virtually unrelenting violence'.[7] Aspects of her femininity are tangled within her ferocious image. Yet she is not without the potential to be seen as a sexual object. Indeed, as the film approaches its climax, San loses her cape and mask in parallel to Ashitaka's gradual removal of clothing. Eboshi, on the other hand, covers her head, hair and shoulders whenever she leaves the safety of the Tataraba. She only adds to her dress, further hiding her skin in order to defend it. The spikes and heavy gates around the Tataraba here extend to Eboshi's body; she presents a resistance to be infiltrated.

In a culture where just 4.9 per cent of women held company director and division chief positions in 2007, this presentation of Eboshi as the successful figurehead of a business is absolutely crucial to remember in conjunction with the multiple roles taken up by Eboshi throughout the film.[8] Miyazaki shows Eboshi as both an inventor and warrior, but also as a kind of nurse and even, perhaps, a messiah. In her secret garden, Eboshi personally tends to lepers who, in turn, work to produce the guns with which she can 'rule the world'. Her treatment of lepers involves a type of care and intimacy that some would shrink from, which is a fascinating idea when compared with the previous scene where San sucks blood from Moro's wound. Miyazaki creates intricate layers of similarity through these details. As Napier argues, he 'defamiliarizes' our ideas of what is acceptable in a woman, challenging the ways in which we would normally categorize them.[9] He brings into question the extent to which anyone could separate the two women as heroine and villain, when they share a markedly similar outlook on life and family in their respective social spheres. Where contemporary Japanese women, particularly those employed in corporations, occupy a liminal space in society, *Princess Mononoke* emphasizes the central status of San and Eboshi in their liminal communities. They exist on the outskirts of civilization, but Miyazaki celebrates their power and influence on wider society.

The main fight between San and Eboshi is one of the most memorable in that it works exclusively to examine the complex relationship between the two women. Indeed, Miyazaki does not present them as enemies with a *mutual* hatred towards each other. San attacks the Tataraba in darkness, with Ashitaka present. She is feral and ferocious, quick-footed and scrabbling her way across the roofs of the Tataraba to stab at Lady Eboshi while her rage possesses her. Eboshi, on the other hand, behaves almost like a long-suffering mother. She trivializes San's rage, disempowering her through her calm, mature appearance. Indeed, when word of San's attack reaches her, Eboshi responds with a rather amusingly non-committal 'oh well'. Subsequently, Eboshi smirks as they clash daggers, seeming to humour San. Her fighting style is more of a performance or a dance, which neutralizes the threat of San's erratic, instinctive stabbing movements. Ashitaka, disturbed by the violence with which San and Eboshi clash, brings their fight to an abrupt end by stunning them with the hilt of his sword. Before he intervenes, however, he says to Eboshi: 'There is a demon inside you. And in her.' This suggests that they are both as destructive and narrowly focused as the *tatarigami* that attacked Ashitaka's village. Here, Miyazaki highlights the similarity between San and Eboshi's capacity for rage. It also demonstrates the way in which neither woman suppresses their anger for the sake of maintaining ideals of gentle femininity. In *Princess Mononoke*, Miyazaki provides space for his main female characters to behave unreservedly and to act on their emotions regardless of intensity.

By including this scene, Miyazaki presents an encapsulation of Eboshi and San's relationship as a whole; it is simply another fight in a timeline of conflict that commenced a long time before the story began. There is a sense of history between them, of endless stalemate that neither seems to *want* to win. This is emphasized by Lady Eboshi's lack of concern at San's infiltration into the Tataraba. Indeed, it is almost as though Lady Eboshi meets with San to accommodate the girl's rage. It could even be argued that Eboshi's crucial 'oh well' suggests that Eboshi fights San because San *needs* to vent her frustration. In this way, Eboshi accepts the roles San assigns her; in San's eyes, Eboshi is the synecdoche for human greed and pollution. In attacking Eboshi, then, San not only attacks the humans who destroy the forest, but also the parents who flung her as a baby at Moro's feet.

An additional way of interpreting the conflict explores San's own feelings of alienation and abandonment. As Eboshi says of San, 'She lives to kill me.' Eboshi, on the other hand, protects and heals the weaker members of society. She provides a haven for sexually abused women, and treats lepers with the care they deserve. The Tataraba, for Eboshi, is a community that welcomes the socially neglected – a community which could very easily include San. Lady Eboshi recognizes San as human, and seems to suggest that she is also concerned with San's condition once she succeeds in destroying the forest. In telling Ashitaka that 'that girl will be human', Eboshi has neither the expression nor the words of a woman similarly living to kill her nemesis. Not only does

Miyazaki show Eboshi as San's adult Other, but rather touchingly presents a kind of unspoken, symbiotic feminine relationship that demonstrates a bond between women that can exist despite and stretch beyond their social positions. The dynamic aligns with what Sarah Appleton Aguiar demonstrates as the female protagonist recognising that the female 'villain' figure is 'a necessary part of herself'.[10] Regardless of their opposed communities, Eboshi as an adult woman represents San's possible future; San both needs and is destined to become Lady Eboshi.

Both San and Lady Eboshi protect the abused. In San's case, this means protecting the forest and its creatures (herself included) from the greedy and destructive ways of humans. Eboshi, for San, seems to represent everything San fears and despises. Eboshi is the ultimate greedy and destructive human. But, again, Miyazaki problematizes what initially appears to be a straightforward struggle. Miyazaki, through Eboshi's character, seems to bring into focus several more recent issues despite the film's historical setting. When Eboshi brings Ashitaka into her secret garden, he is introduced to the Tataraba's community of people suffering with an aggressive disease. Speaking at Tokyo's International Leprosy/Hansen's Disease Symposium on World Leprosy Day (31 January 2016), Miyazaki confirmed that the illness in *Princess Mononoke* is leprosy. In this scene, the more able-bodied are shown to be constructing the very guns that are destroying the gods of the forest, and that will shortly sever the *Shishigami*'s head from its neck. It was only after the first International Conference about Leprosy in 1897 that led Japanese physicians to provide better care and support to leprosy patients and establish leprosarium in Japan.[11] Prior to this, lepers were known to suffer banishment and isolation, wandering endlessly and, according to Sato and Narita, 'making colonies of their own'.[12] Lady Eboshi's garden could be said to be a colony of this sort. The lepers in the film are shown to be grouped together in a hut separate from the rest of the Tataraba. They are bandaged, and some are sleeping or huddled under reed blankets. When Lady Eboshi walks among them, there is a sense of familiarity, mutual respect and gratitude.

The scene in Eboshi's garden is perhaps the most intentionally complicated moment in the film. It problematizes Eboshi's image, not just for the audience but for Ashitaka, too. Eboshi presents to Ashitaka her informal leprosarium, but it is the lepers themselves who, unsolicited, defend Eboshi's character. Osa, the worst afflicted member of the group, strains himself to defend Eboshi's case with the little strength he has. His face is completely covered in bandages, and he coughs as he struggles to speak. He urges Ashitaka not to think badly of the Tataraba's matriarch, explaining that 'she washed [the lepers'] rotting flesh' and was 'the only one who looked upon [them] as human'. Miyazaki is highlighting here the stigma that surrounded leprosy sufferers in Japan. For instance, as Susan L. Burns explains, it was public opinion that leprosy 'threatened the Japanese nation and empire', leading to mass segregation that was only repealed in 1996.[13] It is interesting, then, that Eboshi – who wants to 'rule the world' – is unperturbed by lepers and their supposed threat to civilization. She creates a safe space for them, and allows the more able sufferers to contribute to the progress of her guns. It is a poignant moment in which Miyazaki deliberately makes his audience question their categorization of the film's good and evil characters, and subsequently their culturally dictated opinions of independent women.

In addition to the colony of lepers, for whom Eboshi is a 'nurse' figure, Miyazaki creates a haven for women within the Tataraba. During the scene in which the men of the iron works tell stories of Lady Eboshi to Ashitaka, they speak of her preoccupation with buying up the contracts of 'every brothel girl she finds' and inviting them to work for her in the Tataraba. But this is not a level exchange of ownership; the women are employed in the iron works, but they have freedom and are shown on numerous occasions to be enjoying themselves. Where many women in nineteenth- and twentieth-century Japan were obliged to take piecework (*naishoku*) that demanded exceptionally long hours for little pay,[14] Miyazaki presents a community of women who 'eat their fill' and are financially supported in a comfortable and safe environment. Indeed, whenever Lady Eboshi and the women workers of the Tataraba interact, it is with an interesting blend of familiarity and respect. Eboshi treats the women as her equals, as her friends, and the women seem eager to please, and ferociously quick to defend, their employer. Further to this, Miyazaki presents Eboshi as re-empowering the women through work. Rather than buying their contracts to introduce the women to continued subjugation in a different environment, Eboshi seeks to give them back their dignity by allowing them the use of the guns they help to create.

In fact, she *specifically* creates weapons for the Tataraba's women to hold, as demonstrated in the scene in Eboshi's garden. There, Eboshi holds and tests a newly made gun, but asks its maker to reduce the weight so that the women can use it securely. Miyazaki's narrative decision here could be seen as a criticism of early twentieth-century high-school practices that involved encouraging girls to aim to raise their future sons to become 'strong and powerful soldiers in Japan's military'.[15] In an amusing parody of this idea, Miyazaki shows Eboshi arming the women under her care with guns manufactured by lepers. She raises strong and powerful soldiers, forming a kind of military force within the Tataraba, but it is made of previously disenfranchised members of the culture outside Eboshi's community.

The Tataraba can be analysed in relation to the post-war treatment of women in yet another way. Following Japan's surrender and the end of World War II in August 1945, the US Occupation began with the mission to turn Japan into an American ideal of a 'modern, democratic and enlightened nation'.[16] One of the ways in which General Douglas MacArthur instigated the 'modernization' of Japan was through the introduction of reformed policies regarding women's position in society. On the whole, the relationship between Japanese and American worked well. Indeed, it worked perhaps a little *too* well for the comfort of male occupiers and their heterosexual policies. As Koikari describes:

Japanese middle-class women enthusiastically welcomed the occupiers' reform project and embraced American discourses of democracy and gender equality. On the other hand, however, they also developed a close personal bond with American women reformers, deviating from the Cold War tenet of heterosexual normativity by creating a female homosocial sphere and causing anxiety among American male occupiers. Even Japanese women's resistance often resulted in ambiguous and unpredictable outcomes.[17]

The 'female homosocial spheres' outlined by Koikari could be compared to Eboshi's community of emancipated prostitutes in the Tataraba. On several occasions throughout the film, Miyazaki makes explicit a male anxiety regarding the freedom and independence of the iron works' women. For example, while it is a fairly harmless grumble, the men blame Lady Eboshi for the way the Tataraba's women behave. When Ashitaka joins the men in the hut, they tell him that Eboshi 'spoils' the women by treating them as her equals and ensuring that there is no gender disparity within the community. Miyazaki illustrates that there are culturally influenced dialogues of sexism within the Tataraba, but importantly demonstrates that there is no such limiting hierarchy in place within the community. It is this equal power balance between the sexes that leads Ashitaka to describe the Tataraba as a 'happy town'.

San might see Eboshi as a villain, but Eboshi is also a kind of villain to the rest of Japan. With this in mind, Miyazaki draws yet another parallel between Eboshi and San. San is a human among wolves: a biologically different member of her society. Similarly, Eboshi is a kind of metaphorical wolf among humans – as a figure of power, she stands alone in opposition to the culture she has rejected. For example, during a scene where a representative of the Emperor comes to deliver a message to Eboshi, she allows a group of women to mock and shoot at the men. The purpose of the tall enclosure of the Tataraba, defended with heavy gates and wooden spikes, becomes more understandable; Eboshi has separated her community from the rest of the Japan, and the hostile appearance of the Tataraba represents her unwillingness to be a part of wider society. As she declares to Ashitaka: 'I fear humans more than forest gods.'

There is a third crucial female character in *Princess Mononoke* who presents another critique of culturally constructed femininity: the wolf goddess Moro. As with Lady Eboshi and San, Miyazaki frequently displays an intertwining of femininity and power in Moro's character. On the one hand, Moro is a *yama no kami* – a mountain spirit in the form of a wolf; she is huge and snarling, and her two tails give another uncanny feature to her already threatening presence. But on the other hand, she is as maternal as she is ferocious. This duality relates to Japanese folklore, particularly what John Knight describes as 'the wolf's purpose not to prey but to protect' in stories where a wolf guides a lost traveller through the mountains.[18] During several scenes, Moro is shown to be intensely protective of her two cubs and of San. Talking to Ashitaka, Moro tells him the story of how San came to be her 'daughter': Moro caught two humans defiling the forest, and when threatened by her, the humans 'threw their daughter at [her] feet'. Rather than eat the baby – as the parents intended in order to gain a chance to escape – Moro raises San as her own half-animal, half-human child.

By including this short scene, Miyazaki creates another important criticism of feminine gender roles. He appears to demonstrate that the human preoccupation with fashioning an ideal image of motherhood, and the emphasis on the sanctity of a hetero-normative marriage, as represented in San's birth parents, is a superficial set of expectations that become redundant in the face of danger. When San is being consumed by the demonic rage writhing from within Lord Okkoto – the boar God – Moro snarls, 'Give me back my daughter!' She then buries her muzzle inside the foul corruption erupting from Okkoto's face in order to retrieve San, regardless of the fact that she is exposing herself to the poison.

Moro's relationship with San is, in other words, another ironic presentation of femininity. It further exemplifies the idea that the liminal status of women in *Princess Mononoke* acts as an interrogation of female gender roles in Japanese media and culture. Where Lady Eboshi is independent, childless, and in a position of power, San demonstrates an alternative depiction of girlhood. Neither Eboshi nor San is constricted by ideals of the *shōjo* (young girl, often related to anime and manga characterization) aesthetic.[19] But it is through Moro, the female beast, that Miyazaki celebrates an image of motherhood. It could be argued, then, that Miyazaki represents the mother-identity in Moro to emphasize a *natural* image of the maternal. It is an image of maternity as it should be, discarding the influences of socially constructed expectations and consumerism. In Moro, Miyazaki presents a female creature who is demonstrably more intelligent and wiser than most of humanity, but whose maternal behaviour remains a pure, successful, primal instinct.

As the film progresses, the audience witnesses Lady Eboshi become increasingly drawn to her own damaging ambition. Like the *hamartia* (fatal flaw) of Greek tragedy, the world around Eboshi narrows to the *Shishigami* seen along the barrel of her gun. Ignoring all warnings, she shoots at and severs the head of the powerful forest spirit, plunging the surrounding environment into chaos and decay. While Eboshi's determination echoes the doomed characters of classical theatre, Miyazaki also seems to draw parallels to a hero of Japanese tradition: Yamato Takeru (ca. first century AD). According to the legend as interpreted by Ivan Morris, Takeru climbed a mountain in the province of Shimano, where, while taking a short rest, the mountain god 'took this opportunity to torment the Prince, and, changing himself into a white deer, came and stood before him'.[20] Yamato Takeru does not have as brutal a weapon as Eboshi, but he throws a clove of garlic at the deer, 'hitting the animal in the eye and killing it'.[21] It conjures a remarkably similar image to the scene in which Eboshi finally gets her chance to kill the god of the forest who, like the mountain god who appears before Takeru, takes the shape of a deer. But where this display of human power transcending the gods raises Yamato Takeru to status of 'hero', in Eboshi's case it only serves to reduce her to a powerless fool.

The concluding scenes of *Princess Mononoke*, however, demonstrate a new beginning not only for the forest but for Lady Eboshi and the residents of the Tataraba. Through losing her arm, Miyazaki literally 'disarms' Eboshi, and keeps her from further damaging the environment. But it is crucial to note that he does not destroy her. Indeed, just as the forest sprouts new grass over the wasteland, Eboshi promises to build a new community – a 'good village' – that coexists with nature and the wild creatures that inhabit it. This is a short but important moment. Miyazaki could have ended Eboshi's story with her death or a drastic loss of agency that represents the fall of the power-hungry woman. Instead, he shows Eboshi's recognition that her ambition was misguided, and the audience is presented with a glimpse of a new story for Eboshi and her community.

San and Eboshi's Dynamic in Subsequent Studio Ghibli Films

Before the release of *Princess Mononoke*, many of Studio Ghibli's adult women existed in the margins of the stories. The mother in *My Neighbor Totoro*, for example, not only resides in the liminal space of the hospital, but is also on a threshold between sickness and health. Her role in the film is brief; it is her condition, rather than her character or her personality that is important for the child protagonists Mei and Satsuki. Other adult women before *Princess Mononoke*, including the sky pirate captain Ma Dola in *Tenkū no shiro Lapyuta* (*Castle in the Sky*, 1986) and songstress Gina in *Kurenai no buta* (*Porco Rosso*, 1992) are less ambiguously situated within Miyazaki's narratives: the former functions as an irascible mother, while the latter performs as Marco's love interest. The development of Lady Eboshi as a complex adult woman character, then, showed a development of female representation in Studio Ghibli films.

Despite the emphasis placed on Eboshi's character and her ability to lead a community, Studio Ghibli's focus has largely remained on the young girl protagonist, especially when moving beyond considerations of Hayao Miyazaki's films. The mother in *Neko no ongaeshi* (*The Cat Returns*, Hiroyuki Morita, 2002), for instance, has an incredibly minor part in the film. And while the adults in *Gake no ue no Ponyo* (*Ponyo*, 2008) have a bigger role, they also seem to exist solely in their image as parent-figures. But there are subsequent Studio Ghibli films where significance is given to the adult woman. Within Miyazaki's subsequent films, perhaps the most obvious example is *Hauru no ugoku shiro* (*Howl's Moving Castle*, 2004), in which young Sophie is cursed by the Witch of the Waste into an old woman. Here, the girl and the adult woman collide; although both exist as one person. Horrified by her elderly appearance, Sophie ostracizes herself and stumbles into the company of Howl in his moving castle. Similarly to *Princess Mononoke*, then, *Howl's Moving Castle* depicts its female character surviving in a liminal space, and celebrates Sophie's determination in spite of her curse, although, unlike San and Eboshi, this survival relies upon a more traditionally realized romance narrative.

The 'final' film produced by Studio Ghibli, *Omoide no Mānī* (*When Marnie Was There*, Hiromasa Yonebayashi, 2014), for example, re-emphasizes the most important aspects of girlhood that Studio Ghibli has sought to promote over the years. Anna, a young teenager overwhelmed with depression, is sent to a rural town to recover. There, she meets Marnie, a girl her own age whose similar loneliness seems to soothe Anna's wounds. Adapted from Joan G. Robinson's 1967 children's novel, and directed by Hiromasa Yonebayashi, *When Marnie Was There* constructs a homosocial friendship between Marnie and Anna.[22] While of a very different tone to the dynamic presented in *Princess Mononoke*, the film presents a similarly intense bond to that of San and Lady Eboshi. As suggested earlier in this chapter, Eboshi seems to exist for the benefit of San – as an image of her older self, but also as a scapegoat and target for San's anger regarding both environmental destruction and her own abandonment. Indeed, Eboshi recognizes her own role in San's life. Similarly, just as Marnie understands her obligation to draw Anna out of her depression, Anna comes to realise her role in mitigating Marnie's loneliness.

Further to this, encouraged by her interactions with Marnie, Anna adapts into the role of older sister and role model to Sayaka, who is similarly without a female relationship. Further, it is in the company of an elderly female artist, Hisako, that Anna finds a safe space to practise her painting. San's interactions with Eboshi are intense because Eboshi is the only other human woman with whom she has contact. *When Marnie Was There*, however, demonstrates a host of different female relationships that, transcending age and backgrounds, show a mutual dependence on each other, more akin to the female relationships in *Majo no takkyūbin* (*Kiki's Delivery Service*, Hayao Miyazaki, 1989). Eboshi does not appear to need San with equal ferocity, but *When Marnie Was There* seems to develop the female bond further by presenting a strong web of relationships where women rely on other women for a variety of reasons.

The relationships demonstrated by *When Marnie Was There* stand in contrast to Isao Takahata's masterpiece *Kaguya-hime monogatari* (*The Tale of Princess Kaguya*, 2013). As with most of Studio Ghibli's films, Princess Kaguya, the mythical girl-protagonist, is the pivotal heroine of the story. It is not a happy film, but seems to emphasize Studio Ghibli's theme of social bonding. Kaguya, forced by her parents into a role of nobility away from her childhood friends and community, visibly suffers as a result of her isolation. In the city, she has no strong connection to anyone, much less to a homosocial sphere. It is this loneliness that contributes to her dramatic escape from the confines of nobility.

Where at first it seems difficult to find a similar relationship to that of San and Lady Eboshi in more recent Ghibli films, this character-pairing has influenced a healthier sort of female dynamic. Rather than present female characters in a kind of symbiotic conflict, subsequent Studio Ghibli films appear to have put forward much more mutual, beneficial female relationships (for more, see Chapter 5). Eboshi, in a way, represents an image of San's adult self – demonstrating that her independent girlhood can continue in a similar way to how Lady Eboshi both commands and cares for her people. More recent stories such as *When Marnie Was There*, then, reflect *Princess Mononoke*'s exploration into real, complex femininity but also illustrate the importance of female relationships and social acceptance.

Conclusion

This chapter has explored the symbiotic dimension to the relationship between San and Lady Eboshi in *Princess Mononoke*. As the analysis has demonstrated, Miyazaki gives the adult woman a significant space in which to display autonomy and strength. In *Princess Mononoke*, he makes redundant the tendency to pin demonizing labels to the independent woman. Eboshi might be the film's antagonist because of her attempts to destroy the forest, but Miyazaki problematizes her role as 'villain' by demonstrating her own heroic qualities. On one hand, the community of the Tataraba manufactures iron and guns to spread chaos and pollution, but it also functions as a refuge for the socially ostracized. Miyazaki creates a commentary through Eboshi's character that celebrates the adult woman as leader, worker, inventor and caregiver. In Eboshi, he demonstrates that a woman can have prowess in several roles at once, and in more than just roles that are assigned by gender. Furthermore, while he critiques the object of Eboshi's ambition, through presenting images of the Tataraba community he also shows how progressive and beneficial Eboshi's leadership can be. Eboshi is no friend to the environment, but, with semblance to San's frequently voiced opinion, Miyazaki demonstrates that she has no faith in humanity either. Like San, Eboshi is alone. Throughout the film, and despite the damage their conflict creates, Eboshi exhibits interest – even concern – for San and her place in the world.

This chapter has argued that Eboshi is a future mirror for San; a living vision of the kind of woman she can become in spite of their diametrically opposed positions in culture and despite the social constrictions that continue to oppress women's aspirations. Eboshi is a demonstration of what a woman can achieve when she feeds – rather than stifles – her ambition, and where that ambition is at first misguided, Miyazaki concludes the film by showing Eboshi's determination to re-establish her strong community. As an adult woman, then, Eboshi serves as a kind of handle to which young girls could cling before the anime medium further developed the idea of symbiotic relationships. *Princess Mononoke*, then, highlights space in the medium for successful female representation that emphasizes a progressive view of the options available to women. Through including these characters, Studio Ghibli presents the audience with the idea that autonomous girlhood, developing into autonomous womanhood, is something to be celebrated.

Notes

1 Mayumi Kozo, Barry D. Solomon and Jason Chang, 'The Ecological and Consumption Themes of the Films of Hayao Miyazaki', *Ecological Economics*, vol. 54, no. 1 (2005), p. 6.

2 Gina Marchetti, 'Guests at *The Wedding Banquet*: The Cinema of the Chinese Diaspora and the Rise of the American Independents' in Chris Holmlund and Justin Wyatt (eds), *Contemporary American Independent Film: From the Margins to the Mainstream* (London: Routledge, 2005), p. 185.

3 Christine L. Marran, *Poison Women: Figuring Female Transgression in Modern Japanese Culture* (Minneapolis: University of Minnesota Press, 2007), p. 10–11.

4 Anne Allison, 'Sailor Moon: Japanese Superheroes for Global Girls' in Timothy J. Craig (ed.), *Japan Pop! Inside the World of Japanese Popular Culture* (New York: M. E. Sharpe, 2000), p. 261.

5 Saitō Tamaki, *Beautiful Fighting Girl*, trans. J. Keith Vincent and Dawn Lawson, (Minneapolis, MN: University of Minnesota Press, 2011), p. 57.

6 Anne Allison, *Millennial Monsters: Japanese Toys and the Global Imagination* (Berkeley, CA: University of California Press, 2006), p. 120.

7 Susan J. Napier, *Anime from Akira to Princess Mononoke: Experiencing Contemporary Japanese Animation* (New York: Palgrave Macmillan, 2001), p. 182.

8 Peter Matanle, Kuniko Ishiguro and Leo McCann, 'Popular Culture and Workplace Gendering among Varieties of Capitalism: Working Women and Their Representation in Japanese Manga', *Gender, Work and Organization*, vol. 21, no. 5 (2014), p. 473.

9 Napier, *Anime from Akira to Princess Mononoke*, p. 185.

10 Sarah Appleton Aguiar, *The Bitch Is Back: Wicked Women in Literature* (Carbondale and Edwardsville: Southern Illinois University Press, 2001), p. 6.

11 Hajime Sato and Minoru Narita, 'Politics of Leprosy Segregation in Japan: The Emergence, Transformation and Abolition of the Patient Segregation Policy', *Social Science and Medicine*, no. 56 (2003), p. 2530.

12 Sato and Narita, 'Politics of Leprosy Segregation in Japan , p. 2530.

13 Susan L. Burns, 'Rethinking "Leprosy Prevention": Entrepreneurial Doctors, Popular Journalism, and the Civic Origins of Biopolitics', *The Journal of Japanese Studies*, vol. 38, no. 2 (2012), p. 298.

14 Kathleen Uno, 'One Day at a Time: Work and Domestic Activities of Urban Lower-Class Women in Early Twentieth-Century Japan' in Janet Hunter (ed.), *Japanese Women Working* (London: Routledge, 1993), p. 41.

15 Melanie Czarnecki, 'Bad Girls from Good Families: The Degenerate Meiji Schoolgirl' in Laura Miller and Jan Bardsley (eds), *Bad Girls of Japan* (New York: Palgrave Macmillan, 2005), p. 52.

16 Mire Koikari, *Pedagogy of Democracy: Feminism and the Cold War in the U.S. Occupation of Japan* (Philadelphia: Temple University Press, 2008), p. 2.

17 Koikari, *Pedagogy of Democracy*, p. 5–6.

18 John Knight, 'On the Extinction of the Japanese Wolf', *Asian Folklore Studies*, vol. 56, no. 1 (1997), p. 136.

19 Napier, *Anime from Akira to Princess Mononoke*; Susan J. Napier, 'Vampires, Psychic Girls, Flying Women and Sailor Scouts: Four Faces of the Young

Female in Japanese Popular Culture' in Dolores P. Martinez (ed.), *The Worlds of Japanese Popular Culture: Gender, Shifting Boundaries and Global Cultures* (Cambridge: Cambridge University Press, 1998), pp. 91–109.

20 Ivan Morris, *The Nobility of Failure* (New York: Holt, Rinehart and Winson, 1975), p. 8.
21 Morris, *The Nobility of Failure*, p. 8.
22 Joan G. Robinson, *When Marnie Was There* (London: Harper Collins, 2014 [1967]).

Part 3

A TRANSNATIONAL PRINCESS: THE
ADAPTATION, PROMOTION AND RECEPTION
OF *PRINCESS MONONOKE*

Chapter 7

THE TRANSLATION AND ADAPTATION OF MIYAZAKI'S SPIRIT PRINCESS IN THE WEST

Jennifer E. Nicholson

In 2009, 10 years after the Miramax release of *Princess Mononoke* in dubbed English, author Neil Gaiman was interviewed about a particularly interesting aspect of his involvement in the translation project. When interviewer Steve Biodrowski mentioned 'issues with Miramax' about word choices in the trans-lation, Gaiman responded that they 'got to keep "samurai,"' which had at once point been 'warrior', but that their script 'lost "sake"; "sake" became "wine."'[1] The word is used in passing, once, in the scene where the Lady Eboshi apolo-gises to the men making rifles, and promises to 'have wine sent down later'. If the script had used *sake* instead, what would change? At first glance, any anxiety about the word's translation seems unnecessary. While *sake* is a particular kind of rice wine, different to 'wine' in the way the word is more commonly used in English, Eboshi's offer remains equivalent across the two languages: she will make sure they receive a drink after their work is done. Conversely, *sake*, unlike Western wine, can be served hot or cold, has a much higher alcohol content, and, while it is a specifically Japanese type of wine, can refer to the equivalent English word 'liquor'. If the film's audience is Anglophone, and predominantly American, are these details necessary, or do they detract? What begins as a question of preference – the extent to which Miramax and others wanted to retain what Biodrowski calls a 'Japanese flavour in the dialogue'[2] – becomes a source of anxiety not only about this particular instance of translation, but about translating meaning at all.

Anxiety about translation is a cornerstone of discourse concerning repre-sentations of Japanese media in Anglophone countries. *Princess Mononoke*, or もののけ姫 (*Mononokehime*, Hayao Miyazaki, 1997), displays this even in its title, where *mononoke* (spirit or monster) is left untranslated, and the princess's name left unsaid. This is one of several instances where the film's international publicity relies on an adaptation that drastically alters the refreshing aspects Miyazaki portrays. His work is visually stunning and cinematically advanced for 1997 (as discussed by Rayna Denison in this book's introduction). The film's bildungsroman narrative is familiar yet new for a Western audience, rejecting the tired plotline of a young protagonist's search for a romantic counterpart, alongside the gendered expectations that accompany it. However, Miramax's translation and adaptation of the script greatly affect the film's representation for Anglophone viewers. I suggest that this exemplifies the *mononoke* of translation anxiety. While 'the 21st century is a translation century', and Gaiman's translation work can be commended for its international accessibility, the transformed film is a limited version of the original.[3] However, young viewers particularly have engaged enthusiastically with the film, a fact not unnoticed by Miyazaki himself: 'I realised, ". . . this is something that children must see," because adults, they didn't get it – children understood it.'[4] I propose that the film's unstable status between languages provides a position for spectators, particularly young viewers, to recognize the shifting subjectivities in our translation century.

I will argue that the *mononoke* of translation anxiety is exemplified by the extensive transformation *and* adaptation of both language and culture evident in parallel comparisons between the Ghibli and Miramax versions of Miyazaki's 1997 film. In particular, the final Miramax script, written by Gaiman with assistance from translator Steve Alpert, exemplifies the cultural division between the versions. While *Princess Mononoke* offers interesting commentary on humanity's relationship with nature, it does so differently in its distinctive Anglophone iterations. The two versions, *Mononokehime* and *Princess Mononoke*, create a sense of cultural vertigo for the Anglophone viewer who has seen both, enhancing the sense of instability that is frequently present in translated works. This final point of instability will allow me to draw conclusions concerning the prevalence of uncertainty in what Avadesh K. Singh calls today's 'translation century',[5] through what Susan Napier describes as 'the cinema of deassurance'.[6] Singh suggests that those 'who would survive in this knowledge century . . . [are those] that will learn from others'.[7] As such, the film invites cross-cultural understanding, particularly in young viewers, even as it presents violence and plurality, rather than a fairy tale ending.

Those translating *Princess Mononoke* for an English audience were required to have their work approved by Studio Ghibli prior to its Western release. In an interview only two months after the dubbed film's release in America, Miyazaki told interviewer Toshifumi Yoshida that 'the deal [with Miramax] from the beginning was that there would be no cuts'.[8] While both Alpert and Gaiman strove for a text that would 'give a new identity to this Japanese film', Rayna Denison suggests that 'Miramax undertook . . . a project of indigenisation for *Princess Mononoke*'s American release.'[9] The effect was both translation and adaptation, as the film shifted fluidly between Japanese and American languages *and* cultures.

As mentioned above, *mononoke* is not the princess's name, but to the Anglophone viewer of *Princess Mononoke* this is not immediately evident. The girl's name is San – homonymous with both 三 (three) and さん, an honorific that follows Japanese names[10] – and is separate to her identity as part of the spirit world. In the English title, her name, the marker of identity, is lost because of a difference in the way the two languages work. Having the honorific 'princess', while leaving *mononoke* untranslated, makes the English reader think that her name is 'Princess Mononoke'. As in Jacques Derrida's discussion of Babel, where 'it is in translation that we most often read [the narrative] . . . [so a] proper name retains a singular destiny, since it is not translated in its appearance as proper name',[11] San's name is obscured. Her name marks her as the *third* child of the wolf goddess, Moro, and as the respected princess, soon to be inheritor, of the forest. Although she is human, she is the bridge between humans and nature, seemingly neither one nor the other; San is a *third* category of forest inhabitant, and thereby a spirit-human residing in the natural world. *Mononoke*, by contrast, obscures her actual name with an untranslatable 'name', and thereby obscures her identity by merging it with her role in the narrative. This hindrance to translation exemplifies the overarching effect of the film's English transformation for the West. The title exemplifies a marketing choice that evokes Disney princesses, even though the film is directed at slightly older audiences. While an artful film in its own right, Miramax's *Princess Mononoke* is more prominently an adaptation than a translation of Miyazaki's work.

'What's It Mean?':[12] Translation as Acculturation

The Miramax transformation of *Princess Mononoke* exemplifies the cultural divide between their audience and Ghibli's, alongside the anxiety of translating its language. The result is a script that alters or reduces the narrative in some scenes, and over-explains in others. Gaiman's explanation of his process in interviews reveals how the Miramax translation is a significantly altered version of the film. Given a raw, word-for-word translation by Alpert, Gaiman says that he '*translated the translation* into lines that [voice actors] could say'.[13] This resulted in the differences expected in a translation project, such as when Alpert's literal translation gave the phrase 'his head is mine', and Gaiman 'would be wondering, hang on, does "His head is mine" translate in this context as "He's mine to kill," or do they literally mean, "I'm going to be keeping his head as a trophy?"'.[14] Gaiman also comments that he sometimes wanted to make the translation more elegant, and that jokes in particular had to be changed in order to cross the cultural boundaries between audiences: '*why* something is funny doesn't necessarily translate. You have to go and find something that is the *emotional equivalent*'.[15] This creates an interesting parallel with Napier's review of anime fans at the University of Texas, where she quotes an anonymous student: 'Disney animation is "pretty," but it lacks the emotion of anime'.[16] This question of emotional equivalence in translation greatly affects the Miramax film; the emotional intensity characteristic of Miyazaki's work is altered by changes in the script.

Although credited with the English script, Gaiman says that the final version of the film includes lines and scenes that he did not write, or altered versions of what he wrote. Many of these examples are understandable choices of one word over another, such as when *sake* becomes 'wine', but Gaiman also comments on the fact that both 'Japan' and 'China' are cut from the final English dub script.[17] It is hard to see this as anything but an attempt to displace the film for English-speaking viewers, as if the setting is another fantastical world outside reality, and not Japan's Muromachi period. Gaiman also wonders why, in the Emishi village, Kaya is identified as Ashitaka's sister in his script, saying he does not remember the translation mentioning this, nor making this decision, even though she calls Ashitaka *ani* (brother) in the Japanese dialogue. Most interesting is Gaiman's comment that 'nobody seemed to know where that had come from', which suggests either that the translated script did not include this detail, or that the translation team with whom Gaiman spoke were not aware of it.[18]

These inconsistencies become stranger still when considering Miramax's process in finalizing their script:

> [T]o this day, I don't know where some of the lines in that film came from . . . it's all rather mysterious . . . I got a list of corrections from Studio Ghibli on one script, at the same time as I got the Miramax corrections on that script. And what they wanted were two totally different sets of things . . . I ended up sitting down and writing . . . the Miramax draft and the Ghibli draft, and [said:] . . . Go fight it out amongst yourselves. [*laughs*] And they did.[19]

This conflict exemplifies the anxiety surrounding translation in both the original and target languages' film studios. Vincente L. Rafael suggests that American monolinguism, stemming from its 'historical wishfulness for . . . monolingual citizenship', drives the nation's anxieties about translation.[20] He argues that there is an 'unassailable link between American English and American nationality conceived as synonymous with American democracy', and this appears evident in the transformation of *Princess Mononoke* for American viewers.[21] These script alterations for the largely US North American Anglophone market reveal this anxiety, modifying not just the words but also the narrative progression.

Denison observes a similar national anxiety when commenting on the voice actors chosen for the dub. Though the dress and history related by *Princess Mononoke* may well be Japanese in origin, this nationality is filtered through America, as the film's overall "voice" becomes nationally conflicted. The manner in which audiences hear *Princess Mononoke* therefore deeply impacts on their understanding of the film's cultural and national meanings.[22] Gaiman, Rafael and Denison's comments exemplify the unavoidable tension faced by the writers of both the subtitle *and* dub scripts. Watching the subtitled *Princess Mononoke* allows for the Anglophone viewer to comprehend the narrative, but their aural experience of the film is at odds with the visual. This imbalance, combined with comparative *in*experience with Japanese language and culture, results in a kind of anxiety for the viewer, who has no means by which to fully comprehend the text, filtered as it is by an inevitably imperfect translation. This is perhaps the unconscious reason for why many viewers, unfamiliar with the differences between subtitled and dubbed audio-visual texts, express a preference for dubs. Alternatively, watching the English language dub of the film is less unstable in that the aural and visual cues are more accurately aligned. However, emotional equivalence cannot be directly translated either, and the result is a film with characters reinvented by new voice actors, as well as a different cultural tone. The dubbed text comes at the price of what Denison terms the film's 'indigenization' for America and, more broadly, the Anglophone world.[23] This acculturation could be, conversely, the very reason that viewers who are more familiar with the instability of translation driven by culture prefer subtitled texts. Preferences aside, comparing each of *Princess Mononoke*'s English language versions reveals that Studio Ghibli's subtitles prioritize the overall narrative progression and message of the film, while the Miramax dub does this alongside their project of acculturation for their primarily US audience.

The opening eleven minutes of Miramax's *Princess Mononoke* serves to clarify details for its Western viewers, as well as providing English text that matches the characters' animated mouths. The resulting over-explanation of characters or narrative events continues throughout the film. A noteworthy and striking difference to the original in the film's opening is the addition of a voice-over to slow panning shots of the forest, when no speaker is on-screen. Studio Ghibli's subtitles include a single unspoken sentence: 'In ancient times, the land lay covered in forests where from ages long past dwelt the spirits of the gods'. However, the Miramax version includes this line in voiceover, and adds further details: 'Back then, man and beast lived in harmony, but as time went by, most of the great forests were destroyed. Those that remained were guarded by gigantic beasts who owed their allegiance to the great forest spirit. For those were the days of gods, and of demons.' The final word, 'demons', coincides with a glimpse of the swarming curse surrounding the *tatarigami* (cursed boar god), directly followed by the film's title overlaid on a carved rock face. While this additional prologue material lays foundations for a Western audience, it alters the effect of the film's opening. The *tatarigami* and mystery of the forest are identified prematurely; rather than evoking mystery and suspense, the voiceover clarifies the setting and mythology of the film, at the expense of muddying the revelation of the narrative.

Also early in the film, when Ashitaka speaks with Kaya and the others girls, Ghibli's dub reveals their conversation as heavily reliant on gaps and a lack of knowledge:

Ashitaka:	Oracle says to get back to the village.
Kaya:	The old man, too. He says something's wrong.
Girl 1:	No birds ...

Girl 2:	No animals . . .
Ashitaka:	I'll go to him. You get back home.
Girls:	Okay!

The scene draws in the viewer to wonder what is 'wrong' without identifying what kind of trouble is imminent. Inversely, the Miramax script fills the gaps in the dialogue above with explanatory material. Ashitaka not only tells the girls to return to the village, but says that 'there's something strange going on' and that the girls 'have to hurry' home. Denison suggests that it is not only the alterations and additions to Ashitaka's lines, but also Billy Crudup's 'unremarkable, average voice' that allows Ashitaka to represent the 'most American of heroic types'.[24] What she describes as the figure of an 'average man achieving extraordinary things' exemplifies the way that Ashitaka's character is translated not only through the words he says but also in his role within the narrative.[25] This subtle change characterizes Ashitaka as more protective than in Studio Ghibli. His final words to the girls also reinforce his more protective characterization: 'I'll go to the watch tower and check with Jōsan. Now you three hurry back home, and be quick about it.' Although Miramax's Ashitaka does not know exactly what the demon is, he seems far more assured that there is something physically there, that he should go to the watchtower and that the girls should return to the village. His certainty remains in place when he spots the demon from the watchtower – he is quick to tell his companion that he '[has] to stop it' – but falters, uncertain, when faced with the demon itself: '*whatever you may be*, god or demon, please leave us in peace!'.[26]

Ashitaka's oscillation between complete and incomplete comprehension of the situation mimics the translation process in earlier scenes. The wise woman's prediction that he will die from the curse prompts Ashitaka to leave the Emishi village. In the Ghibli script, Ashitaka shows his arm to the village men, who are shocked. The oracle explains that 'the scar will seep into [his] bones and [he] will die', but that he can seek out the source of the boar's curse, far in the west. The villagers mourn that 'the youth who was one day to lead [them] must journey far to the west'. Ashitaka then cuts his hair as one of the men weeps, and the oracle reminds him that 'the law forbids [them] to watch' as he leaves. However, the Miramax script expands each of these major points. In fact, a side-by-side comparison of any scene shows the Miramax script to be notably longer than the Ghibli translation.

The two most obvious additions are at the beginning and end of this scene. Upon seeing Ashitaka's unwrapped arm, a villager asks, 'What's it mean?', a question answered for the benefit of Ashitaka, the villagers, *and* the non-Japanese viewers; the assumption is made that the visual cues alone are unclear. The village elder and oracle's words explain not only their loss but also the meaning of his departure:

Villager:	Now our last prince must *cut his hair and* leave us, *never to return? Sometimes I think the gods are laughing at us.*

Oracle:	Our laws forbid us from watching you go, Ashitaka. *Whatever comes to pass now, you are dead to us, forever.* Farewell.

The italics above indicate additions to the dialogue that are not present in the Ghibli subtitles. These explanations of spirits and their world continue when Ashitaka rescues the two ox drivers from the river. Kōroku's initial terror at the appearance of a *kodama* is somewhat allayed when Ashitaka explains to him – and, by extension, the audience – that it is a 'tree spirit . . . [that] brings good luck'. This acculturated description evokes a sense of almost mysticism; for viewers whose cultural paradigm generally excludes mythical creatures from the real world, this explains to them not just the spirits' presence in the forest but their presence the narrative. However, in the Ghibli translation, he simply says that the *kodama* are 'a sign the woods are healthy'. This focuses the viewer on the environmental concerns that will become more prevalent as the film progresses, rather than the spirituality of the world in which it is set.

As well as these explanatory lines, the Miramax script has multiple additions that alter the progression of the film's plot. This is particularly evident in the way that this script sometimes anticipates the Ghibli subtitles and explains characters or ideas earlier than in the original film. When Kōroku panics about the *kodama* in the scene above, he is afraid of them '[bringing] their lord . . . a huge monster!', but does not explain that what he fears is the *Shishigami* (Deer God). In the Miramax scene, he explains his fear to Ashitaka and simultaneously reveals the identity and appearance of what he fears: 'it's like a huge enormous deer. Except they say it's got a human face sometimes, and then at night they say it –' he says, before screaming as more *kodama* appear. This introduces the *Shishigami* before Ashitaka sights it in the following scene. Kōroku remains afraid of the *kodama* in both versions, but while Studio Ghibli's script has him afraid of only them, the Miramax Kōroku is afraid of the forest and other spirits, too: 'Did I ever mention that no humans have ever made it through these woods alive?' When they step into the forest clearing, Ashitaka's voice actor Billy Crudup sighs and says, 'this place is magical!', as a panning shot of the forest frames Ashitaka's perspective. This is particularly noteworthy as it does not replace or expand upon an existing line from the Ghibli script, nor does it serve to fill in a 'gap' where a character's mouth moves otherwise silently; this line is added to explain that the clearing is special in some way. The word 'magical' cues Western viewers to treat the film as pure fable, rather than as a historical, though mythical, tale.

The overt explanation exacerbates the effect of earlier Miramax additions to this scene, and detracts from the visual cues already present. As the characters step into the glade, the stillness and the glassy water are immediately obvious as otherworldly. Ghibli's subtitles complement the sense of mystery that pervades the scene, and the contrast between Kōroku's fear and Ashitaka's calmness intrigues the audience without necessitating explanation. After spotting '[fresh] tracks . . . [with] three toes', the audience sees through Ashitaka's eyes, once again panning across the forest to spot the deer walking between the trees, bathed in golden light. At this point in the film, the Studio Ghibli subtitles have revealed almost nothing about the *Shishigami*. This moment is visually beautiful, yet eerie, as Ashitaka gazes at the silhouetted figure only for his cursed arm to spasm painfully and force him to look away.

However, before Miramax's Ashitaka spots the deer, the anxious Kōroku suggests that they 'took a wrong turn somewhere' and calls the clearing 'a place for gods and demons'. This phrase, which appears frequently in the Miramax script as a description for the spirits, implies a black-or-white moral code held by these 'demons' and 'gods', respectively.[27] Furthermore, the Miramax dub has already identified the *Shishigami* prior to this scene, as discussed above. The mysteriousness of the deer between the trees is thereby altered twofold in the Miramax script. When Ashitaka spots the silhouette of the many-antlered deer, the audience also sees the 'monster' that Kōroku greatly fears, *and* hears Ashitaka's cry of pain as his arm suddenly hurts. The above scenes all occur within the first half hour of the film, and reinforce the simultaneous translation and adaptation present in the Miramax dub. The early revelation of the *Shishigami* alters the effect of this scene and, in combination with the implied moralities granted to spirits, seems to indicate this particular spirit's cruel responsibility for the prince's curse, not Eboshi, who first cursed Nago. The audience is already privy to Lady Eboshi's destructive relationship with the forest and the spirits, via a previous scene in which she shoots at the wolf goddess, Moro. It is only once Ashitaka reaches Tataraba, or Iron Town, that a proper explanation is given for Nago's, and thereby Ashitaka's, curse. With these specific additions in mind, I turn to the film's representation of nature and morality side-by-side, and consider how the messages it brings to the fore are different between the two versions of Miyazaki's film.

'This Is How You Kill a God': Translating Morality and Reverence

Both as *Mononokehime* and *Princess Mononoke*, the film offers insightful commentary about humankind's relationship with nature, a theme prevalent in much of Miyazaki's work. Napier argues that the film 'offers a vision of cultural dissonance, spiritual loss, and *environmental apocalypse*' and that the audience floats in a 'liminal, mythic space' as viewers, even though the setting is historical.[28] Miramax once again presents an alternate version of events to the Ghibli subtitles, and this is exemplified by different Japanese and US cultural relationships with both nature and the apocalypse genre. Napier observes how this is evident, saying that 'although Miyazaki can be fruitfully compared with Disney', each studio's use of 'cultural myth' is very different.[29] After the completion of *Majo no takkyūbin* (*Kiki's Delivery Service*, Hayao Miyazaki, 1989), Miyazaki described the creation of *Princess Mononoke* as 'a *huge* risk'.[30] He asked, 'how could we pretend to [children] that we're happy?', and worked to create a film that was pessimistic about humankind's relationship with nature.[31] Nature is portrayed as both calm – as in the spirit glade – and violent – as in the boars' raging stampede – in equal measures. Miyazaki's pessimism about humankind within nature is emphasized through the near-constant presence of weaponry to combat political, but also spiritual, violence, and the latter of these evokes the violence of Miyazaki's, and our, context of environmental destruction.

Ashitaka's tribe, the Emishi, are shown to live alongside nature, such as when, after Nago's death, the Emishi wise woman's respectful promises to build a pyre for his body exemplifies a sense of respect for nature. The contrast with Tataraba is immediate upon Ashitaka's arrival at the town and his tour around the iron works. Eboshi is diametrically opposed to the Emishi oracle and seeks to destroy and disrespect the natural world in favour instead of what nature can provide, by whatever violent means, to maintain the town. Eboshi's disrespect stems from irreverence towards the gods. In the Ghibli subtitles her assertion, 'this is how you kill a god', indicates Eboshi's certainty in being able to kill a deity, and thereby implies her sense of self-importance at odds with the natural world (for more on Eboshi's characterization, see Chapter 6).

In the English dub this conflict is maintained, but in a different light. There are instances in which the translation does not attempt to over-explain, and instead creates gaps in the Western audience's understanding. Eboshi's ruth-lessness is depicted respectfully, as if dominating the forest and suppressing its deities are to be admired in the Miramax script: 'I'm going *to show you how* to kill a god.' This addition of 'to show you how' alters the focus of her words away from her own importance and instead towards the ultimate strength and violence of humankind, represented by the Tataraba and the priests, against the forest, the *Shishigami*, and nature in general. This shift in perspective exempli-fies a difference between the two scripts. Studio Ghibli's subtitles evoke human-ity's disrespect towards nature as something irreverent, while the Miramax dub represents the same disrespect, but with far more emphasis on human war-mongering, rather than the spiritual aspect of this violence.

Analysing American anxiety about remaining a 'monolingual nation', Rafael argues that 'translation is [. . .] weaponised for the sake of projecting American power abroad while insuring security at home'.[32] He suggests that the simulta-neous anxiety to push for 'foreign language acquisition' in America stems par-ticularly from Cold War history.[33] As such, the Miramax adaptation of *Princess Mononoke* represents this anxiety even in its attempts to create an amalgam between cultures that have been historically at odds, particularly since 1941. It signifies Rafael's assertion that 'Babel is the spectre that haunts American English . . . [and reforms] the hierarchy of languages of which monolingual citizenship rests.'[34] America's conflict-riddled transnational relationship with Japan thereby comes inadvertently to the fore in this English language version of the film, as the Ghibli subtitles seem not to be enough for the American audience to comprehend its narrative. The violence of Rafael's theory also infers that there is something to be said for the crossover between 'nature' and '*human* nature'. To a lesser extent than Ghibli's subtitles, Miramax's *Princess Mononoke* conjures images of violence from both 'natures' but allocates different moralities to each of them.

The common comparisons of Studio Ghibli to Disney, also mentioned earlier, become problematic here. The moral perspectives regarding humanity's responsibility towards nature appears to shift: Disney's history of fairy tale films lends itself to portraying morality as concrete, while 'Miyazaki always casts a shadow of doubt over absolutes'.[35] Critic Ernest Hardy observed something similar, suggesting that 'the film's strength lies in its refusal to paint either its arguments or its characters in black and white . . . [with] no pure heroes [or] clearcut villains'.[36] The character closest to what might be considered a moral 'good' is Ashitaka, who displays 'an almost tragic naivety' towards the violence already festering between nature and humankind.[37] His 'grand idealism' presents an exaggeration of a morality that Miyazaki implies is untenable in an apocalyptic setting, juxtaposed against the apparently unstoppable curse that Ashitaka gains from fighting Nago.[38] His cursed scar exemplifies the 'cursed' world into which Miyazaki's young viewers are born.[39] However, Miyazaki has said that *Princess Mononoke* 'is something that children *must* see' because unlike adults, 'they [understand] it'.[40] The scar that spreads over Ashitaka's body forces him to stand against the violence of both humankind and nature towards each other, at the expense of a serious threat to his life. Miyazaki seems to urge his young viewers to do the same.

Napier suggests that 'the film's conclusion . . . is a kind of draw, with neither side triumphant';[41] even though Ashitaka is eventually healed, it is at the cost of the *Shishigami*'s life, sacrificed for the continuation of the forest's life. Tara Judah argues that 'films aimed at audiences still in their formative years have the power to either reinforce or challenge established stereotypes' and that while 'Disney has traditionally done the former, Ghibli engages with the latter.'[42] Unlike a fairy tale ending 'San's refusal to live with Ashitaka and her decision to stay in the forest ensure that a sense of loss or absence inevitably permeates the film's conclusion.'[43] Miyazaki, through *Princess Mononoke*, among his other films, implores his viewers to consider 'plurality and otherness [as] basic [features] of human life', rejecting a clear moral path on which the film's protagonists could tread.[44] Rather, the moral black and white implied in Gaiman's phrase 'gods and demons' is replaced by characters who are 'like us as we really are . . . the good guys have bad qualities and the bad guys have good'.[45]

Miyazaki's antagonists, unlike Disney's, 'aren't *pure* evil', and this applies to each character, antagonist or otherwise, and particularly to San.[46] She represents a true grey area in morality within the narrative, as she is the mediating figure between humans and nature while remaining somewhat disconnected from each side. However, San is 'just as volatile as Eboshi', as the princess is 'unable to exercise control over her emotional responses'.[47] This is evident in contrast with her mother Moro's peace when accepting her death. Although the wolf goddess remains angered by Eboshi and humankind's violence, Moro ultimately maintains that the *Shishigami*'s power to '[give] life, and [take] it away' is as it should be. Judah describes San's actions as '[resembling] those of a petulant child', and it as if this childishness represents humankind's immature and senseless attitude towards nature, as opposed to the attitude held by her mother.[48] However, San is ultimately the mediating figure that 'belongs to both worlds'.[49]

This moral grey area and San's duality are modified through the translation and adaptation of her characterization. When she insists 'I hate humans!', the voice acting in the Miramax script alters the effect of this singular line from San. Claire Danes' delivery is angry, yet seems calm and simply sad in comparison with Yuriko Ishida's enraged, biting tone of voice when she says the equivalent line in Japanese. However, the duality that is apparent in the Japanese translation is dulled in the Miramax script itself, too. Napier argues that this is more typical of Western media, where there is a tendency to '[gloss] over the inconvenient facts of . . . cultural complexity'.[50] The emphasis on magic and fictional otherworldliness, rather than the possibility of a plural reality, means that San is portrayed as wild but determined, rather than possessed by a literal or figurative spirit of nature. While she gains agency as 'a new figure for leadership and hope' after the *Shishigami*'s death, she appears to remain static as she returns to her life in a rejuvenated forest.[51] Judah argues that 'San . . . is the only one who can mediate between species', but in the Miramax script her lower spiritual status, stemming from the fairy tale lens through which the narrative is shown, confines the fluidity of her character.[52] Because 'such fluidity is what allows her to embody this titular role, guiding us spiritually and bridging two worlds', San's characterization as a 'spirit princess' seems flatter and less evocative than in the Ghibli script.[53] However, conversely, her role as an anti-*shōjo*, alongside the other female characters, functions similarly between the two Anglophone scripts.

'The Wild Girl Whose Soul the Wolves Stole': Translating the Voice of an Anti-shōjo

Like much of Studio Ghibli's work under Miyazaki, *Princess Mononoke* rejects stereotypes about femininity that pervade both the East and West in different ways. The film is refreshing in its dismissal of romantic resolution, and the female characters' roles in the plot work against over-feminization and unnecessary sexualization. Napier describes 'the classic *shōjo*', or young girl character, as 'usually characterized by an ultrafemininity that is often passive or dreamy . . . or perhaps ditzy'.[54] San, Moro and Eboshi are all warriors who seek to protect their own and fight for their convictions. Napier suggests that rather than being hyperfeminine, these three 'possess a gender-neutral, or at least deeply ambiguous, characterization compared to traditional female stereotypes'.[55] She also writes that 'San and Eboshi in particular depart from [Miyazaki's] more typical [*shōjo*] heroines in a variety of intriguing ways.'[56] These choices allow Miyazaki to explore 'steadfast, empowered, and independent' characters and in turn force the audience to notice qualities 'at a level of perception that a more conventional male protagonist would be unlikely to stimulate'.[57] In addition to the characters' traits as part of the plot, the Japanese voice acting cast for these three characters successfully evoke strong moments of female power. Additionally, actor and drag queen Akihiro Miwa's role as Moro anticipates the anti-*shōjo* characters, with a deep voice that cuts through the lighter tones of most other characters. For example, when facing the boar invasion, Moro's growling assertion, subtitled 'the Deer God gives life, and takes it away. Have you boars forgotten even that?', utilizes Miwa's deep voice to great effect in the confrontational scene between Moro and Okkoto's clans. Miwa's role as the wolf goddess evokes the ambiguity associated with femininity and the anti-*shōjo* throughout the film.

Furthermore, the physicality of each character adds to their strength and reject oversexualization and hyperfemininity. Moro's strength is first shown in her status as a wolf but also as a deity. From her first appearance charging fearlessly towards Eboshi and her Tataraba men, armed with guns, Moro remains regal even until her death near the conclusion of the film. While the other two wolves, her sons, are drawn as large, but perhaps lifelike, Moro is a giant wolf, much like the other hulking animal-deities in the film. This emphasizes her control over the forest, under the dominion of the *Shishigami*, and visually indicates her authority. Like each of the deities who speak, her mouth does not move with her words and, instead, she growls and bares her teeth, daring her enemies to attack. Even Eboshi observes that harming Moro with one bullet will not kill her, and applies the same idea when trying to kill the *Shishigami*, too. Moro's threatening size and depiction also accentuate her potential violence both as a wolf and as a maternal figure towards San. In the Ghibli subtitles, Moro calls San her 'poor, ugly, lovely daughter', as the camera focuses on Ashitaka's face through Moro's eyes. The frame then shifts to Ashitaka's perspective as Moro asks, derisively, 'can you save her?'. This second shot frames only her face and the fearsome teeth that she bares in Ashitaka's face, emphasizing the potential danger she is to him even as she speaks about the stereotypically gentle idea of motherhood. Moro's characterization, as the embodiment of both potential violence *and* motherhood, draw together multiple ideas that destabilize female stereotypes.

San's first appearance in the film, smeared with blood on her hands and mouth, and cloaked in fur and teeth, evokes a wildness that she maintains throughout the film; 'although she has moments of softness . . . the viewer is most likely to remember [this] first appearance in the film'.[58] The original promotional posters, proclaiming her title in blood-red Japanese script across her mother's white fur, exacerbate the effect of this powerful image, as Ashitaka's *first* sighting of San is the viewer's *second*, and Ashitaka recalls this moment once again when Eboshi first mentions 'the wolf princess' or '*mononoke*', in the Miramax and Ghibli versions respectively. In the latter, Eboshi's words evoke the specifically untameable and non-human aspects of San's character, further alienating her from female stereotyping, and even from her status as a human: 'That girl will *become* human.' San's clothing is loose fitting and, although her body is clearly female, her physicality is animalistic, neither human nor feminine, unlike the 'classic *shōjo*' that Napier identifies.[59] Her anti-*shōjo* status is only further exacerbated by the existing gender fluidity found in Moro's characterization discussed above, and in the fact that San is also characterized *physically* as wolf-like.

However, female characters' autonomies shift with the introduction of the Miramax dub, even though their physical appearances remain the same. The first way in which this occurs is once again through the English language voice actors. As in many of the English versions since *Princess Mononoke*, 'star voices have been used to drastically alter perceptions of Studio Ghibli's films'.[60] Moro's characterization shift in the Miramax script is not unnoticed by Gaiman himself, as he acknowledges the changes he made to Moro's words throughout the film, achieved through a similar effect as in the opening voiceover: 'one of the reasons I love all the Gillian Anderson-Moro stuff so much is it's mine . . . because *we didn't have to match lip movements*, so you could actually hear the rhythms of my dialogue'.[61]

As has already been mentioned, Claire Danes' performance as San produces a critical difference between the Japanese and American versions through her vocal tone. Unlike Moro's lines, Danes' role as San alters the effect of many of her lines. In his 1999 review of the film, Andy Klein describes Danes' voice as 'horribly out of place', and argues that San 'sounds like a whiny suburban teenager'.[62] This is perhaps too harsh, but her delivery of lines like 'I hate humans!' creates the much softer characterization of a San who is unhappy rather than angry, or 'whiny' rather than tough. David Edelstein makes a similarly harsh comment: '[Danes] sounds like a Valley Girl peeved over lack of parking spaces at the mall'.[63] Whether consciously or not, he has recognized the significance of the adaptation, not just the translation, of San's character, proposing that she 'needs a more ragged voice' and that he would be 'interested to hear the original Japanese actress'.[64] Additionally, Minnie Driver's almost-pitying tone implies that San is a victim when she describes her soul stolen by wolves, though critics have generally treated her performance with more regard than Danes'. The Anglophone cast thereby alters the characters even before script differences are taken into account. Denison suggests that the script itself also contributes to this sense of the film being 'no longer Japanese but [instead a] *star-spangled* Japanese-American [co-production]', which 'greatly [aided] Miramax's apparent efforts to indigenise this distinctly Japanese film'.[65] The 'star-spangled' aspect of the film enhances these voice acting alterations, as the casting choices represent the existing Western (American) media expectations. This is particularly evident in light of the female characters' roles in the Miramax film, where

multiple instances of voice acting seem to distort and diminish female characters' agency.

To return to Eboshi's description of San is also to observe another difference in the latter's role in the Miramax film, that of her status as human. When
Ghibli's Eboshi calls her a 'wild girl', she suggests that San has less agency as a
member of the Moro clan because her soul was stolen by the wolves. Studio
Ghibli's script reads as follows:

Eboshi:	That girl will be human.
Ashitaka:	Who?
Eboshi:	Mononoke, the wild girl whose soul the wolves stole.[66]

The small changes to Eboshi's words in the Miramax script alter the secondary
meaning behind her conversation with Ashitaka:

Eboshi:	Princess Mononoke will become human.
Ashitaka:	Princess Mononoke?
Eboshi:	Princess of the spirits of ghouls, beasts and ancient gods. The wolves stole her soul and now she lives to kill me.

In directly identifying San as 'Princess Mononoke' and elaborating on her non-
human characteristics, Driver's role as Eboshi suggests that San is victimized
and lacks agency as a result of her stolen soul.

However, San's agency is in fact found in her non-human identity: 'Shut up!
I'm a wolf!' San's anti-*shōjo* characterization is metaphorically represented by
her insistence that she is a wolf, not a human who is confined by expectations.
In both scripts, when Ashitaka asks for her help to return the *Shishigami*'s head,
Ashitaka identifies that he is human, and that San is too. However, she rejects
not only his plea for help, but also his insistence that she fulfil the role of femininity in their relationship as human boy and human girl. In the Miramax
script she distances herself even further from her humanity: 'I hate *all of you*
humans.' Napier observes that, at the conclusion of the film, while San and the
forest 'do not exactly triumph, they are also not entirely defeated'.[67] She argues
that San and Eboshi 'exist in their own right, independent of any male interloc-
utor . . . [and that] these independent women are not domesticated by marriage
or a happy ending, but are instead interested in living separate but presumably
fulfilling lives'.[68] San, in comparison with other *shōjo* characters from Miyazaki's
oeuvre, overshadows the others in both her strength and liminal qualities, but
as discussed above, translation and voice acting tether her to the role of victim. In doing so, the anxiety found in translating *Princess Mononoke* for the
West does not only exist because of the translation itself. Ghibli's 'princess' is
no Disney princess, but the Miramax adaptation, including the translation, has
produced a kind of hybrid adaptation between the two.

Conclusion

Each of the ideas discussed in the three sections above – those of acculturation, the natural world and gender – result in a sense of linguistic vertigo for a viewer who has seen both versions: in watching one translation, they recall the other. Although the main narrative, characterization and visual aspects of the film remain the same, the cumulative effect of the differences in translation produces an *adaptation* of the Ghibli film, not just another Anglophone version.

Napier suggests that *Princess Mononoke* fits into what she calls 'the cinema of deassurance', and that the film 'creates a world that appears to have some kind of historical basis but then consistently *destabilises* audience expectations'.[69] The film's representations of nature and of gender already embody this destabilization as Studio Ghibli highlights the moral grey areas and uncertainties in the narrative. Montserrat Rifà-Valls proposes that 'the violence of the film [destabilizes] the audience through the construction of identity as otherness, which is presented in . . . multiple layers'.[70] Coupling violence with otherness evokes 'deassurance', as well as emphasizing the plurality between the human and spiritual worlds. Napier suggests this when she asserts that unlike 'American cultural hegemony, Japanese society remains deeply aware of plurality and otherness', and argues that *Princess Mononoke* 'reflects the extraordinary array of pluralities . . . [in the] complex world of the twenty-first century'.[71] This plurality is reflected in the film's conclusion, which is 'the opposite of the inclusionary ending of [a] Disney work'.[72] Moreover, the instability of this cinematic deassurance remains, and is even exacerbated, in the Miramax adaptation.

In an increasingly transnational world, Miyazaki recognizes that his viewers, young and otherwise, live in an uncertain world. His statement on the film's English language website reveals the way that the Muromachi setting embodied an alternative to the current century: 'it was a more fluid period . . . [when] the borders of life and death were more clear-cut . . . without the ambiguity we find everywhere today'.[73] This fluidity and instability reflected in the characters and setting of *Princess Mononoke* is specifically affected by the translation undertaken by Miramax, adding another layer of ambiguity through which to view the film. In Judah's words, while both Anglophone films are titled *Princess Mononoke*, 'the film is not actually about a princess named Mononoke'.[74] Hardy describes the film as 'strung with late-20th-century fear and anxiety'.[75] Twenty years after its original release, in our 'translation century',[76] Gaiman's dialogue has even been retranslated for its Japanese audience and 'become the Japanese sub'.[77] The Miramax adaptation results in an acculturated translation that grapples with the ambiguity both of the princess and *Princess Mononoke* itself. In turn, the fluidity between these *mononoke*-like versions of the film epitomizes the anxiety that pervades all translation.

Notes

1 Steve Biodrowsky, 'Changing Sake into Wine – Neil Gaiman on Adapting "Princess Mononoke" for America', *Cinefantastique Online*, 5 February 2009. http://cinefantastiqueonline.com/2009/02/changing-sake-into-wine-neil-gaiman-on-adapting-princess-mononke-for-america (accessed 9 May 2016).
2 Biodrowsky, 'Changing Sake into Wine'.
3 Avadesh K. Singh, 'Translation Studies in the 21st Century', *Translation Today*, vol. 8, no. 1 (2014), p. 5.
4 Dan Jolin, 'Back Story: Miyazaki on Miyazaki', *Empire*, September 2009, p. 119.
5 Singh, 'Translation Studies in the 21st Century', p. 5.
6 Susan J. Napier, *Anime from Akira to Princess Mononoke: Experiencing Contemporary Japanese Animation* (New York: Palgrave Macmillan, 2001), p. 180.
7 Singh, 'Translation Studies in the 21st Century', p. 6.
8 Miyazaki quoted in: K. Yoshida, 'National Identity (Re)Construction in Japanese and American Animated Film: Self and Other Representation in *Pocahontas* and *Princess Mononoke*', *Electronic Journal of Contemporary Japanese Studies* (September 2011), Article 5. http://www.japanesestudies.org.uk/articles/2011/Yoshida.html (accessed 17 June 2017), p. 6.
9 Rayna Denison, 'Disembodied Stars and the Cultural Meanings of *Princess Mononoke*'s Soundscape', *Scope: An Online Journal of Film Studies*, vol. 3, no. 1, (November 2005). http://www.nottingham.ac.uk/scope/documents/2005/october-2005/denison.pdf (accessed 30 January 2017), p. 2.
10 Tara Judah, '*Princess Mononoke*: Transgressing the Binaries That Bind', *Screen Education*, no.74 (2014), p. 61.
11 Jacques Derrida, '*Des tours de babel*' in Joseph. F. Graham (ed.), *Difference in Translation* (Ithaca, NY: Cornell University Press, 1985), p. 171.
12 Quotations from *Princess Mononoke* are transcribed from the film's DVD via the English subtitles provided by Studio Ghibli, some transcription of the Japanese voice actors, *and* the dialogue of the Miramax dub.
13 Gaiman quoted in: Biodrowski, 'Changing Sake into Wine', my emphasis.
14 Gaiman quoted in: Emru Townsend, 'Neil Gaiman: The *Sandman* Scribe on Anime and Miyazaki', *The Critical Eye*, 8 November 1999. http://purpleplanetmedia.com/eye/inte/ngaiman.php (accessed 9 May 2016).
15 Gaiman quoted in: Biodrowski, 'Changing Sake into Wine', my emphasis.
16 Napier, *Anime from Akira to Princess Mononoke*, p. 251.
17 Biodrowsky, 'Changing Sake into Wine'.
18 Biodrowsky, 'Changing Sake into Wine'.
19 Gaiman quoted in: Townsend, 'Neil Gaiman'.
20 Vincente L. Rafael, 'Translation, American English and the National Insecurities of Empire' in Lawrence Venuti (ed.), *The Translation Studies Reader* (Abingdon: Routledge, 2012), p. 461.
21 Rafael, 'Translation, American English and the National Insecurities of Empire', p. 458.
22 Denison, 'Disembodied Stars', p. 12.
23 Denison, 'Disembodied Stars', p. 2.
24 Denison, 'Disembodied Stars', 8.

25 Denison, 'Disembodied Stars', 8.
26 Throughout the emphasis within quotations is mine, unless otherwise stated.
27 However, the morality that plays out in the film remains ambiguous and grey, and will be further discussed later in this chapter.
28 Napier, *Anime from Akira to Princess Mononoke*, pp. 176, 178.
29 Napier, *Anime from Akira to Princess Mononoke*, p. 282.
30 Jolin, 'Back Story', p. 120.
31 Jolin, 'Back Story', p. 120.
32 Rafael, 'Translation, American English and the National Insecurities of Empire', pp. 455, 453.
33 Rafael, 'Translation, American English and the National Insecurities of Empire', p. 453.
34 Rafael, 'Translation, American English and the National Insecurities of Empire', p. 462.
35 Judah, '*Princess Mononoke*', p. 56.
36 Ernest Hardy, 'Animating the Century', *L.A. Times*, 27 October1999.
37 Judah, '*Princess Mononoke*', p. 57.
38 Judah, '*Princess Mononoke*', p. 57.
39 Miyazaki quoted in: Jolin, 'Back Story', p. 120.
40 Jolin, 'Back Story', p. 120. Miyazaki's desire for children to watch *Princess Mononoke* is evident from its Japanese title; *mononoke* is written in *hiragana* (phonetic characters) so that his younger viewers can read the title for themselves.
41 Napier, *Anime from Akira to Princess Mononoke*, p. 189.
42 Judah, '*Princess Mononoke*', p. 61.
43 Napier, *Anime from Akira to Princess Mononoke*, p. 189.
44 Napier, *Anime from Akira to Princess Mononoke*, p. 192.
45 Anonymous student interviewed in: Napier, *Anime from Akira to Princess Mononoke*, p. 251.
46 Judah, '*Princess Mononoke*', p. 56.
47 Judah, '*Princess Mononoke*', p. 57.
48 Judah, '*Princess Mononoke*', p. 57.
49 Judah, '*Princess Mononoke*', p. 59.
50 Napier, *Anime from Akira to Princess Mononoke*, p. 192.
51 Judah, '*Princess Mononoke*', p. 61.
52 Judah, '*Princess Mononoke*', p. 61.
53 Judah, '*Princess Mononoke*', p. 61.
54 Napier, *Anime from Akira to Princess Mononoke*, p. 124.
55 Napier, *Anime from Akira to Princess Mononoke*, p. 182.
56 Napier, *Anime from Akira to Princess Mononoke*, p. 182.
57 Napier, *Anime from Akira to Princess Mononoke*, p. 126.
58 Napier, *Anime from Akira to Princess Mononoke*, p. 182.
59 Napier, *Anime from Akira to Princess Mononoke*, p. 124.
60 Rayna Denison, 'Star-Spangled Ghibli: Star Voices in the American Versions of Hayao Miyazaki's Films', *Animation: An Interdisciplinary Journal*, vol. 3, no. 2 (2008), p. 144.
61 Gaiman quoted in: Biodrowski, 'Changing Sake into Wine'.
62 Andy Klein, 'Gods almighty', *Dallas Observer*, 4 November 1999. http://www.dallasobserver.com/film/gods-almighty-6396860 (accessed 16 May 2016), p. 3.

63 David Edelstein, 'Machines in the Garden', *Slate*, 29 October 1999. http://www. slate.com/articles/arts/movies/1999/10/machines_in_the_garden.html (accessed 16 May 2016).

64 Edelstein, 'Machines in the Garden'.

65 Denison, 'Star-Spangled Ghibli', p. 144; Denison, 'Disembodied Stars', p. 11.

66 Interestingly, Studio Ghibli's subtitles have Eboshi call San '*Mononoke*' above, as if it is her name. However, this seems to embody Eboshi's misunderstanding rather than a confusion between spiritual role and name.

67 Napier, *Anime from Akira to Princess Mononoke*, p. 189.

68 Napier, *Anime from Akira to Princess Mononoke,* p. 190.

69 Napier, *Anime from Akira to Princess Mononoke*, pp. 180 and 181.

70 Montserrat Rifà-Valls, 'Postwar Princesses, Young Apprentices, and a Little Fish-Girl: Reading Subjectivities in Hayao Miyazaki's Tales of Fantasy', *Visual Arts Research*, vol. 37, no. 2 (2011) http://www.jstor.org/stable/10.5406/ visuartsrese.37.2.0088 (accessed 14 April 2016), p. 94.

71 Napier, *Anime from Akira to Princess Mononoke*, p. 192.

72 Napier, *Anime from Akira to Princess Mononoke*, p. 192.

73 Hayao Miyazaki, 'A Statement by Miyazaki', *Princess Mononoke*, 1999. http:// www.princess-mononoke.com/html/production/miyazaki/06.html (accessed 1 September 2016).

74 Judah, '*Princess Mononoke*', p. 54.

75 Hardy, 'Animating the Century'.

76 Singh, 'Translation Studies in the 21st Century', p. 5.

77 Gaiman quoted in: Townsend, 'Neil Gaiman'.

Chapter 8

MARKETING *MONONOKE*: THE *DAIHITTO* BECOMING DISNEY

Laz Carter

The very existence of this monograph, and indeed the existence of other volumes concerning Studio Ghibli penned in the English language, accords with the fact that a sizable Anglophone audience exists for the studio's canon of films. This market did not simply appear overnight; it has grown organically over time. While other valuable scholarly probes delve into a myriad of complexities, such as the studio's relationship with Japan or a growing international fan base,[1] it is worth taking a moment to reflect upon the influence of an active (and sometimes academic) Anglophone audience as a stimulus for both the craftsmanship of the animators and the Anglophonic marketing strategy sustained over the course of numerous promotional campaigns. On this notable anniversary of one of the true classics of Japanese animation – *Mononokehime* (*Princess Mononoke*, Hayao Miyazaki, 1997) – it is a fitting occasion to cast one's gaze back to where this marketing strategy truly began to take shape.

This chapter focuses on *Princess Mononoke*'s 'paratexts', which is to say certain promotional content such as 'posters, videogames, podcasts, reviews, or merchandise' that function 'not simply [as] add-ons, spinoffs, and also-rans: they create texts, they manage them, and they fill them with many of the meanings that we associate with them'.[2] By deconstructing four such paratexts – a film poster, a theatrical trailer, a DVD featurette and an official website – presented to the Western audience by the then Disney subsidiary, Miramax, this analysis is able to not only track the elements emphasized during marketing, but also draw attention to the marketing practices themselves – including the creation of 'brand-networks'[3] comprised of 'star-images'[4] and authorial 'brand names'[5] – that are intended to elide the cultural divide that lies betwixt the domestic and Anglophone marketplaces. *Princess Mononoke* is a particularly apt case-study for examining this phenomenon as it marks the beginning of the relationship between Ghibli and Disney, and thus provides a unique insight into the US recreation of Ghibli as a 'branded-sub*genre*' of animation.[6]

Before plunging into an analysis of *Princess Mononoke*'s marketing materials, it is worth noting how the paratextuality of this film differs from some of the Ghibli films both preceding and succeeding it. As alluded to earlier, *Princess Mononoke* marks the beginning of the relationship between Ghibli and Disney through the advent of the so-called 'Disney-Tokuma deal' of 1996.[7] Prior to this arrangement, Ghibli films were advertised and distributed in the West on an *ad hoc* basis, with each text being released through different channels. To give some examples prior to 1996, *Kaze no tani no Naushika* (*Nausicaä of the Valley of the Wind*, Hayao Miyazaki, 1984) was infamously recut and released as *Warriors of the Wind* by New World Pictures on VHS in 1985 and *Tonari no Totoro* (*My Neighbor Totoro*, Hayao Miyazaki, 1988) received a later release through Fox Video in 1993. Understandably then, one can read undertones of caution and wariness into the distribution of *Princess Mononoke* in the USA, if only because this distribution of Ghibli films represented a relatively new pathway for US entertainment conglomerates at that time. Near-contemporary successes such as *Kōkaku kidōtai* (*Ghost in the Shell*, Mamoru Oshii, 1995) and *Akira* (Katsuhiro Ōtomo, 1988) had already proved that an Anglophone market for *anime* was available, but these were primarily targeted at specialist, niche consumers and distribution of Japanese animation had yet to reach the mainstream family demographic.

In the US marketplace, Studio Ghibli anime are able to access this mainstream family demographic through their partnership with the multinational giant Walt Disney Studios. Although it was updated over time due to the necessity of addressing various digital and home media rights and although the rights to distribute Ghibli films has now passed to GKids in the United States,[8] the Disney-Tokuma Deal was first crystallized immediately prior to the promotion of *Princess Mononoke*. Yet it is also worth pointing out that this principle of brand-network unification within the stable of Disney-held companies only became commonplace subsequent to the release of *Princess Mononoke*. While Studio Ghibli remains corporately independent of Disney, there remains a strong comparison between their formalized relationship and the fates of the *Star Wars, Marvel* and *Pixar* franchises, which have all since become subject to a restructuring process under the 'unified corporate footprint of [the] conglomerate . . . Disney'.[9] That is to say, the brand names of *Star Wars, Marvel, Pixar,* and, to a lesser extent, *Studio Ghibli,* have had to adapt from being the primary brand name applied to products to, at least in certain marketplaces, merely contributing to the wider brand-network of Disney. Yet back in 1997, during the production and marketing of *Princess Mononoke*, the process of housing and re-distributing content produced by another studio formed a nexus of uncertainty for Disney, especially so given the cultural and linguistic translation challenges present in converting a foreign film for an Anglophone context (see Chapter 7). There existed no straightforward re-marketing strategy to follow and as such the Western promotional campaign for *Princess Mononoke* was inherently bespoke and experimental.

At this juncture I should acknowledge that much of the paratextuality for *Princess Mononoke* refers consumers not directly to the Disney brand name but rather to the brand names of Miramax and Buena Vista International, both of which were Disney subsidiaries at that time. Later in this analysis I will be exploring precisely why I believe this decision was made, but for now it is worth addressing the implications this industrial context has for this study. Writing specifically about Miramax, Alisa Perren states that such 'studio-based subsidiaries . . . operated relatively autonomously from the studio in terms of production and distribution'.[10] Yet in the case of *Princess Mononoke*, due to the freshly signed Disney-Tokuma deal, as well as the parent company's familiarity with the medium of animation, it is my assumption that Disney was at least aware of, and thus complicit in, the re-marketing strategies employed. As such, despite the fact that the Disney brand name is conspicuously absent from *Princess Mononoke*'s paratexts, these tactics can still be discussed in relation to 'Disneyfication', another concept that shall be unpacked below.

In short, while one could make a case that the Disney brand name is absent from the promotional campaign of *Princess Mononoke*, one can still trace the influence of the Disney brand-*network*. Moreover, an anachronous, transhistoric audience viewing Studio Ghibli's canon today may not be aware of the complexities of such intra-industry arrangements and might arguably assume that all of the studio's anime films have undergone the same process of Disneyfication as was applied to Miyazaki's later films. On the basis of these assumptions, this chapter proceeds with the understanding that *Princess Mononoke* experienced at least some degree of Disneyfication and that the associations drawn between Ghibli and Disney through information available to audiences today necessitates a closer look at Disney's role in the anime's Anglophone promotional campaign.

With the benefit of hindsight, the marketing for *Princess Mononoke* also bears a striking resemblance to that undertaken for Miyazaki's later films *Sen to Chihiro no kamikakushi* (*Spirited Away*, Hayao Miyazaki, 2001), *Hauru no ugoku shiro* (*Howl's Moving Castle*, Hayao Miyazaki, 2004), *Gake no ue no Ponyo* (*Ponyo on the Cliff by the Sea*, Hayao Miyazaki, 2008) and *Kaze tachinu* (*The Wind Rises*, 2013). That is to say that the decisions made at this juncture influenced Disney's marketing strategies and voice casting policy for future Ghibli re-productions. Several of the broad themes behind these techniques have been noted by Rayna Denison, including the use of 'star clustering' and brand-networks,[11] but there is still much ground to cover, especially in terms of how specific star-images commingle with and impact upon paratextual materials. This chapter aims to occupy this intellectual space and, by examining the first instance of Disney's involvement with Ghibli, provide a reference point for future re-marketing case studies.

As referenced earlier, previous academics, such as Jonathan Gray and Lisa Kernan,[12] have constructed methodologies for analysing promotional material. In particular, Keith Johnston has contributed greatly to the field through his influential monograph *Coming Soon: Film Trailers and the Selling of Hollywood Technology*, which employs what he terms 'unified analysis' in which he combines textual and contextual concerns.[13] Johnston describes how 'unified analysis places [emphasis] on [both] scrutinizing the individual trailer text, and building a network of the unique historical influences that surrounded its production', going on to comment that '[u]nified analysis begins with the unique and complex trailer text but can expand out to consider the impact of other elements'.[14] This framework has laid the groundwork for my own methodology, yet Johnston and I have differing goals; whereas my goal is to think across the context of *Princess Mononoke*'s promotional campaign in the USA, Johnston utilizes unified analysis to consider the relationship between films and their histories. He comments that 'unified analyses . . . have moved beyond reconstruction and have attempted to understand each text in its historically specific moment'.[15]

As suggested above, my own work, being that it centres on relatively contemporary texts, does not attempt to comprehend historical moments but rather attempts to map how a marketing campaign can continue to have a lasting impact *beyond* the moment of theatrical release. That is to say, my approach, which I term 'campaign analysis', looks across marketing paratexts not only for how they may have affected past demographics but also for how these same paratexts have ongoing effects. Rather than being disposable or time-limited, marketing epiphenomena now have after-lives of their own, thanks to fans and other audience members archiving marketing materials on websites and social media platforms including YouTube. In my previous campaign analysis studies I have found that, by limiting the scope of the study, I am able to elucidate the dissonance created when distributors reframe film texts for the global market.[16] In turn, I am able to highlight the machinations and manoeuvres plotted on an industrial level, while illuminating the cultural gaps and schisms that divide various demographics, marketplaces and, perhaps most importantly, temporalities. In other words, rather than imagining the 'smooth flow of products from one national audience to another',[17] the 'campaign analysis' approach accentuates the 'friction' present between the poles of production and promotion, local and global, contemporaneity and transhistoricism.[18]

Previous academic studies have made comparisons between *Princess Mononoke*'s Japanese and American posters and trailers, including Eriko Ogihara-Schuck's monograph *Miyazaki's Animism Abroad: The Reception of Japanese Religious Themes by American and German Audiences*.[19] While providing a valuable launching pad for this chapter, the theological focus of Ogihara-Schuck's work contrasts with my own methodology, as Ogihara-Schuck is primarily concerned with showing how 'the English poster, trailer, and adaptation of *Princess Mononoke* together downplay animism in the process of converting the film into a magical fantasy'.[20] Yet Ogihara-Schuck findings do highlight several key points and I utilize aspects of her framework to break down the contrasting domestic and Western posters. For instance,

Ogihara-Schuck specifically describes the American *Princess Mononoke* pro-motional campaign as having undergone a process of 'Disneyfication'[21] – a term which has been popularized by a number of academics to denote 'chang-ing an entity into something basic and artificial'.[22] Moving forward with this approach, one can appreciate how every aspect of the Disney re-marketing strategy is characterized by both commodification and an addition of synthetic structures. This chapter builds on Ogihara-Schuck's observation and expends further effort into uncovering evidence of Disneyfication throughout *Princess Mononoke*'s American campaign.

Denison addresses the promotion of *Princess Mononoke* across five key academic studies: a thesis entitled 'Cultural Traffic in Japanese Anime: The Meanings of Promotion, Reception and Exhibition Circuits in *Princess Mononoke*',[23] an article styled 'Disembodied Stars and the Cultural Meanings of *Princess Mononoke*'s Soundscape',[24] a chapter dubbed 'The Language of the Blockbuster: Promotion, *Princess Mononoke* and the *Daihitto* in Japanese Film Culture',[25] an article titled 'Star-Spangled Ghibli: Star Voices in the American Versions of Hayao Miyazaki's Films'[26] and finally her monograph *Anime: A Critical Introduction*.[27] Across these five texts, Denison's analysis constructs a critical framework that addresses how various promotional materials impact a given campaign. In particular, Denison demonstrates how the audiovisual brand of an agent – be they actor or author – plays a significant role in the mar-keting of Studio Ghibli films, a factor which is particularly noticeable through the 'Behind the Scenes' segments included as featurettes on DVDs. Building on this foundation, the following analysis examines precisely how *Princess Mononoke* – a film which, as Denison points out, attained *daihitto* (big hit) status in its domestic setting – was re-marketed for a Western release.[28]

This translation required a concerted effort by the American localizers. Denison notes that 'Japanese films . . . are so reliant on Japanese culture and language',[29] and she goes on to comment that aspects of *Princess Mononoke*'s domestic campaign indicated 'a calculated attempt to key into the national-istic elements of the film's success, appealing directly to patriotic sentiment within potential Japanese audiences'.[30] It follows then that in the Western con-text, Anglophone audiences for *Princess Mononoke* will be less inclined to read patriotic symbolism into the success of the re-dubbed or re-subbed animation, and moreover the stressing of Japanese ideograms and cultural capital in para-textuality will not have the same impact on the American audience members. This chapter addresses Disney as a (re-)branding agent, specifically in terms of the promotional strategies employed when distributing a Ghibli film to an Anglophone audience. While Denison is right to point out that the advertising approaches of Disney 'tend to avoid reference to the blockbuster',[31] the question still remains: upon what *do* Disney promotional campaigns focus?

Denison does examine the Western poster, trailer and website for *Princess Mononoke* in detail.[32] Yet, at least in this instance, her approach is subtly dif-ferent and is concerned with the '*daihitto*' and 'blockbuster' dynamic and academic frameworks such as film *genre*, the 'high concept' film and the 'dispersible text'.[33] My approach throughout this chapter adds three new elements to this existing foundation: a focus on the brand-network of Disney (including the brand names of its subsidiary and partner companies) and how these Disney brand names interact within the broader brand-network of *Princess Mononoke*; a deployment of new techniques and frameworks including campaign analysis and audiovisual synchronous (para)textual analysis; and a deeper inspection of not just the presence and vocal delivery of certain Hollywood stars, as this is covered by Denison's previous work,[34] but also their deployment and significance *within* the promotional paratexts themselves. Taking all of the above into account, this campaign analysis can now begin to unpack how the *daihitto* film culture was transformed into not a blockbuster *per se*, but rather a classic Disney animation.

The campaign analysis methodology utilized in this study focuses on key promotional materials that were not only readily available to the audiences of two decades ago, but that are also available to the contemporary consumer today through various Internet services. An added benefit of analysing posters and trailers is that, because all major film productions have these paratexts, I am better able to compare paratexts across linguistic and cultural contexts, as well as draw contrasts with Ghibli's wider *oeuvre*. In addition to poster and trailer analysis I shall be examining content present on the English language DVD as well as the still operational official website, as these paratexts would not only be influential upon past audiences but will continue to have an impact on consumers viewing *Princess Mononoke* for the first time today. That is to say that my campaign analysis methodology is inherently transhistoric in that it allows consideration of materials produced at the time of the campaign itself as well as the ongoing 'textual poaching' and re-appropriation of these resources by a wide range of fandoms through an ever increasing array of new media technologies, each occurring within individualized moments of (para-)textual consumption and creation.[35]

The following case-study analyses four paratexts: a poster, trailer, featurette and website produced for *Princess* Mononoke, in this specific order, as doing so creates three primary benefits. Firstly, this is close to the chronological order of paratextual release, not just for *Princess Mononoke* but for most contemporary films. The poster is normally released first, followed shortly by the trailer, and then, during or following the release of the film itself, additional content in the form of featurettes and other such ephemera will be released either as DVD special features or through online channels. The only exception within this paratextual release chronology (and the order of the following analysis) is that the website will often be live by the point of the poster release, if not earlier, and run alongside the release all of the above paratexts, often changing on a daily basis to reflect each event within and stage of the campaign. As such, it behoves meaningful examination to discuss it at the end so as to explore how it draws upon all of the previous paratexts. Secondly, this chronology may also loosely mirror the paratextual consumption of an anachronous, transhistoric new audience member watching for the first time today. Such 'new' audiences for *Princess Mononoke* might view the poster or the trailer to decide if they want to watch a given film, and then after consuming the text they might later seek out additional featurettes and other such web-related content. Thirdly, and finally, because this consumption chronology is likely to imitate the paratextual patterns of other mainstream films released at any point during the age of digital home media, following this analytical order allows this study to be less problematically compared to any future studies of film marketing.

Poster Analysis

In her comparison between the two most widely used poster designs, Ogihara-Schuck comments that 'the American poster for *Princess Mononoke* appears more masculine than the Japanese version',[36] pointing out that San is the primary figure in the Japanese design. Indeed, Susan Napier describes this particular image of San as 'an explicit picture of female sexuality that is more ominous than erotic . . . her Otherness [is] not simply female but bestial as well'.[37] Ogihara-Schuck also notes that all other features within the Japanese poster, including the Japanese language title and tagline, act to draw attention to the portentous figure of San.[38] While the Japanese poster perfectly encapsulates the 'female-governed narrative space' of the film,[39] this facet is completely absent from the American design, as Ogihara-Schuck notes: 'Ashitaka becomes the aggressive warrior in the center of the poster . . . with the sentence "The fate of the world rests on the courage of one warrior" newly added . . . [which] immediately foreshadows the warrior's valor'.[40] By performing this paratextual replacement, even the selection of a protagonist becomes subject to Disneyfication. The re-marketing process has removed the complexity of strong female characterization, replacing it with a more straightforward male hero. In fact, one could argue that mislabelling the warrior Ashitaka as the protagonist is deliberately misleading. Denison comments upon this gender substitution, writing that '[t]he central figure is not the warrior on whose shoulders rest the fate of the world: it is the Princess, San. The "warrior's" role too is not to save everyone but to keep striving for peace – Ashitaka does not save the world as a lone hero, in fact he witnesses the end of part of it'.[41] The point is that the American poster as it stands misconstrues what began as a relatively unconventional film driven by a strong female character and the ultimate failure of humanity's battle with nature and, once filtered through the Disneyfication process, it transforms into a more classical Hollywood narrative where a male warrior protagonist must save the world.

Through such alterations, complexity is elided in favour of familiarity. Yet when viewed from an anachronous, transhistoric position, it is difficult to describe this process as characterized by simplification alone. It is worth noting that, while anime critics, reviewers, academics and other informed commentators may well have been aware of the stark differences between the Japanese and American promotional campaigns, this information may not have been as readily available to the mainstream family demographic. A contemporary audience anachronously viewing these paratextual materials today, however, would have full access to all such ephemera and, in this light, these contrasts become more impactful. Thus, for a transhistoric demographic, Disneyfication can be characterized by the addition of an overlaid transparent acetate layer of paratextuality placed on top of the original, wherein, upon close inspection, the two layers are evidently distinguishable from one another, but, at a first brief glance, the campaigns merge into a blended brand-network of signification presumably originating from a single (American) source.

This same process of Disneyfication is applied to every difference between the two posters, including: the reduction of San, the female protagonist, to a coin, the very symbol of commodification; the relegation of the Studio Ghibli and Hayao Miyazaki brand names from prominent positions in the Japanese design to small text at the footer of the American poster; and, perhaps most critically, not only the replacement of the Japanese star cluster for the American one, but also the accentuation of only six specific names in a central position. The Japanese campaign makes use of nine star-images – specifically Yōji Matsuda, Yuriko Ishida, Yūko Tanaka, Kaoru Kobayashi, Masahiko Nishimura, Tsunehiko Kamijō, Akihiro Miwa, Mitsuko Mori and Hisaya Morishige – whereas the American strategy is to focus in detail on just six – Gillian Anderson, Billy Crudup, Claire Danes, Minnie Driver, Jada Pinkett-Smith and Billy Bob Thornton. This limited emphasis is revealing because the film is clearly not comprised of just six, or indeed nine, vocal performances. Indeed, the accentuation of a number of key roles – such as, for example, that of Gonza played by John DiMaggio – are omitted from the Anglophone campaign. This indicates that the star-images listed above have been selected for a specific promotional purpose and that a deeper analysis of their involvement might reveal industrial machinations which target specific audience demographics.

It is worth taking a moment to consider the implications of the deployment of this particular brand-network upon the Western consumer. Finola Kerrigan writes that '[a]s films are made to be watched (consumed), there is a *need* to focus on the audience,'[42] going on to note that 'filmmakers and marketers have an understanding of the different film audiences that exist, and how to engage them.'[43] Yet Kerrigan goes on to posit that, in the case of star clusters, '[e]valuating the impact of stars . . . is problematic as it is often dependent on the star in question, the image that this star has, and how the intended audience for the film receives them.'[44] That is to say, the success of a paratextual promotional strategy hinges not just on the star-image, but also the very individuality of the viewer themselves, and that within collections of consumers there exists variance and diversity.

Given that commentators have described Hayao Miyazaki and Studio Ghibli as having attained a 'cult' status,[45] auteur brand names are almost entirely absent from the marketing campaign and, by contrast, the star cluster is given a large degree of prominence. Such a skewed promotional strategy indicates that in 1997 the Western localizers were less concerned with actively pursuing 'cine-sophisticated audiences' and instead aimed to avoid alienating any aspect of the broadest possible demographic.[46] Moving into the moving-image marketing materials, we shall track how this promotional policy continues throughout *Princess Mononoke*'s marketing campaign.

Trailer Analysis

Having observed that the broad approach for Disney's re-marketing strategy is characterized by Disneyfication and commodification, let us now turn to the moving-image paratextual materials to examine how this policy is executed for the remainder of the Western campaign. When analysing a given film trailer, it is often necessary to specify precisely which paratext is being examined, as often multiple trailers and television 'spots' will be produced for a given linguistic and cultural market. However, in this case, an additional layer of specificity is necessary because there are in fact multiple versions of the primary trailer that I am dissecting: at least one previous version was released with a slightly different narration track. As laid out on The Hayao Miyazaki Web, it appears there exists at least one older version (available at http://www.nausicaa.net/miyazaki/mh/trailers/princessmononoke.mov) where both 'Miyazaki' and 'Mononoke' are incorrectly pronounced by the narrator.[47] While the English pronunciation of Japanese names does not necessarily affect my analysis, this revelation does highlight two points. Firstly, that a study of the specificities of these paratextual materials is worthwhile, as evidently much ongoing attention was allocated to their deployment by those involved in the re-marketing process. Secondly, that precisely because of their revisionary nature, one must be crystal clear when citing a paratext. In this perspicacious spirit, the precise trailer I shall be examining is the one present on the *Princess Mononoke* Region 2 DVD, originally distributed in 2000 by Buena Vista Home Entertainment and Miramax.

As suggested above, the trailer itself encapsulates many of the themes that would come to exemplify Disney's marketing strategies for Ghibli films in the years to come, namely a policy of Disneyfication through a deployment of both auteur brand names, a star cluster of Hollywood talent and a preference for accentuating this brand-network through audiovisual synchronicity present in the voiceover narration. Yet it is worth noting that, as alluded to earlier, such was the state of caution at the time of *Princess Mononoke*'s Western release that Disney deemed it wise to release the film under the Miramax brand name rather than directly through the Disney Company itself. Furthermore, the film's rights were held by Buena Vista International, another Disney subsidiary. This distancing process was repeated for Hayao Miyazaki's final film, *The Wind Rises*, which was distributed in the USA via Touchstone Pictures, despite the fact that the brand names of Ghibli and Disney had appeared together within previous campaigns for such films as *Spirited Away*, *Howl's Moving Castle* and *Ponyo on the Cliff by the Sea*. The common themes tying *Princess Mononoke* and *The Wind Rises* together pertain to more mature source material focusing on war and death, and thus a slightly older desired target audience. In other words, the Disney brand is, on the whole, connected with the children's market and thus when Disney re-distributes and re-brands more adult entertainment the Disney brand name must itself be elided to avoid perpetuating a confused narrative image and uncertain target audience.[48] I argue that such decisions highlight two key points: that the precise brand name attached to a given film is thoughtfully selected on a case-by-case basis and that, as a result, the deployment of a brand name in re-marketing materials is always worth analysing.

In the case of *Princess Mononoke*, I would argue that Miramax was chosen to re-brand the Anglophonic version of the film for a number of reasons. Primarily, as laid out above, the re-production of the early Ghibli films were treated cautiously by Disney and, in an effort to minimize a perceived risk of damage in public perception to the primary Disney brand name, *Princess Mononoke* was thus re-distributed by a subsidiary studio. Yet at the time Disney operated a multitude of secondary label studios, including other well-known brands such as the aforementioned Touchstone Pictures or Hollywood Pictures. To truly comprehend the decision to select Miramax, we must delve deeper to the preconceptions and assumptions which constitute their specific brand identity. As noted by other academics,[49] Miramax was immensely successful in what is problematically termed the 'independent' market. Miramax distributed 'major independent' films – such as *Sex, Lies and Videotape* (Steven Soderbergh, 1989) or *Pulp Fiction* (Quentin Tarantino, 1994) – that were indubitably profitable but, for marketing reasons, were labelled as independent or otherwise distinct from the mainstream blockbuster success.[50] Yet it is worth stressing that the independent label, whether it is applied explicitly or implied more subtly, can be indicative of promotional strategies as much as it can describe a production style. As Biskind writes, ' "Independent film" brings to mind noble concepts like "integrity," "vision," "self-expression," and "sacrifice" … [but] although there is more than a little truth to this conventional notion, it's important to remember that it's not the whole truth.'[51] One can view the major independent status of the Miramax label as a structure employed by multimedia conglomerates like Disney to distribute features that, despite perhaps not being the year's biggest blockbusters, will nevertheless return a sizable profit through combined theatrical and home video releases, while simultaneously holding this canon of independent films as separate from their principal *oeuvre* should they prove unprofitable.

By imbuing certain films with such a major independent status through their Miramax label, Disney is able to suggest that a film is worthy of critical acclaim and moreover that said film text is alternative to the mainstream, despite being deeply entrenched within it. Recalling Kerrigan's point regarding disparate audience appeals, one might argue that the presence of Miramax in the theatrical trailer works to attract a cine-sophisticated audience that had otherwise been forgotten following the decision to limit the deployment of the Studio Ghibli and Hayao Miyazaki as brand names within the promotional campaign. One can see the logic: the use of the Miramax brand name implies a relatively alternative, cinephilic viewing experience without detracting from the otherwise Anglophone linguistic context of the rest of the marketing campaign.

In the very beginning of the Anglophone *Princess Mononoke* trailer, we are presented with the Miramax brand printed in large type, dominating the black screen. The leader fades into the opening imagery of Ghibli's animation, but the Miramax font remains, imprinting English text over the original Japanese animation. This deployment of an American brand name profoundly impacts the signification of the original Japanese animation. Firstly, it allows Disney, by proxy, to stake a claim of ownership over the film. By literally stamping their authority over the text, Disney is able to take credit for, if not the creation of the animation itself, then certainly its widespread Western dissemination. Secondly, it acts to contextualize the images that follow into an Anglophone, American context. Through layering English 'linguistic signs transmitted visually' over the Japanese visuals,[52] Disney can attempt to subtly reposition audience preconceptions away from expectations connected with anime, Otherness and world cinema, and begin to suggest that *Princess Mononoke* can be consumed as domestic, albeit independent, entertainment.

Nowhere is this principle clearer than in a cursory glance at the other brand names the American trailer did choose to deploy. What sets the trailer for *Princess Mononoke* apart from the promos of Miyazaki's later films is the lack of accentuation of the Japanese brand names of Hayao Miyazaki and Studio Ghibli. In fact, Studio Ghibli is not mentioned at all except for a minor footnote in the credits card, the very last image of the trailer. The normal opening credit title card featuring the familiar Totoro figure adorning a blue background is notably absent. As Denison writes, there is the potential that evidence of Japanese language and culture would be relegated to 'nuances and jokes [that] become transcribed into little more than further evidence of the film's Oriental origins',[53] and, continuing this train of thought, one could argue that, even by eliding such industrial evidence, the US distributors might have been seeking to obfuscate the existence of Oriental origins and remove the topics of nationality and culture from the paratext altogether. This Disneyfication process of replacing the Japanese 'odour' with Anglophone linguistic and cultural contexts is evident throughout the localization process and is manifested in the very process of re-dubbing the animation with an English language aurality.[54]

One can also observe that the finale of the trailer features not only, as one might expect, an English language title card but also certain star names from the Hollywood 'star cluster' assembled for *Princess Mononoke*. Their names appear on-screen in an overlaid font, which again, similar to the deployment of the Miramax label, acts to localize the Japanese imagery for the Anglophone audience. The American trailer is where the combined vocal talents of Debi Derryberry, Keith David, Danes, Thornton, Crudup and Driver are showcased to the Anglophone audience, through a script which intercuts clips from the film with elements of narration. The audio transcript of the Disney trailer for *Princess Mononoke* included below, is necessitated by the textual analysis that follows. I highlight particular moments for the sake of clarity: emboldened text pertains to a brand name deployment, underlined text indicates what might be termed an 'inflection' (a qualifier which modifies a given brand name) and italicized text represents the phenomenon that I term 'audiovisual synchronicity' (the marriage between 'verbal signs transmitted acoustically' and 'linguistic signs transmitted visually').[55]

Keith David/Narrator: From master animator **Miyazaki,** <u>one of the most influential filmmakers of all time</u>, comes a ground-breaking motion picture event. In a time when gods walked the earth, an epic battle rages between the encroaching civilisation of man and the gods of the forest.

Minnie Driver/Lady Eboshi: When the forest has been cleared and the wolves wiped out this place will be the richest land in the world.

Narrator: It's a war which threatens to unbalance the forces of nature.

Keith David/Okkoto: It will be a battle the humans will never forget.

Keith David/Narrator: Now the fate of the world rests on the courage of one fearless princess. . .

Claire Danes/San: I'm not afraid to die and I would do anything to get the humans out of here.

Keith David/Narrator: . . . and one brave warrior.

Billy Bob Thornton/Jiko bō: You fight like a demon, boy, like something possessed.

Minnie Driver/Lady Eboshi: What exactly are you here for?

Billy Crudup/Ashitaka: To see with eyes unclouded by hate.

Minnie Driver/Lady Eboshi: Now watch closely everyone. I'm going to show you how to kill a god. Fire!

Debi Derryberry/Hii-sama: You cannot alter your fate. However, you can rise to meet it, if you choose.

Keith David/Narrator: Featuring the voices of *Gillian Anderson, Billy Crudup, Claire Danes, Minnie Driver, Jada Pinkett-Smith* and *Billy Bob Thornton* . . . *Princess Mononoke*.

Even when disregarding the music and sound effect portions of the soundscape for the purpose of concision, the dialogue in the trailer alone makes remarkably little use of audiovisual synchronicity, especially compared to trailers for later Ghibli films like *Howl's Moving Castle*. Indeed, the only auteur brand name is that of Hayao Miyazaki, and even he does not merit the deployment of his full name and is instead reduced to simply 'Miyazaki'. Yet he does receive the inflection of being referred to as 'influential', which is a telling descriptor as it begs the question of whom the director may be influencing. As this is left open to interpretation, one might conclude that Anglophone animators and audiences might feature among this number and thus one is able to quantify the worth of this animation through a context Western consumers can comprehend, displaying yet another example of commodification added by the process of Disneyfication.

Yet, clearly the majority of the audiovisual synchronicity pertains not to auteur brand names, but to star-images. Eagle-eared audience members might observe that the audiovisually synchronous star cluster that is featured on-screen and recited by the narrator at the end of the trailer actually consists of slightly different constituents. That is, the visual star cluster encompasses, in order of appearance, Gillian Anderson, Billy Crudup, Claire Danes, Minnie Driver, Jada Pinkett-Smith and Billy Bob Thornton, yet is missing the presence of Keith David and Debi Derryberry. However, the vocal performances heard within the trailer itself include, in order of appearance: Minnie Driver, Keith David, Claire Danes, Billy Bob Thornton, Billy Crudup and Debi Derryberry, missing out Gillian Anderson and Jada Pinkett-Smith. Only four audiovisual stars – Billy Crudup, Claire Danes, Minnie Driver and Billy Bob Thornton – are fortunate enough to be named on-screen *and* have an extract of their vocal performance present in the trailer paratext. I have produced a table (Table 8.1) that illustrates this dynamic, wherein star-images that fall primarily into a given category are emboldened for clarity. These differences have the effect of creating not one, not two, but three separate star clusters: an aural star cluster of stars whose vocal performances directly feature in the trailer, a visual star cluster of stars whose star-images appear overlaid towards the end of the promo, and an audiovisual star cluster of stars that feature in both of the above.

This critical division between aural, visual and audiovisual stars extends beyond the trailer itself. Recalling the poster analysis presented above, we can

Table 8.1 *Princess Mononoke*'s three star clusters.

Aural Star Cluster	Visual Star Cluster	Audiovisual Star Cluster
Keith David	**Gillian Anderson**	
Debi Derryberry	**Jada Pinkett-Smith**	
(Billy Crudup)	(Billy Crudup)	**Billy Crudup**
(Claire Danes)	(Claire Danes)	**Claire Danes**
(Minnie Driver)	(Minnie Driver)	**Minnie Driver**
(Billy Bob Thornton)	(Billy Bob Thornton)	**Billy Bob Thornton**

see, as one might expect, that the visual star cluster is replicated in the static portion of the Western campaign and the aural stars are omitted entirely, and indeed this preference for this particular visual star cluster continues for the remainder of the campaign. Thus we must assume that the actual star names of the six stars which comprise the visual star cluster were deemed to possess more 'variant audience appeal' for Western audiences than their less well-known star counterparts,[56] David and Derryberry, whose existence in the marketing campaign is linked solely to the quality of their vocal performance.

Writing specifically on Princess Mononoke, Denison goes on to comment that

> It is important to account for the presence of the particular star voices used in *Princess Mononoke* in terms of what they potentially mean to audiences . . . Anderson's massive cult following from *The X-Files*, appeals to 'serious' filmmaking through Crudup and Thornton and appeals to various national, youth and ethnic audiences through the presence of Driver, Danes and Pinkett Smith . . . Thus, the re-recording of *Princess Mononoke* recreated the film not just for a non-specific American audience, but for a series of disparate potential audiences that happen to co-exist within American society.[57]

As we can see, Denison's own taxonomy seems to suggest dividing the star cluster further into differing categories, positing what might be thought of as the star trio of Driver, Danes and Pinkett-Smith; a star pair of Crudup and Thornton;[58] and the stand-alone star of Anderson.[59] In order to discover more about star pairs and other methods of grouping stars, as well as the intricate dynamics created among these stars and the promotional uses to which they were put, it is helpful to examine the complex meta-narrative constructed between comments made by not only the stars themselves but also the voices of Disney producers and uncredited promoters behind the campaign itself.

Featurette Analysis

The 'featurette' video which appears on the Buena Vista Home Entertainment Region 2 release of the *Princess Mononoke* DVD contains a variety of interviews with the cast and producers of the Anglophone dub. One of the intended functions of such paratextual material is to recontextualize the anime for Western audiences and to single out themes and conventions which exemplify Studio Ghibli's canon, such as environmental concerns, moral ambiguity and a focus on animism and spirituality. In such a way, this paratext is able to inform potential audiences of appropriate genre expectations while carrying out its true function: contextualising *Princess Mononoke* in a Western setting, accompanied by English language text and starring American actors. Furthermore, the featurette and other DVD special features satisfy various pragmatic concerns: interviews with stars and producers cost Disney relatively little to produce and this fresh material does not require the payment of rights fees to Ghibli and its partner companies. Moreover, the inclusion of such special features on DVDs acts as a 'sales hook',[60] making them more attractive to potential audiences and thus generating a positive impact upon the sale of DVDs and Blu-rays.

Three segments of the featurette are particularly germane to this study. Firstly, and most straightforwardly, the executive director of the English language dub Jack Fletcher makes the comment that '*Princess Mononoke* was a huge, huge film in Japan. *Titanic* toppled it, but only just'. This has the effect of providing a framework for measuring success through comparison to a Hollywood block-buster, which would be instantly familiar to a Western audience. In such a way, Fletcher can communicate the *daihitto* status of the original text in its domestic context while subtly and simultaneously maintaining the implicit dominance of the Hollywood model and thus Western hegemony. Additionally, for the benefit of audiences watching this film at a later date through home media, this comment places *Princess Mononoke* temporally in the late 1990s.

Secondly, towards the middle of the featurette there exists a segment that consists entirely of lines drawn from the theatrical trailer, fully transcribed as follows:

Minnie Driver/Lady Eboshi: When the forest has been cleared and the wolves wiped out this place will be the richest land in the world.
Keith David/Okkoto: It will be a battle the humans will never forget.
Claire Danes/San: I'm not afraid to die and I would do anything to get the humans out of here.
Minnie Driver/Lady Eboshi: What exactly are you here for?
Billy Crudup/Ashitaka: To see with eyes unclouded by hate.

One could simply argue that these lines were chosen for the purposes of conveying the film's narrative image, yet there are a range of excerpts from outside the theatrical trailer that convey a similar message. Indeed, some of them are utilized later in the featurette, such as the clip of Anderson's line: 'the trees cry out as they die, but you cannot hear them. I lie here, I listen to the pain of the forest'. I posit that these repeated lines primarily act as intratextual references to the theatrical trailer. Indeed, I argue that this cycle of paratextual referencing only confuses a hypothetical consumer into forgetting, at least temporarily, the source of the original animation and instead what lingers in one's memory is the labour of the Disney localizers: the encompassing envelope of paratextuality which fully encircles and encloses the film.

Thirdly and finally, there is evidence supporting the model uncovered by Denison pertaining to Disney's casting policy. Put simply, this formula can be understood as grouping 'stars with experience in voice work with those with little or no experience',[61] a process which tends to create the conditions for 'pairing stars'.[62] In Ghibli's later films one can see a more clear-cut construction of star pairs in, for example, the dynamic between Joseph Gordon-Levitt and

Emily Blunt in *The Wind Rises*. Yet, as *Princess Mononoke* was the first Disney dub of a Ghibli film, this star pair policy had yet to be created and thus what occurred in practice equated more to the 'star cluster' phenomenon. The links created between certain star-images are not uniform across the campaign and as such a range of possible assemblages can be made.

In the following segment from the featurette, four stars – Danes, Crudup, Thornton and Pinkett-Smith – each declare how difficult the dubbing process was to perform. These excerpts are intercut with a comment from Fletcher praising Thornton's experience and performative quality in addition to three audio clips of Thornton delivering lines as Jiko bō. This sequence is fascinating because the placement of the three lines from Thornton in character as Jiko bō – two of which come before Fletcher's statement, foreshadowing the imminent positioning of Thornton as experienced – rhythmically punctuate the meta-narrative, re-affirming the dominance of one star-image over others. Moreover, one can clearly observe how it has the effect of positioning the star-image of Thornton as holding a higher degree of seasoned experience than those of Danes, Crudup and Pinkett-Smith, despite the fact that all four stars are in fact similarly bemoaning the difficulties of the dubbing process.

For experienced stars to be appropriately positioned within the star pair system it is nevertheless necessary to mask the site of labour, or as Barry King writes, 're-site the signification of interiority, away from the actor and onto the mechanism'.[63] This re-siting phenomenon is evident not only in this sequence but several similar behind-the-scenes segments included on Ghibli's later Disney-produced DVDs, which suggests that, seemingly right from the outset of their deal with Tokuma, Disney had a strategy for how they would position certain stars as seasoned or inexperienced, and thus adhere the additional structure of an Anglophone star cluster meta-narrative.

Website Analysis

The seasoned-inexperienced meta-narrative outlined above encompasses just four star-images, yet other star clusters have been suggested allowing for a host of other pairing possibilities. On the official *Princess Mononoke* website (available at http://www.princess-mononoke.com/), the two star-images of the younger actors – Crudup and Danes – seem to consistently be paired as the less experienced performers. Crudup is credited as commenting that 'the movie was such an entirely different experience',[64] with the website going on to clarify that 'Crudup . . . makes his animation debut with PRINCESS MONONOKE.'[65] Similarly, the website positions Danes as a 'rising young star' and stresses that 'Danes had never performed in an animated feature before and was surprised at the depth of the commitment required for this project. "It was surprisingly emotional for me," she admits. "I came in thinking it would be very simple and it turned out to be a very intense and moving experience." '[66] This statement from the star is further accentuated by Fletcher's comment that 'Claire Danes brings an incredible raw anger and passion and righteousness to the role',[67] which emphasizes the relative inexperience of the star through vocabulary with emotional rather than professional characteristics. One could arguably group Crudup and Danes as an inexperienced star pair in that both of these star-images are correspondingly positioned as unproven by the comments that the stars themselves make and by the authoritative 'voice' behind the official website.

By contrast, the deployment of Driver's star-image is characterized by a desire to showcase her experience, as the website praises her 'complex performance'[68] and provides performative context by remarking that 'Lady Eboshi is played by Academy Award nominee Minnie Driver, who also recently provided the voice of Jane in "Tarzan and Jane." ' [*sic*.][69] To a lesser extent, the positioning of Anderson mirrors Driver's experienced status – exemplified by the website's statement that as 'a long-time fan of Miyazaki, she came to PRINCESS MONONOKE knowing what to expect'[70] – and thus one is able to construct a seasoned star pair of Driver and Anderson, as the marketing campaign deems it necessary to highlight their relative experience.

Yet further star pairs are constructed by the structure of the website itself, which is organized into snippets of text linked to one another sequentially rather than longer paragraphs of prose. The extract depicting Crudup as an inexperienced star is immediately succeeded by the following sentence which links his star-image with the section pertaining to Driver, suggesting a more traditional seasoned-inexperienced star pair between the two star-images: 'Ashitaka's main obstacle to fulfilling his mission comes in the form of Lady Eboshi.'[71] This dichotomy is replicated again by the inferred relationship between Danes and Anderson, through the website's comment that 'one of the most intriguing parts of the experience for Danes was that she had to play off Gillian Anderson, who portrays the voice of San's adopted wolf-mother Moro, without ever working with her in person'.[72] In this scenario, the seasoned-inexperienced star pair is made even clearer by linking not only the star-images of Danes and Anderson together, but also stressing the difficulties experienced by the younger star throughout the re-dubbing process.

Conclusion

The formation of star clusters as a promotional strategy lies at the heart of *Princess Mononoke*'s Western campaign, and yet it is certainly confusing to untangle the web of interconnections linking each of these star-images. As referenced earlier, Denison has developed her own taxonomy of examining *Princess Mononoke*'s visual star cluster, dividing the stars into a star trio, a star pair and a stand-alone star. Whether this classification system holds any more veracity than the several hinted at by Disney's various stars, producers and promoters is unclear, but perhaps this ambiguity is the point. That is to say that part of the purpose of constructing an intricate brand-network composed of multiple star clusters is to deliberately distract Western audiences away from the original animation and to instead focus on the American, Anglophone aurality. As Denison comments:

> The range of American (and even British) accents employed detracts from any sense of this film as intrinsically 'Other', or in this case, strips away any sense of this film as a Japanese film. The authority of the animated image could, in this manner, be thought of as undermined by the 'American' voice that narrates it. Though the dress and history related by *Princess Mononoke* may well be Japanese in origin, this nationality is filtered through America, as the film's overall 'voice' becomes nationally conflicted.[73]

Building from this observation, I argue that it is not just the 'voice' of the film which elides the Japanese origin, but also the constructed meta-narratives of paratextuality surrounding the film, particularly those pertaining to star clusters and brand-networks.

Looking across the campaign as a whole, one can see a cohesive strategy that aims to collectively highlight particular meta-narratives and brand-networks across all available paratexts. However, while it would be possible to comment on *Princess Mononoke*'s star cluster(s) by looking at the film poster alone, it would not be possible to demonstrate the complexities of the inexperienced-seasoned star pairing meta-narrative constructed by Disney without also addressing the featurette and official website. Similarly, one might comment that the featurette omits Studio Ghibli's brand name entirely, but without additionally consulting the film poster and theatrical trailer it would not be possible to assess the scale of this obfuscation of the film's Japanese origins. It is by approaching marketing materials through the methodology of campaign analysis that I have been able to read across the paratexts of *Princess Mononoke* and uncover the promotional strategies deployed.

In the case of *Princess Mononoke*, this analysis has shown that the Western promotional strategy emphasized the American star cast above other elements of the production. This can be described by the single concept of Disneyfication, involving the commodification or downright omission of Japanese signifiers and the addition of Anglophone artifice. Rather than following a more traditional '*mukokuseki*', or 'odourless',[74] globalization pattern, the Disneyfication of *Princess Mononoke* is characterized by the layering of American signifiers over the top of the original artwork. At times the Western campaign takes centre stage eclipsing the original paratextual approach, yet at others both campaigns are visible simultaneously. This juxtaposition indicates precisely how uncomfortable Disney found this experimental re-marketing process and that they felt that, for the film to succeed, the promotional paratexts needed to stress not *only* Japaneseness but also, and at times perhaps even more importantly, its

Americanness, recalling Koichi Iwabuchi's description of 'an "Americanization of Japanization." '[75]

It is worth remembering that this 'Americanization of Japanization' globalization pattern is arguably more visible to an anachronous, transhistoric audience, rather than the contemporary mainstream demographics targeted in 1997. Yet by addressing the modern audience through a consideration of campaign analysis, I have been able to acknowledge that an atemporal viewer has easy access to every paratext referenced in this chapter, and that each one is even more relevant today than it has ever been, due to an increasing paratextual presence available online. Accepting the existence of transhistoric, anachronous spectators allows paratextual discussion to move beyond the trappings of contemporaneous availability and 'temporal lag',[76] and address broader strategies that are evident throughout a promotional campaign regardless of paratextual chronology.

As we approach and inevitably move beyond this twentieth anniversary of *Princess Mononoke*, I am moved to reflect not only on the actualities of the individual text itself, as engrossing as the topic may be, but also its connections to the wider Ghibli canon and what phenomena evolved from the crafting of this film. In many ways *Princess Mononoke* acted as a turning point for the future of Ghibli animation, and arguably the success of anime in the global marketplace. Following this film, anime images were introduced to a wider Western audience, Hayao Miyazaki's talent at fantastical world-building only grew, Studio Ghibli's brand name popularity exploded and, of special interest to this author, Disney's promotional strategies for re-marketing Ghibli content continued to develop into the more disciplined and regimented policies still in place to this day.

Notes

1 Susan J. Napier, 'Vampires, Psychic Girls, Flying Women and Sailor Scouts: Four Faces of the Young Female in Japanese Popular Culture' in Dolores P. Martinez (ed.), *The Worlds of Japanese Popular Culture: Gender, Shifting Boundaries and Global Cultures* (Cambridge: Cambridge University Press, 1998), pp. 91–109; and, *From Impressionism to Anime: Japan as Fantasy and Fan Cult in the Mind of the West* (Basingstoke: Palgrave Macmillan, 2007).

2 Jonathan Gray, *Show Sold Separately: Promos, Spoilers, and Other Media Paratexts* (London and New York: New York University Press, 2010), p. 6.

3 Rayna Denison, *Anime: A Critical Introduction* (London: Bloomsbury, 2015), p. 118.

4 Richard Dyer, *Heavenly Bodies: Film Stars and Society* (London: BFI Publishing, 1986), p. 3.

5 Timothy Corrigan, *A Cinema without Walls: Movies and Culture after Vietnam* (New Brunswick, NJ: Rutgers University Press, 1991), p. 103.

6 Denison, *Anime*, p. 11, emphasis in original.

7   Rayna Denison, 'Star-Spangled Ghibli: Star Voices in the American Versions of Hayao Miyazaki's Films', *Animation: An Interdisciplinary Journal*, vol. 3, no. 2 (2008), p. 134.

8   Jennifer Wolf, 'GKids Picks Up Studio Ghibli's "Only Yesterday," ' *Animation World News*, 24 August 2015. https://www.awn.com/news/gkids-picks-studio-ghibli-only-yesterday (accessed 14 April 2017).

9   Derek Johnson, *Media Franchising: Creative License and Collaboration in the Culture Industries* (London and New York: New York University Press, 2013), p. 3.

10 Alisa Perren, 'Sex, Lies and Marketing: Miramax and the Development of the Quality Indie Blockbuster', *Film Quarterly*, vol. 55, no. 2 (2001), p. 30.

11 Denison, 'Star-Spangled Ghibli', p. 142.

12 Gray, *Show Sold Separately* and Lisa Kernan, *Coming Attractions: Reading American Movie Trailers* (Texas: University of Texas Press, 2004).

13 Keith Johnston, *Coming Soon: Film Trailers and the Selling of Hollywood Technology* (North Carolina: McFarland, 2009), p. 11.

14 Johnston, *Coming Soon*, p. 155.

15 Johnston, *Coming Soon*, p. 90.

16 Laz Carter, 'Marketing *Anime* to a Global Audience: A Paratextual Analysis of Promotional Materials from *Spirited Away*', *East Asian Journal of Popular Culture*, vol. 4, no. 1 (2018).

17 Sandra Annett, *Anime Fan Communities: Transcultural Flows and Frictions* (Basingstoke and New York: Palgrave Macmillan, 2014), p. 1.

18 Annett, *Anime Fan Communities*.

19 Eriko Ogihara-Schuck, *Miyazaki's Animism Abroad: The Reception of Japanese Religious Themes by American and German Audiences* (Jefferson, NC: MacFarland, 2014).

20 Ogihara-Schuck, *Miyazaki's Animism Abroad*, p. 77.

21 Ogihara-Schuck, *Miyazaki's Animism Abroad*.

22 Jonathan Matusitz and Lauren Palermo, 'The Disneyfication of the World: A Grobalisation Perspective', *Journal of Organisational Transformation & Social Change*, vol. 11, no. 2 (2014), p. 100; and, David L. Andrews, 'Disneyization, Debord, and the Integrated NBA Spectacle'. *Social Semiotics*, vol. 16, no. 1 (2006), pp. 89–102; Alan Bryman, 'The Disneyization of Society', *The Sociological Review*, vol. 47, no. 1 (1999), pp. 25–47; Alan Bryman, *The Disneyization of Society* (California: Sage, 2004); Henry A. Giroux, 'Animating Youth: The Disneyfication of Children's Culture'. *Socialist Review*, vol. 24, no. 3 (1994), pp. 23–55.

23 Rayna Denison, 'Cultural Traffic in Japanese Anime: The Meanings of Promotion, Reception and Exhibition Circuits in *Princess Mononoke*' (PhD thesis submitted to the University of Nottingham, 2005).

24 Denison, 'Disembodied Stars'.

25 Rayna Denison, 'The Language of the Blockbuster: Promotion, *Princess Mononoke* and the *Daihitto* in Japanese Film Culture' in Leon Hunt and Leung Wing-Fai (eds), *East Asian Cinemas: Exploring Transnational Connections on Film* (London and New York: I. B. Tauris, 2008), pp. 103–22.

26 Denison, 'Star-Spangled Ghibli'.

27 Denison, *Anime*.

28 Denison, 'The Language of the Blockbuster'.

29   Denison, 'The Language of the Blockbuster', p. 105.
30   Denison, 'The Language of the Blockbuster', p. 110.
31   Denison, 'The Language of the Blockbuster', p. 114.
32   Denison, 'Cultural Traffic in Japanese Anime', pp. 182–214.
33   Thomas Austin, *Hollywood, Hype and Audiences: Selling and Watching Popular Film in the 1990s* (Manchester: Manchester University Press, 2002); Justin Wyatt, *High Concept: Movies and Marketing in Hollywood* (Texas: University of Texas Press, 1994).
34   Denison, 'Cultural Traffic in Japanese Anime', pp. 166–81.
35   Henry Jenkins, *Textual Poachers: Television Fans & Participatory Culture* (London and New York: Routledge, 1992).
36   Ogihara-Schuck, *Miyazaki's Animism Abroad*, p. 77.
37   Susan J. Napier, *Anime from Akira to Princess Mononoke: Experiencing Contemporary Japanese Animation* (New York: Palgrave Macmillan, 2001), p. 183.
38   Ogihara-Schuck, *Miyazaki's Animism Abroad*, p. 77.
39   Toshifumi Yoshida, 'Hayao Miyazaki', *Animerica*, no.7 (December 1999), pp. 6, 10–11, 13, 18. http://www.animenostalgiabomb.com/princess-mononoke-hayao-miyazaki-interview-animerica-december-1999/ (accessed 30 December 2016).
40   Ogihara-Schuck, *Miyazaki's Animism Abroad*, p. 77.
41   Denison, 'Cultural Traffic in Japanese Anime', pp. 191–2.
42   Finola Kerrigan. *Film Marketing* (Oxford: Elsevier, 2010), p. 6, my emphasis.
43   Kerrigan, *Film Marketing*, p. 6, my emphasis.
44   Finola Kerrigan, *Film Marketing* (Oxford: Elsevier, 2010), p. 88.
45   Denison, 'Cultural Traffic in Japanese Anime', p. 13; Caroline Ruddell, 'Cutting Edge: Violence and Body Horror in Anime' in Feona Attwood, Vincent Campbell, Ian. Q. Hunter and Sharon Lockyer (eds), *Controversial Images: Media Representations on the Edge* (New York: Palgrave Macmillan, 2013), p. 157; Leigh Singer, 'Hayao Miyazaki: Emperor of Anime', *DazedDigtial.com*, 9 May 2014. http://www.dazeddigital.com/artsandculture/article/19856/1/hayao-miyazaki-emperor-of-anime (accessed 30 January 2017), p. 1.
46   Kerrigan, *Film Marketing*, p. 90.
47   Michael Johnson, ed., 'Miramax English Trailer', *The Hayao Miyazaki Web*. http://www.nausicaa.net/miyazaki/mh/relmedia.html#Miramax (accessed 14 April 2017).
48   Steve Neale, 'Questions of Genre' in Robert Stam and Toby Miller (eds), *Film and Theory: An Anthology* (Malden: Blackwell Publishers, 2000), p. 160.
49   Peter Biskind, *Down and Dirty Pictures: Miramax, Sundance and the Rise of Independent Film* (London: Simon and Schuster Paperbacks, 2004); Perren, 'Sex, Lies and Marketing; Justin Wyatt, 'The Formation of the "Major Independent": Miramax, New Line and the New Hollywood' in Steve Neale and Murray Smith (eds), *Contemporary Hollywood Cinema* (London and New York: Routledge, 1998), pp. 74–90.
50   Wyatt, 'The Formation of the "Major Independent." '
51   Biskind, *Down and Dirty Pictures*, p. 1.
52   Hirofumi Katsuno and Jeffrey Maret, 'Localizing the Pokémon TV Series for the American Market' in Joseph Tobin (ed.), *Pikachu's Global Adventure: The Rise and Fall of Pokémon* (Durham, NC and London: Duke University Press, 2004), p. 82.

53 Rayna Denison, 'The Global Markets for *Anime*: Miyazaki Hayao's *Spirited Away* (2001)' in Alastair Phillips and Julian Stringer (eds), *Japanese Cinema: Texts and Contexts* (London: Routledge, 2007), p. 318.

54 Koichi Iwabuchi, *Recentering Globalization: Popular Culture and Japanese Transnationalism* (Durham, NC and London: Duke University Press, 2002), p. 94.

55 Katsuno and Maret, 'Localizing the Pokémon TV Series for the American Market', p. 82.

56 Denison, 'Star-Spangled Ghibli', p. 141.

57 Denison, 'Disembodied Stars', pp. 12–13.

58 Denison, 'The Language of the Blockbuster', p. 140.

59 Denison, 'Disembodied Stars', pp. 7–12.

60 Nathan Beaman, 'Special Features: DVD Extras', *Videomaker Magazine*, November 2008. https://www.videomaker.com/article/13762-special-features-dvd-extras (accessed 30 January 2017), p. 1.

61 Denison, 'Star-Spangled Ghibli', pp. 140–1.

62 Denison, 'Star-Spangled Ghibli', p. 140.

63 Barry King, 'Articulating Stardom' in Christine Gledhill (ed.), *Stardom: Industry of Desire* (London and New York: Routledge, 1991), p. 180.

64 'The Characters', *Princess Mononoke* [online]. http://www.princess-mononoke.com/html/epic/characters/01.html (accessed 14 April 2017), p. 2.

65 'The Characters', p. 3.

66 'The Characters', pp. 8, 10.

67 '*Princess Mononoke* comes to America', *Princess Mononoke* [online]. http://www.princess-mononoke.com/html/epic/cast/02.html (accessed 14 April 2017), p. 2.

68 'The Characters', p. 6.

69 'The Characters', p. 4.

70 'The Characters', p. 12.

71 'The Characters', p. 4.

72 'The Characters', p. 11.

73 Denison, 'Disembodied Stars', p. 12.

74 Iwabuchi, *Recentering Globalization*, pp. 33, 27.

75 Iwabuchi, *Recentering Globalization*, p. 38.

76 Iwabuchi, *Recentering Globalization*, p. 49; Denison, *Anime*, p. 14.

Chapter 9

HOMER, OVID, DISNEY AND *STAR WARS*: THE CRITICAL RECEPTION AND TRANSCULTURAL POPULARITY OF *PRINCESS MONONOKE*

Emma Pett

The 1999 theatrical release of *Princess Mononoke* in the United States signalled the moment in which many Western audiences became aware of Hayao Miyazaki's films for the first time. *Princess Mononoke*'s early reception in the West was characterized by a focus on the film's provenance and attendant issues of cultural translation. Across the intervening years, however, there has been a distinct shift in the frames of reference employed by Western critics to discuss the film, and in this respect it functions as significant marker of changing attitudes towards anime in Western contexts of reception. This chapter tracks the evolving status of *Princess Mononoke* by considering the fluctuating valuations of the film across a 19-year period. In particular, it explores the ways in which a series of comparisons between Hayao Miyazaki's film and an eclectic mix of popular and high culture reference points, from classical European epics by Homer and Ovid to Hollywood film franchises like *Star Wars*, have been employed to localize, frame and valorize the film for Anglophone audiences. These cultural comparisons also reveal an intersection of discourses around genre, audience and industry, as well as reflecting shifting attitudes towards gender identity, race and media violence. Furthermore, by comparing and contrasting news and magazine reviews of *Princess Mononoke* with those offered by online citizen-critics, this chapter also considers developments and continuities in film reviewing practices across a 20-year period, and reflects on the tensions and overlaps between professional and amateur critics in the digital era.

Methodology

This reception study examines 855 reviews published in the US press and 210 reviews published in British newspapers and magazines between 1997 and 2016.[1] These are considered alongside 570 citizen-critic reviews published on

Internet Movie Database (IMDb) by amateur critics and wider audiences of the film. While a small number of these reviews are posted from outside of Britain and North America, the study is primarily focused on Anglophone contexts of reception, exploring the critical and popular evaluations of the text in the United Kingdom and United States. Drawing on the work of Janet Staiger and Barbara Klinger, I consider reviews of *Princess Mononoke* within the historical, cultural and industrial conditions in which they were produced, and with an awareness of the reviewers' 'constructed identities such as gender, sexual preference, race, ethnicity, class and nationality'.[2] This chapter therefore begins with a brief summary of the discourses circulating around anime in the two principle countries of reception, and then tracks the ways in which these discourses shift over a period of nearly two decades.

The use of citizen-critic reviews also facilitates a consideration of the influence of online amateur reviewing practices on the cultural flow and legitimation of anime between Japan and the West. Broader studies on the impact of citizen-critic reviews on established patterns of film criticism suggest that, while they are challenging traditional cultural hierarchies of taste to a certain degree, there are more continuities than dichotomies between traditional and digital reviewing cultures.[3] In his discussion of online reviewing cultures, Matthias Frey argues that

> online reviews and blogs often allow for an expansion of space for writing. There can be a utopian design to these new forms. Whereas print columns have continued to shrink over the decades in the switch to smaller tabloid formats and to give more space to dwindling advertisement, online reviews and blogging allow at least the possibility of five-thousand-word treatises, unscathed by the machinations of rogue copyeditors or subeditors' mangled titles.[4]

While Frey recognizes the democratic potential of online reviews, he goes on to acknowledge that citizen-critics still face a struggle to achieve significant visibility within the vast public sphere of the Internet.[5] Whilst likewise not adopting a wholly utopian view of citizen-critic reviewing cultures, in this chapter I consider the tensions, interactions and dialogue that occurs between traditional print and online film criticism, and the extent to which one informs or influences the other. This is particularly relevant to the period of time under examination, which begins in 1997 when Internet culture was in its infancy, and concludes in 2016, at a point when the overlap between print and digital reviews has made distinctions between the two increasingly blurred.

Comparisons between the content and style of professional and online film reviews are particularly significant when considered in the light of Shyon Baumann's work on the cultural legitimation of film as art. Baumann argues that the valorization of film as an art form by professional critics has played a significant part in the elevation of film culture more broadly within traditional taste cultures.[6] This has primarily been achieved by drawing on a high art discourse and valorizing the director as an artist, or auteur. However, more recent research on amateur reviewing practices, such as the study conducted by Marc Verboord in 2010, suggests that 'peer-produced content generally draws more on popular aesthetic than on high art discourse'.[7] Similarly, Jodi Holopirek's 2007 study of online reviews suggests that while professional film critics generally offer a comprehensive overview of the films they review, citizen-critics more commonly aim to please a specific audience and focus on the 'entertainment value' of the film in question.[8]

Andrew McWhirter's study of film criticism in the twenty-first century proposes that there are now six distinctive schools of film journalism: academic, sophisticated, populist, trade, consumer and fandom.[9] Of these, he identifies IMDb reviews as falling into the category of 'consumer journalism' in that they primarily aim to attribute a value to the products and convey their personal views on them. This differs, McWhirter suggests, from fan journalism, which he argues is more purposeful and has a bias towards a particular genre, filmmaker or actor.[10] This study of the reception of *Princess Mononoke* in the United States and United Kingdom therefore also includes a consideration of the extent to which these qualities attributed to online fan or consumer reviewers by Verboord, Holopirek and McWhirter can be detected in the amateur reviews of Japanese anime written by IMDb citizen-critics, and to what extent such reviews have shaped or otherwise influenced the cultural legitimization of *Princess Mononoke* in the West.

Transcultural Contexts of Reception

Princess Mononoke was Hayao Miyazaki's first film to be released in the United States following the high-profile deal between Tokuma shoten and Buena Vista International, enabling the media conglomerate to distribute Studio Ghibli films in the United States. The decision to distribute *Princess Mononoke* on the Miramax label, rather than on the more family-oriented Buena Vista distribution arm of Disney, marked the film out for a middlebrow, culturally sophisticated audience.[11] *Princess Mononoke*'s premiere at the New York Film Festival that year further accentuated the way in which the film was being culturally positioned within the US marketplace. Much was also made by professional critics of the quality of the adaption, which the *New York Post* felt had 'been effectively translated (by Neil Gaiman) and dubbed into casual Americanese without losing its Japanese essence and voice-overs'.[12] Discussion of Gaiman's translation, and of the choice of stars cast for the dubbed version (including Clare Danes, Billy Bob Thornton, Gillian Anderson and Minnie Driver) meant that US reviews devoted considerable attention to the process of presenting *Princess Mononoke* in an accessible and appealing way for American audiences. Even the most positive critics, such as Ty Burr in *Entertainment Weekly*, speculated 'I'll be very curious to see if American audiences can handle it',[13] thus compounding the sensitivity swirling around *Princess Mononoke*'s provenance and cultural otherness. Overall, though, the reviews focusing on issues of cultural difference were offset by a number of highly positive evaluations of the film. Although *Princess Mononoke* only took $2.2 million at the US box office (compared with 10.7 billion yen in the home market) is it was widely considered to be a critical success. Roger Ebert, for example, placed *Princess Mononoke* sixth on his top ten movies of 1999.[14]

However, it is worth giving further consideration to the discourse surrounding issues of cultural translation; this is prominent in early reviews of the *Princess Mononoke*, but becomes increasingly less frequent over time and with subsequent Studio Ghibli releases. The discourse is particularly evident in assumptions made concerning the differences between Japanese and American audiences for the film, as evidenced in Michael Atkinson's comment 'we may never grasp what it is about *Princess Mononoke* that made it a smash in Japan, but there's no denying that an enormous amount of something or other got lost in the translation'.[15] The discourse surrounding cultural difference is also manifest in evaluations of Miyazaki's animation style. Writing for the *Washington Post*, Stephen Hunter critiques Miyazaki with the following comment: 'The animation is – well, Japanese. That is to say, it's completely vivid and exquisitely detailed and convincing – almost. Somehow the Japanese haven't quite mastered the one trick remaining in the animation bag, which Disney aced years back, and that's the sense of motion. These creatures are fanciful, even beautiful, but somehow when they move they don't seem fully alive.'[16] What makes *Princess Mononoke*'s US release significant, then, is the way in which professional critics respond to its 'Japaneseness', often framing this discussion with comparative comments about Disney films. Koichi Iwabuchi has argued that the proliferation of Japanese culture in the West during the 1990s was partly due to the way products had been rendered 'culturally odourless'.[17] However, as Susan Napier contends – and reviews for *Princess Mononoke* illustrate – this argument does not fully explain the discursive context of the film's US reception. Napier argues instead that it is Miyazaki's 'willingness to entertain a worldview that acknowledges the ambiguity of life, but at the same time exists in a moral framework', that explains the popularity of *Princess Mononoke*.[18] The transcultural context of *Princess Mononoke*'s US release therefore raises questions around the extent to which concerns voiced by the professional critics relating to the cultural translation of the film were justified.

In a marked contrast to the US scenario, *Princess Mononoke* did not obtain a theatrical release in the United Kingdom until 2001, and even then it was extremely limited. The film was first screened at the Barbican in London as part of their 'Studio Ghibli – The Art of Japanese Animation' season in the autumn of that year. The reticence of British distribution and exhibition chains to pick up *Princess Mononoke* before 2001 was echoed in the press response to the film's eventual release; only six newspapers (the *Independent*, the *Times*, the *Sunday*

Times, the *Guardian,* the *Telegraph* and the *Daily Mail*) reviewed the film, and many of these reviews, as discussed throughout this chapter, were both brief and unfavourable. James Christopher in the *Times,* for example, describes the film as 'slurpy and pretty enough, but also total hogwash'.[19] Only Cosmo Landesman in the *Sunday Times* praises *Princess Mononoke* as 'first-class family entertainment'.[20]

The reluctance of UK distributors to pick up *Princess Mononoke* for a British release reflects an on-going uneasiness towards Japanese anime on the part of film critics in the United Kingdom. This hesitancy was a specifically British issue, as identified by Andrew Osmond in the *Guardian* at the time, who wrote:

> Over in France, Cahiers du Cinema compared it to the Kurosawa classics *Rashomon* and *Hidden Fortress.* So why won't Britain see *Princess Mononoke*? The answer may not be unconnected to the fact that *Mononoke* is animated. In Britain, Japanese animation is seen as either schlocky 'manga' that clogs up the shelves in video stores, or the cheap factory animation that ruins children's television.[21]

This dominant discourse circulating in the United Kingdom throughout the 1990s around 'schlocky manga' arose from a confluence of issues surrounding the distribution and reception of anime films. This was, in part, a result of the marketing tactics and distribution decisions made by Island Entertainment, who owned the Manga label. Manga's release of a number of violent and sexually violent anime feature films in the late 1980s and early 1990s had shaped broader perceptions of the genre and earned it a dubious reputation. Attempts to release the *Urotsukidoji* series, though partially thwarted by the British Board of Film Classification (BBFC), fuelled the perception that Japanese animation was warped and twisted, eventually leading to a campaign run by the *Sunday Mail* to close down a London-based mailing list supplying anime films.[22] Both the British and American contexts of reception for *Princess Mononoke*'s theatrical release thus reveal that the cultural flow between Japan and the West was, in the late 1990s, marked by a broad suspicion of anime and reluctance to legitimate Miyazaki's work. This chapter now turns to consider the industrial and generic discourses that shaped this distrust, and the ways in which they manifested in both professional and amateur film criticism.

Generic Expectations: Disney, Ghibli and the Issue of Violence

The shadow of Disney looms large over any reception study of Miyazaki for a number of reasons, not least the rights acquired by the media conglomerate in the 1996 to distribute Studio Ghibli films in the United States. However, in terms of the critical and popular reception of *Princess Mononoke,* it is Disney's cultural domination of the animation genre that makes it an important context for analysing the Western reception of *Princess Mononoke*. As Rayna Denison observes, 'US animation studios, principally Disney, but to a lesser extent, studios like Warner Brothers, Pixar and Dreamworks, have come to define US animation. Their proprietary film cycles so dominate the market for feature film animation in the USA that they offer an alternative to the concept of subgenres: proprietary or branded subgenres.'[23] Denison argues that studio brands, such as Disney and Warner Brothers, organize the gentrification processes of US animation and compete among each other to dominate the 'family' animation picture.[24] Disney's decision to release *Princess Mononoke* on the Miramax label therefore suggests that there was an awareness that the film might be more readily received as an arthouse product than as family fare.

Early reviews of *Princess Mononoke* in the United States speculate fairly explicitly about Disney's decision to release the film with Miramax. Ken Tucker, writing for the *New York Times*, observes that 'Miramax is betting that the audience that made *The Blair Witch Project* a hit still thirsts for something other than the standard blockbuster, and will respond to the pleasant shock of seeing another genre – in this case, the cartoon – reinvented for the end of the century.'[25] Discussions such as these thus revolve around the innovative and slightly subversive qualities of *Princess Mononoke*, framing it in the context of the horror genre. Tucker goes on to describe the more violent elements of the narrative, and concludes: 'Right away, an American viewer gets the message: Walt Disney and *Tarzan* this ain't.'[26] Even those reviews of *Princess Mononoke* appearing in the US press that do not *directly* reference Disney nevertheless draw on the same discourse:

> Flying in the face of popular Western animation, *Princess Mononoke* is not a musical, nor is it primarily directed at preteens, even if that group can readily embrace it. The film represents a bold experiment for Miyazaki, whose earlier work, including *Kiki's Delivery Service*, *The Red Pig* and *My Neighbor Totoro*, had more gentle, youthful themes. The new film, which has grossed more than $150 million in Japan, is not only more sharply drawn, it has an extremely complex and adult script.[27]

Leonard Klady's review highlights the obvious differences between *Princess Mononoke* and Western animation films, thus reflecting Denison's observation that, regardless of whether an American animation film is produced by Disney, Warner Brothers or Pixar, it is invariably aimed at the family audience.

What marks *Princess Mononoke* out as culturally different is not just its violent content. As Susan Napier and Helen McCarthy both discuss, the narrative structure and resolution of *Princess Mononoke*, in which the central characters agree to live apart, offers an important alternative to the inclusionary endings common to Disney films.[28] These adult themes also prompted several US journalists to direct their reviews at parents and guardians, writing 'let parents consider themselves warned. Anyone expecting a clawless cartoon fairy tale they can just dump the kids at while slipping off to see *Fight Club* will be sorely disappointed.[29] A significant number of reviews published for the film in the late 1990s and early 2000s strongly emphasize that *Princess Mononoke* is 'not a film for the kids.'[30] Indeed, if there is one point that professional critics share a general consensus on, it is that *Princess Mononoke* is unsuitable for children.

The initial reception of *Princess Mononoke* in the United Kingdom was likewise informed by discussions around generic expectations of animation films; again, these were guided by the assumption that animation films were primarily intended for children. A precedent had already been set for the regulation of Japanese anime at the BBFC around the classification of *Urotsukidoji*, during which one examiner had stated: 'In this country (plainly not in contemporary Japan) the cartoon is regarded as a visual art form of pure entertainment, and intended principally for children. No-one expects an animated film to be a didactic exploration of major human themes; its audience plans to be entertained, so whatever is presented is received as entertainment.'[31] Advance reviews of *Princess Mononoke* in the British press focused on the violent content of the film. Reporting in the *Guardian* on the box office success of the film in its home market, Jonathan Watts observed that 'as well as being morally complex, *Princess Mononoke* is at times extremely violent: humans and animals spill buckets of each other's blood in the battle for survival.'[32] Similarly, shortly after *Princess Mononoke*'s UK release, Rupert Mellor observes in the *Times* that 'some of the more controversial areas of adult-orientated anime mean that many consumers consider the entire genre as off-limits.'[33] These cultural frameworks serve to highlight the reluctance on the part of professional British film critics to legitimize anime as a culturally *bona fide* product.

As in the United States, the problematic issue of violence and adult themes in a genre 'intended principally for children' also sits alongside comparisons between *Princess Mononoke* and Disney. Writing in the *Independent*, Anthony Quinn summarizes that 'I can't see this knocking Disney off its perch over here: the animation has no great subtlety, the script is almost entirely humourless, and at 134 minutes, it will test the patience of the staunchest eco-warrior.'[34] Yet, despite the obvious differences between the animation styles of Disney and Miyazaki, there was a tendency amongst some British critics in the early 2000s to frame Studio Ghibli films within this comparative context, as evidenced in an article published in the *Independent on Sunday* a few years later that refers to *Princess Mononoke* as 'a technically astounding animation by the Ghibli Studio, sometimes referred to in the West as "the Disney of the East." '[35] The inability of many professional British and American film critics to locate Japanese animation within a recognizable generic framework thus begat a slew of comparisons attempting to position the products using their own cultural markers. As *Princess Mononoke* was the first Miyazaki film to be distributed by Disney and promoted in a Western context, these cultural touchstones are perhaps more evident in the late 1990s, and, over a period of almost 20 years, reveal shifting attitudes around transcultural media consumption and the valorization of Miyazaki as an East Asian auteur.

While professional film critics in both the United States and United Kingdom frame and problematize their evaluations of *Princess Mononoke* in the context of the Disney brand, amateur reviews of the film posted on IMDb often employ the Disney comparison in a different way. When Disney is discussed on IMDb, citizen-critics more frequently take an oppositional stance to this industrial and cultural positioning of the text. For example, one contributor argues that 'some say he is the Japanese Disney, but I don't like that. His work has a depth and sophistication that goes beyond Disney cute. There is no other animation like it. This is truly an adult work: children might like some of the visuals, but I doubt that many kids below teen age will have any idea what it is all about, and even adults will get more out of this each time you see it again.'[36] Other citizen-critic reviews of the film posted on IMDb also reflect an appreciation of the sophistication of *Princess Mononoke*'s narrative when compared to animation films produced in the United States; however, these citizen-critics tend to adopt a slightly different position to the professional critics on the film's suitability for children. One reviewer comments that 'the complexity of this movie is something never seen in the United States in an animated movie and even exceeds that of most live action movies as well . . . this is truly an adult movie but my children, ages 12 to 15 all loved it and talked about it for days later. Even my wife who holds a strong prejudice against Japanese animation enjoyed this movie.'[37] In this respect, amateur reviews are far less likely to be characterized by a distrust of the 'Japaneseness' of *Princess Mononoke*.

References made to Disney by IMDb users are thus more frequently employed to demonstrate an appreciation of *Princess Mononoke*'s complexity and cultural sophistication. For example, one comment posted by a British citizen-critic suggests that for some amateur reviewers, *Princess Mononoke* carries a subcultural capital.[38] For this reviewer, the cultural value of the film lies in the way it functions as an alternative to mainstream or 'commercial' American products like Disney:

> In England we grow up on an unappealing diet of Disney tripe, but we don't realise it is so shoddy because it's all we have. This is because we don't have a strong animation industry of our own really, with the possible exception of Aardman Animations, and we are gripped by America's commercial stranglehold. The lower classes in this country love America and anything it produces, because they are ignorant, pure and simple. The sad fact is that the average person in the street has not heard of Studio Ghibli or Miyazaki.[39]

This review of *Princess Mononoke* reveals how the Disney brand can also be used as a marker for expressing distaste for American animation and 'low culture' as much as for an appreciation of Miyazaki's film. While both the professional and amateur reviewers are largely in agreement that Miyazaki's film is more 'adult' and 'sophisticated' than a Disney feature, the extent to which this comparison operates as a positive or negative evaluation of the film varies. Evidence suggests that citizen-critics are more likely to reference Disney as a means to elevate Miyazaki's cultural status, whilst professional reviewers, such as Mathews,[40] Files, Howell and Quinn use the same comparative framework to critique the violence of *Princess Mononoke* and imply that it is unsuitable for children. These on-going valuations around high- and low-cultural markers can be traced back to the 1999 US release of the film, and its contextual ties with the *Star Wars* franchise.

Beyond Generic Frameworks: Star Wars, *Fantasy and the 'Quality' Debate*

The US release of *Princess Mononoke* in October 1999 arrived just a few months after that of *Star Wars: Episode 1 – The Phantom Menace* (George Lucas, 1999), which received its theatrical premiere in May 1999. For those film critics attempting to convey the fantasy elements of *Princess Mononoke* to their readers, it was therefore perhaps inevitable that they would turn to one of the most popular film franchises of recent times as a point of reference. Writing in the *New York Post*, Jonathan Foreman references the latest *Star Wars* instalment as a means to offer a favourable valuation of *Princess Mononoke,* claiming that 'it's the *Star Wars* of animated features, a haunting, beautiful film that holds your attention despite its length and its complex plot, which is rooted in Japanese folk tales and animist mythology'.[41] Though Foreman's influential review was later used as an endorsement on the *Optimum Asia* DVD release of the film, other professional critics employed the *Star Wars* comparison differently. Andrew O'Hehir's review suggested that 'maybe George Lucas would make a movie like this if he had the dramatic chops or the largeness of spirit to pull it off; next to the beauty and tragedy of *Princess Mononoke, Star Wars: Episode I* looks like dim radiation from a dull and distant galaxy.[42] This valuation of *Princess Mononoke* resonates with several critics, such as Ty Burr in *Entertainment Weekly*, who concludes that 'when it's over, you realize you've witnessed a vision with the cumulative, mythic power of a *Lord of the Rings*, a *Narnia* Chronicles, or a *Star Wars*. In fact, George Lucas can only wish *The Phantom Menace* was as good – as wondrous and otherworldly – as this.'[43]

While the professional critics employ the *Star Wars* reference in quite different ways, online critics, such as blogger Daniel Mumby, directly address the *New York Post* review, offering the oppositional view that '*Princess Mononoke* is not "the *Star Wars* of animation" – because it's arguably a whole lot better than *Star Wars*'.[44] This blog is interesting in that it is written twelve years after the original review, illustrating how Internet reviews provide more than merely the opportunity to post instant responses to films. In this case they facilitate an ongoing dialogue between professional and amateur film critics about their evaluations of particular film titles. Similarly, an IMDb review poster in May 2016 writes 'this is NOT the *Star Wars* of animation . . . no matter what the *New York Post* said about it'.[45] Citizen-critic reviewing cultures thus function a space for fans and amateur reviewers to question the validity of the professional critics' interpretations, and create an on-going dialogue that extends beyond the initial reception of the film.

Many professional film critics rely on *Star Wars*, *The Lord of the Rings* and *Narnia* to provide recognizable fantasy fiction frameworks with which they can evaluate *Princess Mononoke*. These generic comparisons vary slightly from one critic to another, but draw on a similar canon of reference points, which are evident in a review published in the *Independent on Sunday* which describes *Princess Mononoke* as 'an eco-adventure that felt like Tolkien storyboarded by Kurosawa'.[46] However, there are some notable exceptions to this dominant critical pattern, one being Peter Bradshaw's review in *The Guardian*, in which he writes: 'I must admit to being agnostic about the animation: particularly the humans' saucer-eyed moppet faces: but the story has simplicity and force, with captivating images and gutsy narrative ideas recalling Kipling, Ovid and Homer'.[47] Bradshaw offers an elevated estimation of Miyazaki's film by likening it to classical Greek mythology and other high art touchstones that position *Princess Mononoke* as culturally superior to Disney and other animation films. In this way, Bradshaw follows the tradition of film criticism discussed by Baumann that seeks to position certain texts as culturally legitimate through a series of art and literature references to 'othered' subjects.[48]

Interestingly, online citizen-critics and amateur reviewers are, like Bradshaw, also more likely to deviate from using dominant cultural touchstones, instead preferring to employ a more eclectic range of comparisons. One amateur reviewer writes that

> no animated film had ever moved me as much as a *Godfather* [Francis Ford Coppola, 1972] or *Unforgiven* [Clint Eastwood, 1992] or *Dr. Strangelove* [*Dr. Strangelove or, How I Learned to Stop Worrying and Love the Bomb*, Stanley Kubrick, 1974], that is until one fine day in 1999. I was in high school, and *Princess Mononoke* was premiering at the Coolidge Theater in Brookline, I was pumped as I really enjoyed *Castle in the Sky* and *Totoro*, so I went to the theater with a few friends and was absolutely blown away.[49]

This amateur reviewer moves beyond traditional generic boundaries, drawing parallels between *Princess Mononoke* and a gangster movie, a western and a political satire as a means underscore the autobiographical significance of the film. Framing memories of watching the film within a personal life narrative is a feature of citizen-critic reviews that is not observed as frequently in the discourses of professional critics, and offers an alternative framework of valuation.

Similarly, another IMDb reviewer likens the characters to those found in *Citizen Kane* (Orson Welles, 1941), *Raging Bull* (Martin Scorsese, 1980) and *Metropolis* (Fritz Lang, 1927), noting that

Ashitaka especially, the main character of the film, is so nuanced that he has become in my mind one of the great characters in film, up there with Charles Foster Kane and Jake La Motta. I would compare him to Freder, the main character of Fritz Lang's *Metropolis*. His role in the film is a mediator between the forces of humans and the gods of nature.[50]

Rather than employ references to popular genre films a means to evaluate *Princess Mononoke*, this reviewer instead discusses *Citizen Kane* and *Metropolis*. In this respect the citizen review eschews the parameters of popular film criticism as defined by Verboord and McWhirter, and instead invokes the 'quality' debate. This tendency amongst anime fans and amateur critics has also been observed by Susan Napier, who notes that 'what may be most surprising to those unfamiliar with anime is that for most fans, the important difference is not between cultures per se, but between the quality of cultural products'.[51] Napier's observation clearly reflects the characteristics of amateur reviews offered by IMDb users in relation to *Princess Mononoke* considered in this study. These findings imply that, in the case of the transcultural reception of Japanese anime, fan or amateur reviews differ from those analysed in the broader studies of citizen-critic practices undertaken by Verboord, McWhirter and Holopirek, in that they do not merely make reductive value statements about how much they like or dislike the film. This 'quality' debate therefore propels *Princess Mononoke* beyond discourses linked to cultural provenance, and demonstrates the significant role the film has played historically in challenging Western preconceptions of animation.

Miyazaki as Auteur: Festivals, Awards and Critical Accolades

Discourses around auteurism have long been recognized as instrumental in elevating the status and cultural capital of a film director. Recent studies of film criticism in the United States and United Kingdom suggest that, despite increasing variances in reviewing cultures facilitated by the Internet, 'critically acclaimed films tend to be appraised with a strong emphasis on auteurism'.[52] This valorization of a director as an auteur is facilitated by a number of commercial institutions and industrial framings. The evaluation of *Princess Mononoke* alongside *The Godfather, Unforgiven* and *Dr. Strangelove* by citizen-critics on IMDb positions Miyazaki's film next to three feature films that have garnered widespread critical recognition and numerous accolades on the awards circuit.

These amateur evaluations were also evident in a small number (though certainly not all) of the American and British professional reviews considered. Writing in the *Chicago Sun-Times*, Roger Ebert notes that

Princess Mononoke was the top-grossing film in Japanese history until it was dethroned by *Titanic*. It was preceded in the American market by two of Miyazaki's magical family oriented films, *My Neighbor Totoro* and *Kiki's Delivery Service*. This one transcends everything else he has done, and is being given a major push by Miramax, with an opening Oct. 29. If the Motion Picture Academy truly does seek out the five best features of the year, then it is hard to see how it can fail to nominate this one.[53]

Ebert's review registers the implications of the film being distributed by Miramax, and speculates about its potential to receive an Oscar nomination – which it did not. However, the potential for *Princess Mononoke* to receive this kind of critical accolade was clearly considered to be a possibility. Rayna Denison observes that 'from the first Miramax-produced trailer for *Princess Mononoke*, claims were made about Hayao Miyazaki being a "master animator" and subsequent trailers continued this pattern'.[54] These observations acknowledge not just the brand-genre awareness that Disney were building around Studio Ghibli, but also the significance of Miyazaki as a 'master animator'. A subsequent step, then, in Miyazaki's elevation within transcultural contexts of film reception, was his on-going valorization as an auteur. This was instigated not just by Disney and a minority of professional critics, but more significantly by amateur online reviewers.

Key to the elevation of several East Asian auteurs within western contexts of reception has been their status on the festival circuit. The precedent set by Kurosawa's *Rashomon* (1950), which won the Golden Lion at the 1951 Venice Film Festival and an Academy Award in 1952, has shaped the trajectory of Asian film promotion within a western context across the intervening decades. Joanne Bernardi notes, in her summary of the international reception of Japanese cinema between 1951 and 1985, that when Kurosawa's period film *Kagemusha* (1980) won the Golden Palm at Cannes in 1980 there was immediately discussion of a 'long-awaited new dawn of the Japanese film'.[55] *Princess Mononoke* was initially screened as part of the New York Film Festival programme in 1999, and its critical reception in the United States was thus informed by this high culture acknowledgement. Janet Maslin's review of the film in the *New York Times* reflects this discourse, and focuses on Miyazaki's status with other successful directors of animation feature films:

> 'Not a day goes by that I do not utilize the tools learned from studying his films,' John Lasseter (*Toy Story*, *A Bug's Life*) has said. Barry Cook and Tony Bancroft, whose *Mulan* shows string evidence of Mr. Miyazaki's influence, are on the record with 'Miyazaki is like a god to us.' *Princess Mononoke*, which was shown over the weekend as part of the New York Film Festival (an unusual distinction for an animated feature), explains what they mean.[56]

This framing of the film reinforces the significance of film festivals in establishing the auteur status of international directors. Wikanda Promkhunthong's research on the international reception of East Asian directors such as Wong

Kar Wai and Kim Ki-duk similarly observes the role played by film festivals in establishing their auteur status, which she argues leads to wider commercial exposure within the international marketplace.[57] While the UK release of *Princess Mononoke* was not accompanied by a screening at a high-profile film festival, its promotion as part of the Studio Ghibli season at the Barbican in London, an arts venue long associated with high culture, was inevitably part of the reason behind the limited coverage it received in the national press, particularly where the tabloid newspapers were concerned.

In the time that has elapsed since *Princess Mononoke* was first released in the United States, a narrative has subsequently been repeated on both sides of the Atlantic surrounding Miyazaki's relationship with Miramax. Interviewing Miyazaki in the *Guardian*, Xan Brooks speculates on the relationship between Disney and Studio Ghibli, repeating the story that 'Disney wields no creative control. There is a rumour that when Harvey Weinstein was charged with handling the US release of *Princess Mononoke*, Miyazaki sent him a samurai sword in the post. Attached to the blade was a stark message: "No cuts." '[58]

Miyazaki reportedly responds to Brooks with the comment: ' "Actually, my producer did that. Although I did go to New York to meet this man, this Harvey Weinstein, and I was bombarded with this aggressive attack, all these demands for cuts." He smiles. "I defeated him." '[59] The director is thus complicit in the construction of his auteur image and the 'no cuts' narrative, which is re-told in other articles about Miyazaki appearing in the Western press.[60] In a number of ways, then, the critical reception and marketing hype that has accompanied *Princess Mononoke* in the United States and United Kingdom has served to elevate the cultural status of the film within a Western context. The mythologizing discourse surrounding Miyazaki in particular has propelled the film beyond the usual reception frameworks for discussing animation, and has facilitated re-evaluations of *Princess Mononoke's* broader cultural significance in the light of what could be termed 'the Miyazaki effect'.

The Miyazaki Effect: The Wider Cultural Influences and Legacy of Princess Mononoke

A final perspective from which to consider the changing status of *Princess Mononoke* within western contexts of film reception are the recent references made by professional and amateur critics to the growing legacy of the film. Writing a review of *Snow White and the Huntsman* (Rupert Sanders, 2012) in the *Daily Mail*, Chris Tookey suggests that Sanders' influences include 'strong echoes of Guillermo del Toro's *Pan's Labyrinth*, Peter Jackson's *Lord Of The Rings* trilogy and Hayao Miyazaki's dreamlike cartoon *Princess Mononoke*'.[61] Tookey's review indicates that, just as Ovid and Homer were used to elevate the cultural status of *Princess Mononoke* in earlier reviews of films, the film has now itself become an established cultural touchstone within a canon of creative fantasy films by auteur directors. A similar use of *Princess Mononoke* is also made in a recent review of *Kubo and the Two Strings* (Travis Knight, 2016) in the *Chicago Tribune*: 'Kubo feels like a gorgeously illustrated Japanese fable, with gloriously crafted images serving strong narrative points. It resembles an intelligent, strong-scripted mash-up of *Harry Potter* and Hayao Miyazaki's dazzling fantasy *Princess Mononoke*, balancing a childlike sense of wonderment with subjects possessing a much more complex, mature and serious tone.'[62] In both the United States and the United Kingdom, then, there is a sense in which *Princess Mononoke* has become a legitimate part of the animation canon, and functions to define the 'high culture' end of the animation spectrum.

This re-evaluation of the cultural significance of *Princess Mononoke* is also evident in a 2014 *Guardian* review of *Kaze tachinu* (*The Wind Rises*, Hayao Miyazaki, 2014), which opens with this assessment of Miyazaki's legacy:

> It seems like yesterday that Hayao Miyazaki, the master of Japanese anime, was making his US debut with *Princess Mononoke*, a lush, deeply imagined environmental allegory. That 1997 movie was the first time many American filmgoers entered Miyazaki's world of myth, magic and lyrical, finely detailed imagery; happily, there are now generations of children who have grown up cherishing such Miyazaki classics as *My Neighbour Totoro, Kiki's Delivery Service, Spirited Away* and *Howl's Moving Castle* the way their parents did *Snow White, 101 Dalmatians* and *The Aristocats*.[63]

In her reflection on Miyazaki's career and influence, Ann Hornaday, who also reviews for the *Washington Post*, positions *Princess Mononoke* as a turning point in the western reception of his work. Although returning to Disney as a cultural reference point, she positions Miyazaki's films as a 'classics' that have shaped a generation of children, thus suggesting the significance and reach of his cultural influence.

Princess Mononoke's cultural influence has also informed a number of academic discussions moving beyond film scholarship. In her comparative analysis of the heroines found in Miyazaki and Disney films, religious studies scholar Christine Hoff Kraemer discusses representations of romantic love and observes that, unlike Disney films such as *Mulan*, the relationship between Ashitaka and San is established as a relationship between equals. Hoff Kraemer concludes that 'in terms of providing strong female role models for our children, however, the choice between Disney and Miyazaki is clear: the future of feminism in animated films is undoubtedly Japanese.'[64] This observation constitutes one of the earliest re-evaluations of San as a feminist heroine, foreshadowing a number of popular feminist evaluations of her significance as a role model for young girls.

Moving beyond the world of academic criticism, Miyazaki's influence is also apparent in a number of diverse cultural contexts, spanning from popular music to more highbrow art forms. Linda Stein, a New York sculptor, has a developed her critical reputation around references to provocative and inspiring female figures from mythical and popular culture; one of these is the heroine of Miyazaki's blockbuster film, *Princess Mononoke*.[65] However, it is not just a New York artist who is engaging in a feminist appropriation of *Princess Mononoke*. In her article 'Kickass Feminists on Film: *Princess Mononoke*', for the digital magazine *Lip*, Jade Bate argues that Miyazaki's female characters, and in particular San from *Princess Mononoke*, were offering cinematic visions of female empowerment long before Disney produced *Brave* (Brenda Chapman and Mark Andrews, 2012) and *Frozen* (Chris Buck and Jennifer Lee, 2013).[66] Similarly, and despite the early negative reviews that focused on the violence of the film and its inappropriateness for children, *Princess Mononoke*'s rehabilitation in the United Kingdom has centred on the positive role model the film offers to young girls. In a recent article discussing online resources for women, for example, it is noted that '*Times* journalist Wendy Ide has compiled a series of alternatives to the films kids obsess over – she suggests Japanese animation *Princess Mononoke* as a break for mums exhausted by repeat views of *Frozen*.'[67] This feminist reframing of *Princess Mononoke* thus provides a final discursive context for understanding the changing cultural value and status of the film, though undoubtedly there will be many more.

Conclusion

This overview of the reception of *Princess Mononoke* in the United States and United Kingdom does not cover all critical evaluations of the film, and there are clearly many individual reviewers whose responses do not reflect the broader trends identified here. However, analysing reviews from across the professional and amateur spectrum reveals some significant patterns. Early professional reviews of *Princess Mononoke* published between 1997 and 2002, though mixed in tone and levels of appreciation, tend to query the violent content of the film and speculate about its potential audience; these professional reviewers are largely united in their view that *Princess Mononoke* is not a film for children. Alongside this discourse centring on violence and audience suitability, the Disney brand is repeatedly employed as a point of comparison. While professional critics tend to make this comparison in a way that elevates Disney and challenges the cultural legitimacy of *Princess Mononoke*, the citizen-critic reviews posted on IMDb frequently do the reverse.

Citizen-critics also take an oppositional perspective to some of the professional reviewers in relation to comparisons made with *Star Wars*, sometimes openly challenging specific newspapers. This suggests that the advent of online amateur reviewing practices has produced tensions and dialogues between professional and amateur film critics. However, while McWhirter, Holopirek and Verhooven have argued that citizen-critics tend to employ less aesthetic and culturally sophisticated forms of appreciation than professional reviewers, in many cases the amateur reviews of *Princess Mononoke* imply that this is not the case. What becomes apparent in later reviews for *Princess Mononoke* and other Miyazaki films is that the tradition of valorizing and legitimizing film directors, as discussed by Baumann, is very much evident amongst both professional and amateur film critics alike.

Perhaps the most interesting shift in discourses circulating around *Princess Mononoke*, however, involves her celebration as a feminist icon. Whereas the film's violent content meant that the early reception of *Princess Mononoke* saw it designated as unsuitable for children, its re-evaluation in the context of contemporary feminist discourse means it is now recommended viewing for young girls in conservative parenting circles, and advocated by *Times* journalist Wendy Ide. This diachronic examination of the way in which both high- and low-cultural touchstones have been employed in Western contexts of reception to denigrate, interrogate and valorize the cultural status of *Princess Mononoke* therefore reveals the significance of the film in a number a contexts: as a reminder of the on-going hegemonic dominance of Western cultural markers, be they Homer, Ovid, Disney or *Star Wars*; as a case study for capturing the changing attitudes towards animation in the West; and perhaps most importantly, as a revealing insight into shifting attitudes towards gender, and the designation and legitimization of positive role models for girls in the early twenty-first century.

Notes

1 These reviews were sourced using the Nexis database and by conducting online searches for 'Princess Mononoke'.

2 Janet Staiger, *Interpreting Film: Studies in the Historical Reception of American Cinema* (Princeton, NJ: Princeton University Press, 1992), p. xiii.

3 Marc Verboord, 'The Impact of Peer-Produced Criticism on Cultural Evaluation: A Multilevel Analysis of Discourse Employment in Online and Offline Film Reviews', *New Media and Society*, vol. 16, no. 6 (2014), p. 921.

4 Matthias Frey, 'Introduction: Critical Questions' in Matthias Frey and Cecilia Sayed (eds), *Film Criticism in the Digital Age* (New Brunswick, NJ: Rutgers University Press, 2015), p. 8.

5 Matthias Frey, 'The New Democracy? Rotten Tomatoes, Metacritic, Twitter and IMDb' in Matthias Frey and Cecilia Sayed (eds), *Film Criticism in the Digital Age* (New Brunswick, NJ: Rutgers University Press, 2015), p. 95.

6 Shyon Baumann, 'Intellectualization and Art World Development: Film in the United States', *American Sociological Review*, vol. 66, no. 3 (2001), pp. 404–26.

7 Verboord, 'The Impact of Peer-Produced Criticism on Cultural Evaluation', p. 935.

8 Jodi A. Holopirek, 'Online Journalism: The Transformation of the Film Review' (PhD thesis submitted to the University of Kansas, 2007), p. iii.

9 Andrew McWhirter, 'Film Criticism in the Twenty-First Century', *Journalism Practice*, vol. 9, no. 6 (2015), p. 897.

10 McWhirter, 'Film Criticism in the Twenty-First Century', p. 899.

11 This decision might also have been informed by Studio Ghibli's insistence that they retained the licensing rights to their merchandise. See: Rayna Denison,

'Transcultural Creativity in Anime: Hybrid Identities in the Production, Distribution, Texts and Fandom of Japanese Anime', *Creative Industries Journal*, vol. 3, no. 3 (2010), pp. 223–4 for further discussion of this.

12 Janet Maslin, 'Waging a Mythic Battle to Preserve a Pristine Forest', *The New York Times*, 27 September 1999.

13 Ty Burr, 'Here's the Next *Star Wars*-like Epic', *Entertainment Weekly*, 3 November 1999. http://www.ew.com/article/1999/11/03/heres-next-star-wars-epic (accessed 18 September 2016).

14 Roger Ebert, 'The Best 10 Movies of 1999', *Roger Ebert's Journal*, 31 December 1999. http://www.rogerebert.com/rogers-journal/the-best-10-movies-of-1999 (accessed 20 September 2016).

15 Michael Atkinson, '*Princess Mononoke* Review', *Mr. Showbiz*, 29 October 1999.

16 Stephen Hunter, 'The Bland Violence of *Mononoke*', *Washington Post*, 5 November 1999.

17 Koichi Iwabuchi, 'How "Japanese" is Pokémon?' in Joseph Tobin (ed.), *Pikachu's Global Adventure: The Rise and Fall of Pokémon* (Durham, NC: Duke University Press, 2004), pp. 53–79.

18 Susan J. Napier, 'The World of Anime Fandom in America' in Frenchy Lunning (ed.), *Mechademia: Emerging Worlds of Anime and Manga* (Minneapolis, MN: University of Minnesota Press, 2006), p. 60.

19 James Christopher, 'Another Fine Mess', *Times*, 18 October 2001.

20 Cosmo Landesman, 'This Week's Films', *The Sunday Times*, 21 October 2001.

21 Andrew Osmond, 'Beauty and the Beastly: It's Gorgeous, It's Japan's Biggest Hit Ever, and It's not *Pokemon*. But Will Prejudice against Violent Manga Cartoons Prevent us from Seeing *Princess Mononoke*?', *The Guardian*, 14 April 2000.

22 Emma Pett, '"Blood, Guts and Bambi Eyes": *Urotsukidoji* and the Transcultural Reception and Regulation of Anime', *Journal of British Cinema and Television*, vol. 13, no. 3 (2016), pp. 390–408.

23 Rayna Denison, *Anime: A Critical Introduction* (London: Bloomsbury, 2015), p. 118.

24 Denison, *Anime*, p. 119.

25 Ken Tucker, 'Cute Characters, But No Comic Relief', *New York Times*, 12 September 1999.

26 Tucker, 'Cute Characters, But No Comic Relief'.

27 Leonard Klady, *Daily Variety*, 30 January 1998.

28 Susan J. Napier, *Anime from Akira to Howl's Moving Castle* (New York: Palgrave Macmillan, 2005), p. 248.

29 Gemma Files, '*Mononoke* – Warrior Princess: Powerful Japanese Anime Takes First Dip in North America Mainstream', *Eye*, 28 October 1999.

30 Burr, 'Here's the Next *Star Wars*-like Epic'; Files, '*Mononoke*'; Peter Howell, 'Animated Feature a Bit Dark for the Kids', *Toronto Star*, 29 October 1999; Joe Morgenstern, 'John Malkovich Is Weird, and We Mean That in a Good Way', *Wall Street Journal*, 29 October 1999.

31 British Board of Film Classification, 'Examiner's Report on *Urotsukidoji: Legend of the Overfiend*', 8 October 1992.

32 Jonathan Watts, 'Japan in Grip of Blood-soaked Cartoon Film: E.T. Sent Packing; The Queues Are Starting at Dawn for an Animated Feature Film Breaking all Box Office Records', *The Guardian*, 5 November 1997.

33 Rupert Mellor, 'Film Profile: Japanimation', *The Times*, 19 October 2002.

34 Anthony Quinn, 'Also Showing', *Independent*, 21 October 2001.

35 James McNair, 'The Life Aquatic: When Bjork Started Going Out with American Artist Matthew Barney', *Independent on Sunday*, 17 July 2005.

36 IMDb review 2006. All reviews have been anonymized.

37 IMDb review, 2000.

38 Sarah Thornton, *Club Cultures: Music, Media and Subcultural Capital* (Cambridge: Polity, 1995).

39 IMDb review, 2007.

40 Jack Mathews, 'This Dark "Princess" Isn't for Kids', *New York Daily News*, 29 October 1999.

41 Jonathan Foreman, 'A Very Pretty "Toon"', *New York Post*, 29 October 1999.

42 Andrew O'Hehir, '*Princess Mononoke*: After the Success of Disney's Mulan, Miramax Does Its Parent Company One Better'. *Salon*, 27 October 1999.

43 Burr, 'Here's the Next *Star Wars*-Like Epic'.

44 Daniel Mumby, 'Film Review: *Princess Mononoke*', *Three Men on a Blog*, 15 March 2001. http://threemenonablog.blogspot.co.uk/2011/03/film-review-princess-mononoke-1997.html (accessed 19 September 2016).

45 IMDb review 2016.

46 Jonathan Romney, 'Arts: Film – Watch Out for the Stink God', *Independent on Sunday*, 14 September 2003.

47 Peter Bradshaw, 'Film: *Princess Mononoke*', *The Guardian*, 19 October 2001.

48 Baumann, 'Intellectualization and Art World Development'.

49 IMDb review 2003.

50 IMDb review 2005.

51 Susan J. Napier, *From Impressionism to Anime: Japan as Fantasy and Fan Cult in the Mind of the West* (Basingstoke: Palgrave Macmillan, 2007), p. 176.

52 Annemarie Kersten and Denise D. Bielby, 'Film Discourse on the Praised and Acclaimed: Reviewing Criteria in the United States and United Kingdom', *Popular Communication*, vol. 10, no. 3 (2014), p. 196.

53 Ebert, 'The Best 10 Movies of 1999'.

54 Denison, *Anime*, p. 120.

55 Joanne.R. Bernardi, 'Catching a Film Audience Abroad,' *Japan Quarterly*, vol. 32, no. 3 (1985), p. 290.

56 Janet Maslin, 'Waging a Mythic Battle to Preserve a Pristine Forest', *New York Times*, 27 September 1999.

57 Wikanda Promkhunthong, 'Wong Kar-wai: "Cultural Hybrid", Celebrity Endorsement and Star-auteur Branding', *Celebrity Studies*, vol. 5, no. 3 (2014), p. 351.

58 Xan Brooks, 'A God among Animators: Hayao Miyazaki's Hand-Crafted Fables Have Made Him Japan's Most Successful Film-Maker Ever', *The Guardian*, 14 September 2005.

59 Brooks, 'A God among Animators'.

60 Robbie Collin, 'Goodbye Studio Ghibli, Your Genius Will Endure', *Daily Telegraph*, 4 August 2014.

61 Christopher Tookey, 'Charlize Makes a Mean Queen: Theron's Evil Stepmother Will Leave You Quaking in Your Boots', *Daily Mail*, 1 June 2012.

62 Colin Covert, '*Kubo and the Two Strings* Review: A Thrilling Action-Adventure for All', *Chicago Tribune*, 19 August 2016.
63 Ann Hornaday, 'Hayao Miyazaki Offers Anime Enthusiasts a Final Flight of Fancy', *The Guardian*, 23 February 2014.
64 Christine Hoff Kraemer, 'Disney, Miyazaki and Feminism: Why Western Girls Need Japanese Animation', *Christine Hoff Kraemer*, 2000. http://www.christinehoffkraemer.com/miyazaki.html (accessed 20 September 2016).
65 Chael Needle, 'Artist Linda Stein Talks to Lester Strong about Gender, AIDS and Self-Empowerment', *A&U America's Aids Magazine*, 4 June 2015. http://www.aumag.org/2015/06/04/linda-stein/ (accessed 16 September 2016).
66 Jade Bate, 'Kickass Feminists on Film: *Princess Mononoke*', *Lip*, no.13 (September 2014). http://lipmag.com/arts/film-arts/kickass-feminists-on-film-princess-mononoke/ (accessed 20 September 2016).
67 Ian Burrell, 'The Digital World for Women is Breaking New Ground', *The Independent*, 14 November 2014.

A GUIDE TO FURTHER RESEARCH

The publishing world around manga and anime has exploded in recent years, making a guide like this one far more of a challenge than in the past. The aim here is to highlight the major resources (in English) that students and researchers might find helpful, so it is not an exhaustive list. Rather, this guide is intended as a starting point for future bibliographies, and as a recommended set of readings for those interested in finding out more about *Princess Mononoke*, Hayao Miyazaki or anime in general. There is also a filmography at the end of this book, for suggestions for further viewing.

Mononokehime and *Princess Mononoke*

Denison, Rayna. 'The Language of the Blockbuster: Promotion, *Princess Mononoke* and the *Daihitto* in Japanese Film Culture' in Leon Hunt and Leung Wing-Fai (eds), *East Asian Cinemas: Exploring Transnational Connections on Film* (London and New York: I. B. Tauris, 2008a), pp. 103–22.
   This chapter in East Asian Cinemas is one of the first to tackle Miyazaki's success in Japan. In it, I build on the work of Chris Berry (2003) to suggest that the *daihitto* film culture in Japan has helped to turn Miyazaki's *Mononokehime* into a 'local' blockbuster film.

Hoff Kraemer, Christine. 'Between the Worlds: Liminality and Self-Sacrifice in *Princess Mononoke*', *Journal of Religion & Film*, vol. 8, no. 2 (2016), Article 1. http://digitalcommons.unomaha.edu/jrf/vol8/iss2/1 (accessed 16 June 2017).
   In this article, Hoff Kraemer explores the relationship between the protagonists of *Princess Mononoke*. She infers the use of religious allegory in the positioning of Ashitaka as saviour/mediator between the warring factions of *Princess Mononoke*.

McCarthy, Helen. *Hayao Miyazaki: Master of Japanese Animation* (Berkeley, CA: Stone Bridge Press, 1999).
   McCarthy's book was the first English-language work on Hayao Miyazaki, and even though it was not written as an academic textbook, the meticulous research and careful attention to detail mean that it is still a treasure trove of information. Although the chapter on *Princess Mononoke* is just one among many, McCarthy expertly argues that this film needs to be understood in

relation to Miyazaki's history and oeuvre of films, but also covers the film's major themes.

Napier, Susan. Anime from *Akira* to *Howl's Moving Castle* (New York: Palgrave, 2005). [Specifically Chapter 12, 'Princess Mononoke: Fantasy, the Feminine, and the Myth of Progress', pp. 231–48.]
 Napier's book is one of the first to tackle anime as an academic subject, and it remains one of the best. Napier contends that there are three differing modes of anime storytelling: the apocalyptic, the carnival and the elegiac. In chapter 12, she argues that *Princess Mononoke* fits two of these modes, functioning as an apocalyptic elegy for a lost period in Japanese history, and for the potential it offered women. Napier's deep engagement with women's representations in *Princess Mononoke* is matched by her concern to investigate Miyazaki's environmental theme, which is where she locates the apocalyptic elegy within the film.

Tucker, John A. 'Anime and Historical Inversion in Miyazaki Hayao's *Princess Mononoke*', *Japan Studies Review*, vol. 7, no. 1 (2003), pp. 65–102.
 This article offers a great introduction to the historical time periods that Miyazaki palimpsests in *Princess Mononoke*. Tucker's wide-ranging, thoughtful analysis repeatedly demonstrates how carefully Miyazaki approached the representation of history in *Princess Mononoke*.

Yoshida, Koari. 'National Identity (Re)Construction in Japanese and American Animated Film: Self and Other Representation in *Pocahontas* and *Princess Mononoke*', *Electronic Journal of Contemporary Japanese Studies*, September 2011. http://www.japanesestudies.org.uk/articles/2011/Yoshida.html (accessed 16 June 2017).
 This is a much newer essay on the representations of marginalized people in *Princess Mononoke* that interrogates the way identity is constructed through notions of the self and other. Yoshida's analysis is built upon a thoroughly researched understanding of the Japanese context for *Princess Mononoke* and is therefore very useful to anyone looking to make connections between the characters and Japanese culture or history.

Primary/Reference Sources: Industry and Commentary

Biodrowsky, Steve. 'Changing Sake into Wine – Neil Gaiman on Adapting "Princess Mononoke" for America', *Cinefantastique Online*, 5 February 2009. http://cinefantastiqueonline.com/2009/02/changing-sake-into-wine-neil-gaiman-on-adapting-princess-mononke-for-america/ (accessed 9 May 2016).
 This is a fascinating interview with Neil Gaiman in which Biodrowsky teases out the difficulties inherent in trying to localize *Princess Mononoke*.

Clements, Jonathan and Helen McCarthy. *The Anime Encyclopedia: Revised & Expanded Edition* (Berkeley, CA: Stone Bridge Press, 2006).
	Written by two of the world's most knowledgeable anime critics, this ever-expanding encyclopaedia of anime has seen many updates and expansions, something that scholars should hope that the authors are willing to keep doing. With insightful overviews and very helpful film analyses, this is the perfect reference work for those with an interest in anime.

Drazen, Patrick. *Anime Explosion! The What? Why? and Wow! of Japanese Animation* (Berkeley, CA: Stone Bridge Press, 2003).
	While not an academic book, Drazen's account of anime offers loving attention to the details of its history and reveals much about the way it moved between Japan and the United States. It contains some very useful background information about Miyazaki, Isao Takahata and the production culture at Studio Ghibli.

Miyazaki, Hayao. *Starting Point 1979–1996*, trans. Beth Cary and Frederik L. Schodt (San Francisco, CA: VIZ Media, 2009 [1996]).
	Miyazaki, Hayao. *Turning Point 1997–2008*, trans. Beth Cary and Frederik L. Schodt (San Francisco, CA: VIZ Media 2014 [2009]).
	These two volumes of translated interviews are a goldmine for any student of Hayao Miyazaki's filmmaking. They give you access to materials never-before translated into English, including Miyazaki's initial production pitches, interviews from throughout his career and also talks about how he sees the world beyond filmmaking. These two volumes were originally published in Japanese, and have been painstakingly translated for the English market by Beth Cary and Frederik L. Schodt. Schodt is already well-known to manga and anime fans as the author of *Manga! Manga! The World of Japanese Comics* (1983).

Patten, Fred. *Watching Anime, Reading Manga: 25 Years of Essays and Reviews* (Berkeley, CA: Stone Bridge Press, 2004).
	A witty, insightful commentary on anime and manga from one of the commentators who saw anime's introduction to the United States. Vital reading for anyone who wants to understand the background to how Miyazaki's films ended up being distributed to the United States.

Hayao Miyazaki and Studio Ghibli

Cavallaro, Dani. *The Anime Art of Hayao Miyazaki* (Jefferson, NC: McFarland, 2006).
	This book contains a history of Studio Ghibli and analyses of its major films, including *Princess Mononoke*. Cavallaro is one of the few scholars to point to

the CG animation in *Princess Mononoke*, and her analyses of the films are wide ranging.

Denison, Rayna. *Anime: A Critical Introduction* (London: Bloomsbury, 2015). [Specifically chapter 7, 'Ghibli Genre: Toshio Suzuki and Studio Ghibli's Brand Identity', pp. 117–32.]

My introduction to anime is part of a film genres series at Bloomsbury Press, so it focuses on the history of genres in anime from the earliest moments of anime to the contemporary period. Chapter 7 looks at the way Studio Ghibli has taken on different meanings at home and abroad; essentially becoming a animation genre in the United States, while becoming a powerful brand name in other parts of the world. The chapter looks at Toshio Suzuki's role in turning Ghibli into one of Japan's most powerful animation studios.

Hu, Tze-Yue. *Frames of Anime: Culture and Image-Building* (Hong Kong: Hong Kong University Press, 2010). [Specifically chapter 6, 'Miyazaki and Takahata Anime Cinema', Kindle Edition.]

Although it does not mention Studio Ghibli in its title, Hu's use of Miyazaki and his Studio Ghibli partner, Isao Takahata, to tell the story of anime's development and rapid change from the 1980s onwards is an excellent introduction to Miyazaki's studio. She moves from studying authorship and style through to Takahata and Miyazaki's shared themes, particular ecology, which would be useful to those studying *Princess Mononoke*.

Lamarre, Thomas. *The Anime Machine: A Media Theory of Animation* (Minneapolis, MN: University of Minnesota Press, 2009).

Lamarre's book presents a strong analysis of anime's techniques and production processes in an effort to reveal what is unique to, and special about, anime. Within this discussion, Miyazaki is a favoured example, and there is extensive analysis of films like *Castle in the Sky* (which is even featured as the cover image). While this book is useful just in terms of making sense of anime as a kind of animation, it is therefore also a great introduction to the way Miyazaki makes films. Lamarre is careful to show how Miyazaki's films generate movement, use framing and colour to produce new, often fantastic, worlds.

Napier, Susan J. *From Impressionism to Anime: Japan as Fantasy and Fan Cult in the Mind of the West* (New York: Palgrave Macmillan, 2007). [Specifically chapter 8, 'In Search of Sacred Space? Anime Fandom and MiyazakiWorld', pp. 191–204.]

In this book, Napier explores the flow of high and popular art from Japan to the rest of the world. By charting European and US interactions with Japanese culture, she contends that there has been a longer history of Japan-related fandom than previously acknowledged. As part of this study, Napier undertakes an audience study surveying fans of Miyazaki's filmmaking via the Hayao Miyazaki Web, which is the first such study of online Ghibli fandom.

Odell, Colin and Michelle Le Blanc. *Studio Ghibli: The Films of Hayao Miyazaki and Isao Takahata* (Harpenden: Kamera Books, 2009).
This short book on Studio Ghibli offers overviews/reviews of Miyazaki and Takahata's films, with some useful observations and history produced along the way. It is not focused on the academic market, but provides an inclusive introduction to Miyazaki's studio and uses primary Japanese sources to support its points.

Yoshioka, Shiro. 'Heart of Japaneseness: History and Nostalgia in Hayao Miyazaki's *Sprited Away*' in Mark W. MacWilliams (ed.), *Japanese Visual Culture: Explorations in the World of Manga and Anime* (Armonk, NJ: M. F. Sharpe, 2008), pp. 256–73.
This is a really useful chapter for anyone wanting to know more about how Miyazaki has positioned himself within Japanese filmmaking since *Princess Mononoke*. Yoshioka's analysis takes in Miyazaki's philosophical stance as a filmmaker, and relates that to the sometimes didactic messages contained in Miyazaki's films.

Anime

Annett, Sandra. *Anime Fan Communities: Translcutural Flows and Frictions* (New York: Palgrave, 2014).
Annett's book thinks about how fans have helped to make anime a global phenomenon, sharing texts and information across geographic and linguistic borders. Her study is impressively broad and includes fan communities in North America, Japan and South Korea.

Azuma, Hiroki. *Otaku: Japan's Database Animals*, trans. Jonathen E. Abel and Shion Kono (Minneapolis, MN: University of Minnesota Press, 2009).
It is not often that whole scholarly books on anime written by Japanese scholars get translated, and Azuma's is proving to be very influential. Though not focused on Studio Ghibli, Azuma discusses anime fandom in Japan in enlightening ways, contending that anime is so dispersed and expansive there that it operates like a database of texts that fans can access however they like. His approach uses psychology and philosophy to frame the decisions fans make and to argue for an understanding of anime as an affective construct in the minds of fans, not just films and television shows that they happen to watch.

Brown, Steve T., ed. *Cinema Anime* (New York: Palgrave, 2006).

Even though none of the chapters in Brown's collection are about Studio Ghibli, there is a wealth of coverage within the essays collected in this volume that would benefit those wanting to understand the context in which Miyazaki makes films. There are particularly good essays in this collection about the way anime has been appreciated in the United States (Levi), and also about science fiction in anime films. Brown's introduction also does a wonderful job setting up the field and thinking through the impact of new technologies on and in anime.

Clements, Jonathan. *Anime: A History* (London: BFI and Palgrave, 2013).

A tour-de-force exposition of Japan's animation history. Clements covers everything from the earliest moments in Japanese animation, through to the rise of its studio system and its current digital era. While Studio Ghibli and Miyazaki are not a particular focus on this book, any student or researcher of anime (or, indeed, animation studies) would hugely benefit from reading *Anime: A History*.

Condry, Ian. *The Soul of Anime: Collaborative Creativity and Japan's Media Success Story* (Durham, NC: Duke University Press, 2013).

Condry is an ethnographer, and as part of this project he gained access to a variety of anime production studios. He followed the activities of their staff members in order to think about anime as an industry that contains a wide range of different production styles, different types of media (from film to advertising) and different production philosophies. The result is a magnificent overview of Japan's animation industry as a creative community. While Ghibli does not feature, again, this book is a must-read for anyone interested in finding out how anime are made.

Lunning, Frenchy, ed. *Mechademia* (Minneapolis, MN: University of Minnesota Press, 2006–15).

Frenchy Lunning's ten-volume book series on manga and anime never had a special issue on Ghibli, but there is a plethora of highly researched scholarly work available through this series that would be highly beneficial to students and researchers alike. The series includes specific work on *Porco Rosso* (vol. 2) and *Howl's Moving Castle* (vol. 3), but Ghibli's presence is acknowledged in far more instances than can be listed here.

Steinberg, Marc. *Anime's Media Mix: Franchising Toys and Characters in Japan* (Minneapolis, MN: University of Minnesota Press, 2012).

For anyone interested in how anime became a dominant cultural force in Japan, Steinberg's book is a key text. His elegant analysis includes an analysis of anime aesthetics, as well as a cogent argument about how anime came to sit at a nexus point in production that extends from manga to live action film, while including everything from branded stickers and chocolates to whole empires of ancillary production. In treating anime textually and industrially, Steinberg has helped inculcate a fundamental shift in the study of anime.

Yokota, Masao and Tze-Yue G. Hu, eds, *Japanese Animation: East Asian Perspectives* (Jackson, MS: University of Mississippi Press, 2013).

This collection of essays, largely by Asian scholars, offers a corrective to US- and UK-centred studies of anime consumption and fandom. In so doing, it challenges many of the myths about, and assumptions regarding, the dominant flows of anime from Japan to the rest of the world. The collection includes translated articles from some of Japan's most famous anime scholars, as well as fascinating essays that track the exchanges between mainland Asia and Japanese animators.

BIBLIOGRAPHY

Alaimo, Stacy. *Bodily Natures* (Bloomington, IN: Indiana University Press, 2010).

Allison, Anne. 'Sailor Moon: Japanese Superheroes for Global Girls' in T. J. Craig (ed.), *Japan Pop! Inside the World of Japanese Popular Culture* (New York: M. E. Sharpe, 2000), pp. 259–78.

Allison, Anne. *Millennial Monsters: Japanese Toys and the Global Imagination* (Berkeley, CA: University of California Press, 2006).

Amino, Yoshihiko. '*"Shizen" to "ningen," 2 tsu no seichi ga shōtotsu suru higeki*' [Nature and Humanity: The Tragedy When Two Sacred Places Collide], in *Mononokehime Pamfuletto* [*Princess Mononoke* Theatre Programme] (Tokyo: Tokuma shoten, 1997), p.15.

Amino, Yoshihiko. *Nihon no rekishi o yominaosu (zen)* [Rewriting the History of Japan (Complete)] (Tokyo: Chikuma shobō, 2005).

Anderson, Hans Christian. *Den Lille Havfrue* [The Little Mermaid], trans. H. B. Paull (USA: Hythloday Press, 2014 [1836]).

Andrews, David L. 'Disneyization, Debord, and the Integrated NBA Spectacle'. *Social Semiotics*, vol. 16, no. 1 (2006):89–102.

Animage, 225, March 1997, pp. 14–17.

Animage, 230, August 1997, pp. 6–31.

Annett, Sandra. *Anime Fan Communities: Transcultural Flows and Frictions* (Basingstoke and New York: Palgrave Macmillan, 2014).

Ansen, David. '"Princess" Ride'. *Newsweek*, vol. 134, no. 18 (1 November 1999):87.

Appleton Aguiar, Sarah. *The Bitch Is Back: Wicked Women in Literature* (Carbondale and Edwardsville: Southern Illinois University Press, 2001).

Atkinson, Michael. '*Princess Mononoke* Review'. *Mr. Showbiz*, 29 October 1999.

Austin, Thomas. *Hollywood, Hype and Audiences: Selling and Watching Popular Film in the 1990s* (Manchester: Manchester University Press, 2002).

Backus, Robert L., trans. *The Riverside Counsellor's Stories: Vernacular Fiction of Late Heian Japan* (Paolo Alto, CA: Stanford University Press, 1985).

Barthes, Roland. *Camera Lucida: Reflections on Photography*, trans. Richard Howard (London: Cape, 1982).

Bate, Jade. 'Kickass Feminists on Film: *Princess Mononoke*'. *Lip*, no.13 (September 2014). http://lipmag.com/arts/film-arts/kickass-feminists-on-film-princess-mononoke/ (accessed 20 September 2016).

Baumann, Shyon. 'Intellectualization and Art World Development: Film in the United States'. *American Sociological Review*, vol. 66, no. 3 (2001):404–26.

Beaman, Nathan. 'Special Features: DVD Extras'. *Videomaker Magazine*, November 2008. https://www.videomaker.com/article/13762-special-features-dvd-extras (accessed 30 January 2017).

Beeck, Nathalie op de. 'Anima and Animé: Environmental Perspectives and New Frontiers in *Princess Mononoke* and *Spirited Away*' in Mark I. West (ed.),

The Japanification of Children's Popular Culture: From Godzilla to Miyazaki (Lanham: Scarecrow Press, 2009), pp. 267–84.

Bernard, Rosemarie. 'Shintō and Ecology: Practice and Orientations to Nature'. *Forum on Religion and Ecology at Yale*. 1998. http://fore.yale.edu/religion/Shintō/ (accessed 15 April 2017).

Bernardi, Joanne.R. 'Catching a Film Audience Abroad'. *Japan Quarterly*, vol. 32, no. 3 (1985):290–5.

Berry, Chris. '"What's Big about the Big Film?": "De-Westernizing" the Blockbuster in Korea and China' in Julian Stringer (ed.), *Movie Blockbusters* (London: Routledge, 2003), pp. 217–30.

Biodrowsky, Steve. 'Changing Sake into Wine – Neil Gaiman on Adapting "Princess Mononoke" for America'. *Cinefantastique Online*, 5 February 2009. http://cinefantastiqueonline.com/2009/02/changing-sake-into-wine-neil-gaiman-on-adapting-princess-mononoke-for-america (accessed 9 May 2016).

Biskind, Peter. *Down and Dirty Pictures: Miramax, Sundance and the Rise of Independent Film* (London: Simon and Schuster Paperbacks, 2004).

Bradshaw, Peter. 'Film: *Princess Mononoke*'. *The Guardian*, 19 October 2001.

British Board of Film Classification. 'Examiner's Report on *Urotsukidoji: Legend of the Overfiend*'. 8 October 1992.

Brooks, Xan. 'A God among Animators: Hayao Miyazaki's Hand-Crafted Fables Have Made Him Japan's Most Successful Film-Maker Ever'. *The Guardian*, 14 September 2005.

Bryman, Alan. 'The Disneyization of Society'. *The Sociological Review*, vol. 47, no. 1 (1999):25–47.

Bryman, Alan. *The Disneyization of Society* (California: Sage, 2004).

Buell, Lawrence. *The Environmental Imagination: Thoreau, Nature Writing, and the Formation of American Culture* (Cambridge, MA: Harvard University Press, 1996).

Buell, Lawrence. *The Future of Environmental Criticism: Environmental Crisis and Literary Imagination* (Oxford: Blackwell Publishing, 2005).

Buljan, Katherine and Carole M. Cusack. *Anime, Religion and Spirituality Profane and Sacred Worlds in Contemporary Japan* (Sydney: Equinox, 2015).

Burns, Susan L. 'Rethinking "Leprosy Prevention": Entrepreneurial Doctors, Popular Journalism, and the Civic Origins of Biopolitics'. *The Journal of Japanese Studies*, vol. 38, no. 2 (2012):297–323.

Burr, Ty. 'Here's the Next *Star Wars*-Like Epic'. *Entertainment Weekly*, 3 November 1999. http://www.ew.com/article/1999/11/03/heres-next-star-wars-epic (accessed 18 September 2016).

Burrell, Ian. 'The Digital World for Women Is Breaking New Ground', *The Independent*, 14 November 2014.

Callenbach, Earnest. *Ecotopia: The Notebooks and Reports of William Weston* (New York: Bantam, 1975).

Campbell, Joseph. *The Hero with a Thousand Faces* (New York: Pantheon, 1949).

Carr, Jay. 'Epic Mononoke Simply Breathtaking'. *Boston Globe*, 29 October 1999.

Carson, Rachel. *Silent Spring* (Boston, MA: Houghton Mifflin, 1962).

Carter, Laz. 'Marketing *Anime* to a Global Audience: A Paratextual Analysis of Promotional Materials from *Spirited Away*'. *East Asian Journal of Popular Culture*, vol. 4, no. 1 (2018).

Cavallaro, Dani. *Hayao Miyazaki's World Picture* (Jefferson, NC: McFarland & Co., 2015).

Chan, Melanie. 'Environmentalism and the Animated Landscape in *Nausicaä of the Valley of the Wind* (1984) and *Princess Mononoke* (1997)' in C. Pallant (ed.), *Animated Landscapes: History, Form and Function* (New York: Bloomsbury, 2015), pp. 93–108.

'The Characters'. *Princess Mononoke* [online]. http://www.princess-mononoke.com/html/epic/characters/01.html (accessed 14 April 2017).

Chihiro to Fushigi no machi: Sen to Chihiro no kamikakushi tettei kōryaku gaido [Chihiro and the Mysterious Town: A Complete Guide to Spirited Away] (Tokyo: Kadokawa shoten, 2001).

Christopher, James. 'Another Fine Mess'. *The Times*, 18 October 2001.

Chute, David. 'Organic Machine: The World of Hayao Miyazaki'. *Film Comment*, vol. 34, no. 6 (1998):62–65.

Clarke, James. 'Ecology and Animation: Animation Gone Wild: *Bambi* vs *Princess Mononoke*'. *Imagine*, no.31 (May2010), pp. 36–9.

Clements, Jonathan. *Anime: A History* (Basingstoke: Palgrave Macmillan, 2013).

Clements, Jonathan and Helen McCarthy. *The Anime Encyclopedia*, 2nd edn (Berkeley, CA: Stone Bridge Press, 2011).

Collin, Robbie. 'Goodbye Studio Ghibli, Your Genius will Endure'. *Daily Telegraph*, 4 August 2014.

Corrigan, Timothy. *A Cinema without Walls: Movies and Culture after Vietnam* (New Brunswick, NJ: Rutgers University Press, 1991).

Covert, Colin. '*Kubo and the Two Strings* Review: A Thrilling Action-Adventure for All'. *Chicago Tribune*, 19 August 2016.

Cubbit, Sean. *Eco Media* (Amsterdam: Rodopi, 2005).

Czarnecki, Melanie. 'Bad Girls from Good Families: The Degenerate Meiji Schoolgirl' in Laura Miller and Jan Bardsley (eds), *Bad Girls of Japan* (New York: Palgrave Macmillan, 2005), pp. 49–64.

'Dakota Pipeline: What's Behind the Controversy?'. *BBC News* [online], 7 February 2017. http://www.bbc.co.uk/news/world-us-canada-37863955 (accessed 21 June 2017).

Dale, Peter. *The Myth of Japanese Uniqueness* (London: Routledge, 1986).

Danner, Chas. 'Standing Rock Protesters Declare Victory after Construction of Dakota Access Oil Pipeline Suspended'. *Daily Intelligencer*, 4 December 2016. http://nymag.com/daily/intelligencer/2016/12/report-construction-of-dakota-access-pipeline-halted.html (accessed 16 June 2016).

Deleuze, Gilles and Félix Guattari. *A Thousand Plateaus: Capitalism and Schizophrenia*, trans. Brian Massumi (Minneapolis, MN: University of Minnesota Press, 1987).

Denison, Rayna. 'Cultural Traffic in Japanese Anime: The Meanings of Promotion, Reception and Exhibition Circuits in *Princess Mononoke*' (PhD thesis submitted to the University of Nottingham, 2005).

Denison, Rayna. 'Disembodied Stars and the Cultural Meanings of *Princess Mononoke*'s Soundscape'. *Scope: An Online Journal of Film Studies*, vol. 3, no. 1, (November 2005). http://www.nottingham.ac.uk/scope/documents/2005/october-2005/denison.pdf (accessed 30 January 2017).

Denison, Rayna. 'The Global Markets for *Anime*: Miyazaki Hayao's *Spirited Away* (2001)' in Alastair Phillips and Julian Stringer (eds), *Japanese Cinema: Texts and Contexts* (London: Routledge, 2007), pp. 308–21.

Denison, Rayna. 'The Language of the Blockbuster: Promotion, *Princess Mononoke* and the *Daihitto* in Japanese Film Culture' in Leon Hunt and Leung Wing-Fai (eds),

East Asian Cinemas: Exploring Transnational Connections on Film (London and New York, NY: I.B. Tauris, 2008), pp. 103–22.

Denison, Rayna. 'Star-Spangled Ghibli: Star Voices in the American Versions of Hayao Miyazaki's Films'. *Animation: An Interdisciplinary Journal*, vol. 3, no. 2 (2008):129–46.

Denison, Rayna. 'Transcultural Creativity in Anime: Hybrid Identities in the Production, Distribution, Texts and Fandom of Japanese Anime'. *Creative Industries Journal*, vol. 3, no. 3 (2010):221–35.

Denison, Rayna. 'Anime Fandom and the Liminal Spaces between Fan Creativity and Piracy'. *International Journal of Cultural Studies*, vol. 14, no. 5 (2011):449–66.

Denison, Rayna. *Anime: A Critical Introduction* (London: Bloomsbury, 2015).

Denison, Rayna. 'Before Ghibli Was Ghibli: Analysing the Historical Discourses Surrounding Hayao Miyazaki's *Castle in the Sky* (1986)'. *East Asian Journal of Popular Culture*, vol. 4, no. 1 (2018).

Derrida, Jacques '*Des tours de babel*' in Joseph. F. Graham (ed.), *Difference in Translation* (Ithaca: Cornell University Press, 1985), pp. 165–206.

Drazen, Patrick. *Anime Explosion! The What? Why? & Wow! of Japanese Animation* (Berkeley, CA: Stone Bridge Press, 2003).

Dyer, Richard. *Heavenly Bodies: Film Stars and Society* (London: BFI Publishing, 1986).

Ebert, Roger. 'Drawing Success'. *Chicago Sun-Times*, 6 September 1999.

Ebert, Roger. 'The Best 10 Movies of 1999'. *Roger Ebert's Journal*, 31 December 1999. http://www.rogerebert.com/rogers-journal/the-best-10-movies-of-1999 (accessed 20 September 2016).

Edelstein, David. 'Machines in the Garden'. *Slate*, 29 October 1999). http://www.slate.com/articles/arts/movies/1999/10/machines_in_the_garden.html (accessed 16 May 2016).

7×7 Editors. 'Hayao Miyazaki Contemplates Dreams, the Environment, and the Elegant Simplicity of "Ponyo" '. *7×7*, 2016. http://www.7x7.com/hayao-miyazaki-contemplates-dreams-the-environment-and-the-elegant-sim-1779168535.html (accessed 10 December 2016).

Ettinger, Ben. 'Two Pioneer Women Animators'. *Anipages*, 11 November 2006. http://www.pelleas.net/aniTOP/index.php/notable_women_animators (accessed 2 January 2017).

Files, Gemma. '*Mononoke* – Warrior Princess: Powerful Japanese Anime Takes First Dip in North America Mainstream'. *Eye*, 28 October 1999.

Fishzon, Anna. 'The Fog of Stagnation: Explorations of Time and Affect in Late Soviet Animation'. *Cahiers du monde russe*, vol. 56, no. 2 (2006). http://www.cairn.info.ezp-prod1.hul.harvard.edu/revue-cahiers-du-monde-russe-2015-2-page-571.htm#pa65 (accessed 14 September 2016).

Foreman, Jonathan. 'A Very Pretty 'Toon'. *New York Post*, 29 October 1999.

Foster, Michael Dylan. *Pandemonium and Parade: Japanese Monsters and the Culture of Yōkai* (Berkeley, CA: University of California Press, 2009).

Frazer, James George. *The Golden Bough: A Study in Magic and Religion* (London: MacMillan, 1890).

Frey, Matthias. 'Introduction: Critical Questions' in Matthias Frey and Cecilia Sayed (eds), *Film Criticism in the Digital Age* (New Brunswick, NJ: Rutgers University Press, 2015), pp. 1–20.

Frey, Matthias. 'The New Democracy? Rotten Tomatoes, Metacritic, Twitter and IMDb' in Matthias Frey and Cecilia Sayed (eds), *Film Criticism in the Digital Age* (New Brunswick, NJ: Rutgers University Press, 2015), pp. 81–98.

Friday, Karl F. 'Pushing beyond the Pale: The Yamato Conquest of the Emishi and Northern Japan'. *Journal of Japanese Studies*, vol. 23, no. 1 (1997):1–24.

Gale, Thomson. 'Ecology and Religion: Ecology and Shintō'. *Encyclopedia of Religion* (2005). http://www.encyclopedia.com/environment/encyclopedias-almanacs-transcripts-and-maps/ecology-and-religion-ecology-and-Shintō (accessed 15 April 2017).

Garrard, Greg. *Ecocriticism* (New York: Routledge, 2012).

Gilbey, Ryan. '*Kiki's Delivery Service*: Japanese classic returns in time for Christmas'. *The Guardian*, 28 November 2016. https://www.theguardian.com/stage/2016/nov/28/kikis-delivery-service-japanese-classic-christmas-show-southwark-playouse-london (accessed 17 April 2017).

Giroux, Henry A. 'Animating Youth: The Disneyfication of Children's Culture'. *Socialist Review*, vol. 24, no. 3 (1994):23–55.

Graves, Robert. *The White Goddess: A Historical Grammar of Poetic Myth* (London: Faber and Faber, 1948).

Gray, Jonathan. *Show Sold Separately: Promos, Spoilers, and Other Media Paratexts* (London and New York: New York University Press, 2010).

Haraway, Donna. *Primate Visions: Gender, Race, and Nature in the World of Modern Science* (New York and London: Routledge, 1989).

Haraway, Donna. *The Haraway Reader* (New York: Routledge, 2004).

Haraway, Donna. *When Species Meet* (Minneapolis, MN: University of Minnesota Press, 2008).

Hardy, Ernest. 'Animating the Century'. *L.A. Times*, 27 October 1999.

Heise, Ursula. 'Plasmatic Nature: Environmentalism and Animated Film'. *Public Culture*, vol. 26, no. 2 (2014):301–18.

Hersher, Rebecca. 'Protesters Leave Dakota Access Pipeline Area; Some Stay and Are Arrested'. *National Public Radio* (NPR), 22 February 2017. http://www.npr.org/sections/thetwo-way/2017/02/22/516448749/protesters-leave-dakota-access-pipeline-area-some-stay-and-are-arrested. (accessed 16 June 2017).

Hills, Matt. *Fan Cultures* (London: Routledge, 2002).

Hoff Kraemer, Christine. 'Disney, Miyazaki and Feminism: Why Western Girls Need Japanese Animation'. *Christine Hoff Kraemer*, 2000. http://www.christinehoffkraemer.com/miyazaki.html (accessed 20 September 2016).

Hoff Kraemer, Christine. 'Between Worlds: Liminality and Self-Sacrifice in *Princess Mononoke*'. *Journal of Religion and Film*, vol. 8, no. 2 (2004), Article 1. http://digitalcommons.unomaha.edu/jrf/vol8/iss2/1/ (accessed 15 April 2017).

Holopirek, Jodi A. 'Online Journalism: The Transformation of the Film Review' (PhD thesis submitted to the University of Kansas, 2007).

Hornaday, Ann. 'Hayao Miyazaki Offers Anime Enthusiasts a Final Flight of Fancy'. *The Guardian*, 23 February 2014.

Howell, Peter. 'Animated Feature a Bit Dark for the Kids'. *Toronto Star*, 29 October 1999.

Hu, Tze-Yue G. *Frames of Anime: Culture and Image-Building* (Hong Kong University Press, 2010).

Hunter, Stephen. 'The Bland Violence of *Mononoke*'. *Washington Post*, 5 November 1999.

ICMN Staff. 'Dakota Access Pipeline Springs a Leak'. *Indian Country Today*, 16 May
   2017. https://indiancountrymedianetwork.com/news/environment/dakota-access-
   pipeline-leak/ (accessed 21 June 2017).
Inaba, Shinichirō. *Naushika kaidoku: Yūtopia no rinkai* [Deciphering Nausicaä:
   A Critique of Utopia] (Tokyo: Madosha, 1996).
'Interview with Hayao Miyazaki'. *Young Magazine*, 20 February, reprinted in Archives
   of Studio Ghibli, 1, 1996, p. 54.
Ivy, Marilyn. *Discourses of the Vanishing: Modernity, Phantasm, Japan*
   (Chicago: University of Chicago Press, 1995).
Iwabuchi, Koichi. *Recentering Globalization: Popular Culture and Japanese
   Transnationalism* (Durham, NC and London: Duke University Press, 2002).
Iwabuchi, Koichi. 'How "Japanese" Is Pokémon?' in Joseph Tobin (ed.), *Pikachu's
   Global Adventure: The Rise and Fall of Pokémon* (Durham, NC: Duke University
   Press, 2004), pp. 53–79.
Jenkins, Eric S. 'Another *Punctum*: Animation, Affect, and Ideology'. *Critical Inquiry*,
   vol. 39, no. 3 (2013):575–91.
Jenkins, Henry. *Textual Poachers: Television Fans & Participatory Culture* (London and
   New York: Routledge, 1992).
Johnson, Derek. *Media Franchising: Creative License and Collaboration in the Culture
   Industries* (London and New York: New York University Press, 2013).
Johnson, Michael, ed. 'Miramax English Trailer'. *The Hayao Miyazaki Web*. http://www.
   nausicaa.net/miyazaki/mh/relmedia.html#Miramax (accessed 14 April 2017).
Johnston, Keith. *Coming Soon: Film Trailers and the Selling of Hollywood Technology*
   (North Carolina: McFarland, 2009).
Jolin, Dan. 'Back Story: Miyazaki on Miyazaki'. *Empire*, September 2009, pp. 114–23.
Jones, Diana Wynne. *Howl's Moving Castle* (New York: Harper Collins, 1986).
Judah, Tara. '*Princess Mononoke*: Transgressing the Binaries That Bind'. *Screen
   Education*, no.74 (2014), pp. 52–61.
'*Kakie Sovetskie multfilmi ochen' populyarni za rubezhom?*' [Which Soviet Animations
   Are Very Popular Abroad?]. *Kino-Expert*. http://kino-expert.info/articles/
   kakie-sovetskie-multfilmi-ochen-populyarni-za-rubezhom.html (accessed 14
   September 2016).
Kalland, Arne. 'Culture in Japanese Nature' in Ole Bruun and Arne Kalland (eds),
   Asian Perception of Nature: A Critical Approach (London: Curzon Press, 1995), pp.
   243–57.
Kanō, Seiji. *Miyazaki Hayao zensho* [The Complete Hayao Miyazaki] (Tokyo: Firumu
   āto sha, 2006).
Karahashi, Takayuki. 'The Whimsy and Wonder of Hayao Miyazaki', trans. Takashi
   Oshiguchi, *Animerica Magazine*, August 1993.
Katsuno, Hirofumi and Jeffrey Maret. 'Localizing the Pokémon TV Series for the
   American Market' in Joseph Tobin (ed.), *Pikachu's Global Adventure: The Rise and
   Fall of Pokémon* (Durham, NC and London: Duke University Press, 2004), pp.
   80–107.
Kayano, Terumi. 'The World of Spirituality: *Princess Mononoke* Interpreted through
   Shinto' (M.A. Dissertation submitted to the Hawaii Pacific University, 2009).
Kermode, Mark. 'The Red Turtle Review – Rapturous Minimalism from Studio Ghibli'.
   The Guardian, 28 May 2017.

Kernan, Lisa. *Coming Attractions: Reading American Movie Trailers* (Texas: University of Texas Press, 2004).

Kerrigan, Finola. *Film Marketing* (Oxford: Elsevier, 2010).

Kersten, Annemarie and Denise D. Bielby. 'Film Discourse on the Praised and Acclaimed: Reviewing Criteria in the United States and United Kingdom'. *Popular Communication*, vol. 10, no. 3 (2014):183–200.

Kikuchi, Minoru. '*Sūpāburando toshite no Miyazaki anime: naze Mononokehime genshō*' [Miyazaki Anime as a Super Brand: Why Has *Princess Mononoke* Become a Phenomenon?]. *New Media*, no.180, September 1998, pp. 46–50.

King, Barry. 'Articulating Stardom' in Christine Gledhill (ed.), *Stardom: Industry of Desire* (London and New York: Routledge, 1991), pp. 169–85.

Kingston, Jeff. *Contemporary Japan: History, Politics and Social Change since the 1980s* (London: Wiley Blackwell, 2013).

Klady, Leonard. *Daily Variety*, 30 January 1998.

Klein, Andy. 'Gods almighty'. *Dallas Observer*, 4 November 1999. http://www.dallasobserver.com/film/gods-almighty-6396860 (accessed 16 May 2016).

Knight, John. 'On the Extinction of the Japanese Wolf'. *Asian Folklore Studies*, vol. 56, no. 1 (1997):129–59.

Kōgyō tsūshinsha. '*Rekidai ranking*' [Historical Rankings], *CINEMA Ranking Tsūshin*, 2016. http://www.kogyotsushin.com/archives/alltime/ (accessed 11 May 2016).

Koikari, Mire. *Pedagogy of Democracy: Feminism and the Cold War in the U.S. Occupation of Japan* (Philadelphia: Temple University Press, 2008).

Kozo, Mayumi, Barry D. Solomon and Jason Chang. 'The Ecological and Consumption Themes of the Films of Hayao Miyazaki'. *Ecological Economics*, vol. 54, no. 1 (2005):1–7.

Lamarre, Thomas. *The Anime Machine: A Media Theory of Animation* (Minneapolis, MN: University of Minnesota Press, 2009).

Landesman, Cosmo. 'This Week's Films'. *Sunday Times*, 21 October 2001.

MacFadyen, David. *Yellow Crocodiles and Blue Oranges: Russian Animated Film since World War II* (Montreal: McGill-Queen's University Press, 2005).

Marchetti, Gina. 'Guests at *The Wedding Banquet*: The Cinema of the Chinese Diaspora and the Rise of the American Independents' in Chris Holmlund and Justin Wyatt (eds), *Contemporary American Independent Film: From the Margins to the Mainstream* (London: Routledge, 2005), pp. 182–95.

Marran, Christine L. *Poison Women: Figuring Female Transgression in Modern Japanese Culture* (Minneapolis, MN: University of Minnesota Press, 2007).

Maslin, Janet. 'Waging a Mythic Battle to Preserve a Pristine Forest'. *New York Times*, 27 September 1999.

Matanle, Peter, Kuniko Ishiguro and Leo McCann. 'Popular Culture and Workplace Gendering among Varieties of Capitalism: Working Women and their Representation in Japanese Manga'. *Gender, Work and Organization*, vol. 21, no. 5 (2014):472–89.

Mathews, Jack. 'This Dark "Princess" Isn't for Kids'. *New York Daily News*, 29 October 1999.

Matsumura, Hirofumi and Yukio Dodo. 'Dental Characteristics of Tohoku Residents in Japan: Implications for Biological Affinity with Ancient Emishi'. *Anthropological Science*, vol. 117, no. 2 (2009):95–105.

Matusitz, Jonathan and Lauren Palermo. 'The Disneyfication of the World: A Gobalisation Perspective'. *Journal of Organisational Transformation & Social Change*, vol. 11, no. 2 (2014):91–107.

McCarthy, Helen. *Hayao Miyazaki: Master of Japanese Animation* (Berkeley, CA: Stone Bridge Press, 1999).

McCarthy, Helen. *500 Essential Anime Movies: The Ultimate Guide* (Lewes: Ilex Press, 2008).

McHugh, Susan. 'Animal Gods in Extinction Stories: *Power* and *Princess Mononoke*' in Jeanne Dubino, Ziba Rishidian and Andrew Smyth (eds), *Representing the Modern Animal in Culture*, Kindle edn (Gordonsville: Palgrave Macmilla, 2014).

McNair, James. 'The Life Aquatic: When Bjork Started Going Out with American Artist Matthew Barney'. *Independent on Sunday*, 17 July 2005.

McWhirter, Andrew. Film Criticism in the Twenty-first Century'. *Journalism Practice*, vol. 9, no. 6 (2015):890–906.

Mellor, Rupert. 'Film Profile: Japanimation'. *The Times*, 19 October 2002.

Mes, Tom. 'Hayao Miyazaki'. *Midnight Eye*, 11–23 December 2001. http://www.midnighteye.com/interviews/hayao-miyazaki/ (accessed 22 December 2016).

Mihailova, Misha. 'Animating Global Realities in the Digital Age' (PhD thesis submitted to Yale University, 2017).

Miyazaki, Hayao. 'Discarding the Future? Conversation with Ernest Callenbach'. *Asahi Journal*, 6 July 1985.

Miyazaki, Hayao. *Mononokehime* [*Princess Mononoke*] (Tokyo: Tokuma shoten, 1993).

Miyazaki, Hayao. *Shuppatsu ten* [Starting Point] (Tokyo: Tokuma shoten, 1996).

Miyazaki, Hayao. '*Gendai ni oite kotenteki bōken katsugeki wa ariuruka*' [Are there Classic Adventure Stories Today?]. *Yuriika* [Eureka], August 1997, pp. 138–50.

Miyazaki, Hayao. '*Mori to ningen*' [The Forest and the Human-Being]. *Mononokehime o yomitoku* [Reading *Princess Mononoke*], Comic Box, 2 (August 1997), pp. 74–81.

Miyazaki, Hayao. '*Doitsu berurin eigasai intabyū: kaigai no kisha ga miyazaki kantoku ni tou "mononokehime" e no 44 no shitsumon*' [An Interview at Germany's Berlin Film Festival: 44 Questions about *Princess Mononoke* to Miyazaki from Foreign Reporters]. *Roman Album Animage Special: Miyazaki Hayao to An'no Hideaki* [Roman Album Animage Special: Hayao Miyazaki and Hideaki Anno], 1997, pp. 48–54.

Miyazaki, Hayao. 'A Statement by Miyazaki'. *Princess Mononoke*, 1999. http://www.princess-mononoke.com/html/production/miyazaki/06.html (accessed 1 September 2016).

Miyazaki, Hayao. *Kaze no kaeru basho* [The Place Where the Wind Changes] (Tokyo: Rokkingu on, 2002).

Miyazaki, Hayao. *Starting Point 1979-1996*, trans. Beth Cary and Frederik L. Schodt (San Francisco, CA: VIZ Media, 2009 [1996]).

Miyazaki, Hayao. '*Miyazaki Hayao kantoku intai kaiken*' [Hayao Miyazaki Retirement Interview]. *Neppū: Sutajio jiburi no kōkishin* (October 2013), pp. 56–87.

Miyazaki, Hayao. *Turning Point 1997-2008*, trans. Beth Cary and Frederik L. Schodt (San Francisco, CA: VIZ Media 2014 [2009]).

Miyazaki, Hayao. *Princess Mononoke: The First Story*, trans. Jocelyne Allen (San Francisco, CA: VIZ Media) 2014 [1993]).

Miyazaki, Hayao and Ernest Callenbach. '*Hi o suteru?* "*Naushika*" *to Reizoko no aru "Ecotopia*"' ["Nausicaä" without Fire? and "Ecotopia" with Refrigerator] in Studio

Ghibli and Bunshun Bunko (ed.), *Jiburi no Kyōkasho 1: Kaze no Tani no Naushika* [Ghibli Textbook 1: Nausicaä of the Valley of the Wind] (Tokyo: Bungei Shunju, 2013), pp .276–91.

Miyazaki, Hayao and Yasuo Ōtsuka. '*Ikihaji o sarashite ikiru otoko to shite no rupan*' [Lupin Is a Man Who Is Living in Disgrace], in *Animēju* (*Animage*) (ed.), *Eiga Tenkū no shiro Lapyuta Guide Book* [Castle in the Sky Guide Book] (Tokyo: Tokuma shoten, 1986), pp. 184–95.

Mononokehime o yomitoku [Reading *Princess Mononoke*]. Comic Box, 2 (August 1997).

Mononokehime Pamfuletto [*Princess Mononoke* Theatre Programme] (Tokyo: Tokuma shoten, 1997).

Morgenstern, Joe. 'John Malkovich Is Weird, and We Mean That in a Good Way'. *Wall Street Journal*, 29 October 1999.

Mori, Takuya. '*Sovieto manga eiga no keifu: Shuusaku "Yuki no Joou" o chūshin ni*' [The Genealogy of Soviet Animated Films: Focus on the Masterpiece *The Snow Queen*]. *Eiga Hyouron* [Film Criticism], vol. 17, no. 5 (1960):82–95.

Morris, Ivan. *The Nobility of Failure* (New York: Holt, Rinehart and Winson, 1975).

Mumby, Daniel. 'Film Review: *Princess Mononoke*'. *Three Men on a Blog*, 15 March 2001. http://threemenonablog.blogspot.co.uk/2011/03/film-review-princess-mononoke-1997.html (accessed 19 September 2016).

Murakami, Ryū. 'Murakami Ryū in Conversation with Hayao Miyazaki'. *Animage*, November 1988, reprinted in *Shuppatsuten* [Starting Point] (Tokyo: Tokuma shoten, 1996). http://www.nausicaa.net/miyazaki/interviews/heroines.html (accessed 17 April 2017).

Murdock, Maureen. *The Heroine's Journey* (Boston, MA: Shambhala, 1990).

Nakao Sasuke. *Saibai shokubutsu to nōkō no kigen* [The Origins of Cultivate Plants and Farming] (Tokyo: Iwanami shoten, 1966).

Napier, Susan Joliffe. 'Vampires, Psychic Girls, Flying Women and Sailor Scouts: Four Faces of the Young Female in Japanese Popular Culture' in Dolores P. Martinez (ed.), *The Worlds of Japanese Popular Culture: Gender, Shifting Boundaries and Global Cultures* (Cambridge: Cambridge University Press, 1998), pp. 91–109.

Napier, Susan Joliffe. *Anime from Akira to Princess Mononoke: Experiencing Contemporary Japanese Animation* (New York: Palgrave Macmillan, 2001).

Napier, Susan Joliffe. 'Confronting Master Narratives: History as Vision in Miyazaki Hayao's Cinema of De-assurance'. *East Asian Cultures Critique*, vol. 9, no. 2 (2001):467–93.

Napier, Susan Joliffe. *Anime from Akira to Howl's Moving Castle* (New York: Palgrave Macmillan, 2005).

Napier, Susan Joliffe. 'The World of Anime Fandom in America' in Susan J. Lunning (ed.), *Mechademia: Emerging Worlds of Anime and Manga* (Minneapolis, MN: University of Minnesota Press, 2006), pp. 47–63.

Napier, Susan Joliffe. *From Impressionism to Anime: Japan as Fantasy and Fan Cult in the Mind of the West* (Basingstoke: Palgrave Macmillan, 2007).

'*Nazo no monogatari ninki no nazo*' [The Mystery of the Popularity of Mystery Stories]. *Asahi Shimbun*, 12 April 1997 (morning issue), p. 18.

Neale, Steve. 'Questions of Genre' in Robert Stam and Toby Miller (eds), *Film and Theory: An Anthology* (Malden: Blackwell Publishers, 2000), pp. 157–78.

Needle, Chael. 'Artist Linda Stein Talks to Lester Strong about Gender, AIDS and Self-empowerment'. *A&U America's Aids Magazine*, 4 June 2015. http://www.aumag.org/2015/06/04/linda-stein/ (accessed 16 September 2016).

Ng, Kazna. 'Miyazaki on Creating Kiki's Delivery Service', *Vimeo.com*. https://vimeo.com/45200524 (accessed 20 June 2017).

Nicol, Clive W. *Tree*, illustrator Hayao Miyazaki (Tokyo: Tokuma shoten, 1991).

Nishijima, Tateo. '*Anime: Gendai no shin'wa: Nazo ga umidasu kaishaku no kōzui*' [Anime: Modern Myths: A Flood of Interpretations That Creates Myths], *Asahi shimbun*, 16 August 1997, (morning issue), p.11.

Niskanen, Eija. '*Kalalapsi, joka halusi olla ihminen*' [The Little Fish, Who Wanted to Become Human). *Helsingin Sanomat*, 19 September 2009. http://www.hs.fi/kulttuuri/art-2000004680111.html (accessed 15 April 2017).

O'Hehir, Andrew. '*Princess Mononoke*: After the Success of Disney's Mulan, Miramax Does Its Parent Company One Better'. *Salon*, 27 October 1999.

Ogihara-Schuck, Eriko. *Miyazaki's Animism Abroad: The Reception of Japanese Religious Themes by American and German Audiences* (Jefferson, NC: MacFarland, 2007).

Okada, Eriko, trans. *The Princess Who Loved Insects*, no.18, Kindle edn (Kiiroitori Books, 2016).

Okuyama, Yoshiko. *Japanese Mythology in Film: A Semiotic Approach to Reading Japanese Film and Anime* (Lanham: Lexington Books, 2015).

Ōmori, Shunji. '*Sutaffu intabyū bijutsu Yamamoto Nizō ni kiku: kuraku shizunda minasoko to akarui midori no koke wo egaku no ga muzukashikatta*' [Staff Interview: Nizō Yamamoto: It was difficult to draw the depths of a dark river bed and bright green moss]. *Kinema Junpo*, no. 1233 (1997), pp. 83–7.

Ōmori, Shunji. '*Sutaffu intabyū Yasuda Michiyo-shi ni kiku: Miyazakisan no mezasu sekai wo hageshiku, yasashiku, "iro" de sasaeru*' [We talk to colour designer Michiyo Yasuda: The world that Miyazaki is aiming for is supported by colour, intensely, gently]. *Kinema Junpo*, no. 1233 (1997), pp. 91–3.

Osmond, Andrew. 'Beauty and the Beastly: It's Gorgeous, It's Japan's Biggest Hit Ever, and It's not *Pokemon*. But Will Prejudice against Violent Manga Cartoons Prevent Us from Seeing *Princess Mononoke*?'. *The Guardian*, 14 April 2000.

Ōtsuka, Eiji. '"*Mononokehime*" *kaidai*' [Modern Times in *Princess Mononoke*] in Studio Ghibli and Bunshun Bunko (eds), *Jiburi no kyōkasho 13: Mononokehime* [Ghibli Textbook 13: *Princess Mononoke*] (Tokyo: Bungei shinjū, 2016), pp. 256–78.

Ōtsuki, Takahiro. '*Kotoba ni sarenu "riaru": 'Shinseiki evangerion' no shinshō fūkei*' [The Word 'Real': The Imagined Landscape of *Neon Genesis Evangelion*]. *Mainichi shinbun*, 28 November 1996, (evening issue), p. 8.

Perren, Alisa. 'Sex, Lies and Marketing: Miramax and the Development of the Quality Indie Blockbuster'. *Film Quarterly*, vol. 55, no. 2 (2001):30–9.

Pett, Emma. '"Blood, Guts and Bambi Eyes": *Urotsukidoji* and the Transcultural Reception and Regulation of Anime'. *Journal of British Cinema and Television*, vol. 13, no. 3 (2016):390–408.

'*Princess Mononoke* Comes to America'. *Princess Mononoke* [online]. http://www.princess-mononoke.com/html/epic/cast/02.html (accessed 14 April 2017).

Promkhunthong, Wikanda. 'Wong Kar-wai: "Cultural Hybrid", Celebrity Endorsement and Star-Auteur Branding'. *Celebrity Studies*, vol. 5, no. 3 (2014):348–53.

Quinn, Anthony. 'Also Showing'. *The Independent*, 21 October 2001.

Romney, Jonathan. 'Arts: Film – Watch Out for the Stink God'. *Independent on Sunday*, 14 September 2003.

Rafael, Vincente L. 'Translation, American English and the National Insecurities of Empire' in Lawrence Venuti (ed.), *The Translation Studies Reader* (Abingdon: Routledge, 2012), pp. 451–68.

Rendell, James. 'Bridge Builders, World Makers: Transcultural Studio Ghibli Fan Crafting', *East Asian Journal of Popular Culture*, vol. 4, no. 1 (2018).

Rifà-Valls, Montserrat. 'Postwar Princesses, Young Apprentices, and a Little Fish-Girl: Reading Subjectivities in Hayao Miyazaki's Tales of Fantasy'. *Visual Arts Research*, vol. 37, no. 2 (2011):88–100. http://www.jstor.org/stable/10.5406/visuartsrese.37.2.0088 (accessed 14 April 2016).

Robinson, Joan G. *When Marnie Was There* (London: Harper Collins, 2014 [1967]).

Rose, Steve. 'Studio Ghibli: Leave the Boys Behind'. *The Guardian*, 14 July 2011. https://www.theguardian.com/film/2011/jul/14/studio-ghibli-arrietty-heroines (accessed 21 June 2017).

Rots, Aike P. 'Sacred Forests, Sacred Nation: The Shinto Environmentalist Paradigm and the Rediscovery of "Chinju no Mori."' *Japanese Journal of Religious Studies*, vol. 42, no. 2 (2015):205–33.

Ruddell, Caroline. 'Cutting Edge: Violence and Body Horror in Anime' in Feona Attwood, Vincent Campbell, Ian Q. Hunter and Sharon Lockyer (eds), *Controversial Images: Media Representations on the Edge* (New York: Palgrave Macmillan, 2013), pp. 157–69.

Saitani, Ryo. '*Mori to ningen*' [Miyazaki's interview: The Forest and the Human-being]. *Princess Mononoke o yomutoku*. Comic Box, 2 (August 1997), pp. 72–81.

Sandler, Kevin S. and Gaylyn Studlar, eds, *Titanic: Anatomy of a Blockbuster* (New Brunswick, NJ: Rutgers University Press, 1999).

Sasaki, Kōmei. *Shōyō jurin bunka towa nanika* [What Is Commercial Forest Culture?] (Tokyo: Chūō Kōron Shinsha, 2007).

Sato, H. and M. Narita. 'Politics of Leprosy Segregation in Japan: The Emergence, Transformation and Abolition of the Patient Segregation Policy'. *Social Science and Medicine*, no.56 (2003), pp. 2529–39.

Schatz, Thomas. 'The New Hollywood' in John Collins, Hilary Radner and Ava Preacher Collins (eds), *Film Theory Goes to the Movies* (New York: Routledge, 1993), pp. 8–36.

'*Sen to Chihiro no kamikakushi*' *o yomi 40 no me* [40 Viewpoints to Read Spirited Away] (Tokyo: Kinema junpōsha, 2001).

'*Senden keikakusho*' [Advertising Plan] in Studio Ghibli (ed.), *Sutajio jiburi sakuhin kanren shiryōshū IV* [The Works of Studio Ghibli Collection IV] (Tokyo: Tokuma shoten, 1996), pp. 48–9.

Sherman, Paul. '*Princess Mononoke* gets Pretty Monotonous'. *Boston Herald*, 29 October 1999.

Shibuya, Tomoko. 'Excavation Sheds Light on Jomon Life'. *Japan Times*, 10 Nov–16 Nov, vol. 37, no. 45 (1997):15.

Shikibu, Murasaki. *The Tale of Genji*, trans. Edward G. Seidensticker (New York: Knopf, 1008 [1985]).

Shimamura, Tomio and Yoshinori Sugano. '*Honkakuteki dejitaruka ni idonda Mononokehime no CG genba kara*' [From the site of *Princess Mononoke*'s CG which defied standard digitalization]. *Kinema Junpo*, no.1233 (1997), pp. 74–82.

Shiraki, Midori. '*Kyokō no jidai ni michisuji shimesu: messēji "ikiro" ni wakamono han'nō*' [Showing the path to a Fictional Age: Young People's Reactions to the Message to 'Live'] in Studio Ghibli and Bunshun Bunko (eds), *Jiburi no kyōkasho 10: Mononokehime* [Ghibli Textbook 10: *Princess Mononoke*] (Tokyo: Bungei shinjū, 2015), pp. 176–80.

Shouse, Eric. 'Feeling, Emotion, Affect'. *M/C Journal: A Journal of Media and Culture*, vol. 8, (6 December 2005) http://journal.media-culture.org.au/0512/03-shouse.php (accessed 15 September 2016).

Singer, Leigh. 'Hayao Miyazaki: Emperor of Anime'. *DazedDigtial.com*, 9 May 2014. http://www.dazeddigital.com/artsandculture/article/19856/1/hayao-miyazaki-emperor-of-anime (accessed 30 January 2017).

Singh, Avadesh K. 'Translation Studies in the 21st Century'. *Translation Today*, vol. 8, no. 1 (2014):5–44.

Smith, Michelle J. and Elizabeth Parsons. 'Animating Child Activism: Environmentalism and Class Politics in Ghibli's *Princess Mononoke* (1997) and Fox's *Fern Gully* (1992)'. *Continuum: Journal of Media and Cultural Studies*, vol.26 (1 February 2012), pp. 25–37.

'*Snezhnaya Koroleva 55: Kholod' i krasota*' [Snow Queen 55: Cold and Beauty]. *Animator: Site ob animatsii v rossii i ne tolko* [Site on Russian Animation, Etc], 7 December 2012. http://www.animator.ru/?p=show_news&nid=1501 (accessed 14 September 2016).

Sonoda, Minoru. 'Shintō and the Natural Environment' in John Breen and Mark Teeuwen (eds), *Shintō in History: Ways of the Kami* (Richmond: Curzon Press, 2000), pp. 32–46.

Staiger, Janet. *Interpreting Film: Studies in the Historical Reception of American Cinema* (Princeton, NJ: Princeton University Press, 1992).

Steinberg, Marc. *Anime's Media Mix: Franchising Toys and Characters in Japan* (Minneapolis, MN: University of Minnesota Press, 2012).

Stringer, Julian, ed. *Movie Blockbusters* (London: Routledge, 2003).

Studio Ghibli. *Naushika no 'shinbun kōkoku' tte mitakoto arimasuka: jiburi no shinbun kōkoku 18 nenshi* [Have You Seen the Newspaper Advertisements for Nausicaä?: The 18 year History of Ghibli's Newspaper Advertisments] (Tokyo: Tokuma shoten, 2002).

Studio Ghibli. '*Sutajio jiburi monogatari: Mizou no taisaku "Mononokehime"*' [The Story of Studio Ghibli: The Unprecedented Masterpiece *Princess Mononoke*] in Studio Ghibli and Bunshun Bunko (eds), *Jiburi no kyōkasho 10: Mononokehime* [Ghibli Textbook 10: *Princess Mononoke*] (Tokyo: Bungei shinjū, 2015), pp. 25–55.

Sutcliff, Rosemary. *The Mark of the Horse Lord* (Oxford: Oxford University Press, 1965).

Sugimoto, Yoshio. 'Making Sense of *Nihonjinron*'. *Thesis Eleven*, vol. 57, no. 1 (1999):81–96.

Suzuki, Toshio. *Eiga Dōraku* [My Film Hobby] (Tokyo: Pia, 2005).

Suzuki, Toshio. '*Chie to dokyō no ōbakuchi! Mizou no "Mononokehime daisakusen"*' [A Huge Gamble Taking Real Courage and Wisdom!: The Epic 'Operation Mononoke'] in Studio Ghibli and Bunshun Bunko (eds), *Jiburi no kyōkasho 10: Mononokehime* [Ghibli Textbook 10: *Princess Mononoke*] (Tokyo: Bungei shinjū, 2015), pp. 56–77.

Takahata, Isao. '*Rongu intabyū: Takahata Isao*' [Long Interview: Isao Takahata].
Hōhokekyo tonari no Yamadakun o yomitoku!? [Reading My Neighbors the
Yamadas], Comic Box (1999), pp. 19–27.
Takai, Hideyuki, Masaru Yabe, Minami Ichikawa, Shinpei Ise, Seiji Okuda and Toshio
Suzuki. '*Tokushū "Jiburi no dai hakurnkai Tōhō no rekidai purodūsā ga ōi ni kataru*',
[Special Feature: The Great Ghibli Exhibition: Current and Previous Producers
of Tōhō Tell Everything about Their Work]. *Neppū*, vol. 13, no. 9 (September
2015):4–32.
Tamaki, Saitō. *Beautiful Fighting Girl*, trans. J. Keith Vincent and Dawn Lawson,
(Minneapolis, MN: University of Minnesota Press, 2011).
Taniguchi, Hideko J. 'The Representation of the Child and Childhood in *The Princess
Who Loved Insects*'. Conference Paper, *22nd Biennial Congress of IRSCL*, University
of Worcester, 8–12 August 2015. http://www.irscl.com/pdf/2015_IRSCL_congress_
programme_individual_papers.pdf (accessed 18 December 2016).
Thornton, Sarah. *Club Cultures: Music, Media and Subcultural Capital*
(Cambridge: Polity, 1995).
Tobin, Joseph, ed. *Pikachu's Global Adventure: The Rise and Fall of Pokémon* (Durham,
NC: Duke University Press, 2004).
Tookey, Christopher. 'Charlize Makes a Mean Queen: Theron's Evil Stepmother Will
Leave You Quaking in Your Boots'. *Daily Mail*, 1 June 2012.
Townsend, Emru. 'Neil Gaiman: The *Sandman* Scribe on Anime and Miyazaki'. *The
Critical Eye*, 8 November 1999. http://purpleplanetmedia.com/eye/inte/ngaiman.
php (accessed 9 May 2016).
'Trailer'. *Hakujaden* [The White Serpent], Toei, 1958. https://www.youtube.com/
watch?v=cN0i8v9VTWE (accessed 21 June 2017).
Tuana, Nancy. 'Viscous Porosity: Witnessing Katrina' in Stacy Alaimo and Susan
Heckman (eds), *Material Feminisms* (Bloomington, IN: Indiana University Press,
2008), pp. 188–213.
Tucker, John A. 'Anime and Historical Inversion in Miyazaki Hayao's *Princess
Mononoke*'. *Japan Studies Review*, vol. 7, no. 1 (2003):65–102.
Tucker, Ken. 'Cute Characters, But No Comic Relief'. *New York Times*, 12 September 1999.
Turan, Kenneth. 'Mononoke a Haunting Magical World of Fantasy: Writer-Director
Hayao Miyazaki Brings a Different Sensibility to Anime in His Fairy Tale That
Fuses Lyricism with Terror'. *Los Angeles Times*, 29 October 1999.
Udagawa, Hidetada. '*Mononokehime sekai dōji kōkai no ōshōbu*' [The Great Game of
Princess Mononoke's Simultaneous Worldwide Release]. *The Weekly Toyo Keizai*, 13
April 1996, pp. 26–9.
Umehara, Takeshi. '*Mori no shisō' ga jinrui o sukuu* [Forest Ideology Will Save
Mankind] (Tokyo: Shōgakukan, 1991).
Umehara, Takeshi. '*Nihon no shinsō*' [The Depth of Japanese Ideology] in
Umehara Takeshi choaskushū [Collected Works of Hiroshi Umehara], no. 6
(Tokyo: Shōgakukan, 2000), pp. 21–238.
Uno, Kathleen. 'One Day at a Time: Work and Domestic Activities of Urban Lower-
Class Women in Early Twentieth-century Japan' in Janet Hunter (ed.), *Japanese
Women Working* (London: Routledge, 1993), pp. 37–68.
Usai, Elena. '*L'epoca delle donne: Miyazaki e le principesse selvagge*'. *Lundici*, no.87
(October 2015). http://www.lundici.it/2015/10/lepoca-delle-donne-miyazaki-e-le-
principesse-selvagge/ (accessed 17 April 2017).

Verboord, Marc. 'The Impact of Peer-Produced Criticism on Cultural Evaluation: A Multilevel Analysis of Discourse Employment in Online and Offline Film Reviews'. *New Media and Society*, vol. 16, no. 6 (2014):921–40.

Watts, Jonathan. 'Japan in Grip of Blood-soaked Cartoon Film: E. T. Sent Packing; The Queues are Starting at Dawn for an Animated Feature Film Breaking All Box Office Records'. *The Guardian*, 5 November 1997.

Wells, Paul. 'Smarter Than the Average Art Form: Animation in the Television Era' in Carole A. Stabile and Mark Harrison (eds), *Prime Time Animation: Television Animation and American Culture* (London: Routledge, 2003), pp. 15–32.

Wolf, Jennifer. 'GKids Picks Up Studio Ghibli's "Only Yesterday."' *Animation World News*, 24 August 2015. https://www.awn.com/news/gkids-picks-studio-ghibli-only-yesterday (accessed 14 April 2017).

Wright, Lucy. 'Forest Spirits, Giant Insects and World Trees: The Nature Vision of Hayao Miyazaki', *Journal of Religion and Popular Culture*, vol. 10, no. 1 (Summer 2005). http://www.jurn.org/ejournal/art10-miyazaki.html (accessed 17 June 2017).

Wyatt, Justin. *High Concept: Movies and Marketing in Hollywood* (Texas: University of Texas Press, 1994).

Wyatt, Justin. 'The Formation of the "Major Independent": Miramax, New Line and the New Hollywood' in Steve Neale and Murray Smith (eds), *Contemporary Hollywood Cinema* (London and New York: Routledge, 1998), pp. 74–90.

Yardley, William. 'Construction to Resume on Dakota Access Pipeline'. *Los Angeles Times*, 9 February 2017. http://www.latimes.com/politics/washington/la-na-essential-washington-updates-construction-resumes-on-dakota-access-1486673813-htmlstory.html (accessed 17 June 2017).

Yoshida, Kaori. 'National Identity (Re)Construction in Japanese and American Animated Film: Self and Other Representation in *Pocahontas* and *Princess Mononoke*'. *Electronic Journal of Contemporary Japanese Studies* (September 2011), Article 5. http://www.japanesestudies.org.uk/articles/2011/Yoshida.html (accessed 17 June 2017).

Yoshida, Toshifumi. 'Hayao Miyazaki'. *Animerica*, no.7 (December 1999), pp. 6, 10–11, 13, 18. http://www.animenostalgiabomb.com/princess-mononoke-hayao-miyazaki-interview-animerica-december-1999/ (accessed 30 December 2016).

Yoshioka, Shiro. 'Memory, Nostalgia and Cultural Identity in the World of Miyazaki Hayao' (PhD Thesis submitted to the International Christian University, 2009).

Yuriika [Eureka], vol. 33, no. 7 (August 2001).

Zipes, Jack. *Fairy Tale as Myth/Myth as Fairy Tale*, Kindle edn (Lexington: University of Kentucky Press, 2013).

FILMOGRAPHY

Akira (1988), [Film] Dir. Katsuhiro Ōtomo, Japan: Tōhō.

Bambi (1942), [Film] Dir. David Hand, James Algar, Samuel Armstrong, Graham Heid, Bill Roberts, Paul Satterfield, Norman Wright, USA: Disney.

Gake no ue no Ponyo/Ponyo (2008), [Film] Dir. Hayao Miyazaki, Japan: Studio Ghibli.

Hauru no ugoku shiro/Howl's Moving Castle (2004), [Film] Dir. Hayao Miyazaki, Japan: Studio Ghibli.

Heisei tanuki gassen Ponpoko/Pompoko (1994), [Film] Dir. Isao Takahata, Japan: Studio Ghibli.

Kagyua-hime no monogatari/The Tale of Princess Kaguya (2013), [Film] Dir. Isao Takahata, Japan: Studio Ghibli.

Karigurashi no Ariettī /Arietty (2010), [Film] Dir. Hiromasa Yonebayashi, Japan: Studio Ghibli.

Kaze no tani no Naushika/Nausicaä of the Valley of the Wind (1984), [Film] Dir. Hayao Miyazaki, Japan: Topcraft.

Kaze tachinu/The Wind Rises (2013), [Film] Dir. Hayao Miyazaki, Japan: Studio Ghibli.

Kimi no na wa/Your Name (2016), [Film] Dir. Makoto Shinkai, Japan: Amuse, Answer Studio, CoMix Wave Films, East Japan Marketing & Communications, Kadokawa, Lawson HMV Entertainment,Tōhō, Vogue Ting.

Kōkaku kidōtai/Ghost in the Shell (1995), [Film] Dir. Mamoru Oshii, Japan: Production I.G.

Kurenai no buta/Porco Rosso (1992), [Film] Dir. Hayao Miyazaki, Japan: Studio Ghibli.

Lupin III: Caguriosutoro no shiro/Castle of Cagliostro (1979), [Film] Dir. Hayao Miyazaki, Japan: TMS Entertainment.

Majo no takkyūbin/Kiki's Delivery Service (1989), [Film] Dir. Hayao Miyazaki, Japan: Studio Ghibli.

Mimi o sumaseba/Whisper of the Heart (1995), [Film] Dir. Yoshifumi Kondō, Japan: Studio Ghibli.

Meitantei Holmes/Sherlock Hound (1984), [TV] Dir. Hayao Miyazaki, Japan/Italy: TMS Entertainment & RAI.

Mononokehime/Princess Mononoke (1997), [Film] Dir. Hayao Miyazaki, Japan: Studio Ghibli.

Mononokehime wa kōshite umareta/This Is How Mononokehime Was Born (2000), [DVD] Dir. Not listed, Japan: Buena Vista International.

Neko no ongaeshi/The Cat Returns (2002), [Film] Dir. Hiroyuki Morita, Japan: Studio Ghibli.

Omoide no Mānī/When Marnie Was There (2014), [Film] Dir. Hiromasa Yonebayashi, Japan: Studio Ghibli.

Pulp Fiction (1994), [Film] Dir. Quentin Tarantino, US: Miramax.

The Red Turtle (2016), [Film] Dir. Michaël Dudok de Wit, Japan-France: Studio Ghibli.

Sen to Chihiro no kamikakushi/Spirited Away (2001), [Film] Dir. Hayao Miyazaki, Japan: Studio Ghibli.
Sex, Lies and Videotape (1989), [Film] Dir. Steven Soderbergh, US: Outlaw Productions.
Shin seiki Evangerion/Neon Genesis Evangelion (1995–96), [TV] Dir. Hideaki Anno, Japan: Gainax.
Shitsuraken/A Lost Paradise (1997), [Film] Dir. Yoshimitsu Morita, Japan: Ace Pictures, Kadokawa shoten, Mitsui Company, Nihon Shuppan Hanbai and Tōei.
Snezhnaya Koroleva/The Snow Queen (1957), [Film] Dir. Lev Atamanov, Russia: All-Union Animated Cartoon Film Studios, Soyuzmultfilm.
Snow White and the Seven Dwarfs (1937), [Film] Dir. David Hand, William Cottrell, Wilfred Jackson, Larry Morey, Perce Pearce, Ben Sharpsteen, USA: Disney.
Tarzan (1999), [Film] Dir. Chris Buck and Kevin Lima, US: Walt Disney Pictures.
Tarzan & Jane (2002), [Film] Dir. Steve Loter and Lisa Schaffer, US: Walt Disney Pictures.
Tenkū no shiro Rapyūta/Castle in the Sky (1986), [Film] Dir. Hayao Miyazaki, Japan: Studio Ghibli.
Tonari no Totoro/My Neighbor Totoro (1988), [Film] Dir. Hayao Miyazaki, Japan: Studio Ghibli.
Yadosagashi/House Hunting (2006), [Short Film] Dir. Hayao Miyazaki, Japan: Studio Ghibli.
Yume to kyoki no okoku/The Kingdom of Dreams and Madness (2013), [Film] Dir. Mami Sunada, Japan: Ennet Dwango.

NOTES ON CONTRIBUTORS

Julia Alekseyeva is finishing her PhD in Comparative Literature at Harvard University, and teaches Cinema Studies at Brooklyn College. Her dissertation analyses the avant-garde documentary traditions of Japan, France and the former USSR. Her articles on 1960s cinema have appeared in the *Journal of Japanese and Korean Cinema* and *The Cine-Files*. Concurrently with her academic work, Julia is an author-illustrator whose debut graphic novel, *Soviet Daughter: A Graphic Revolution* (Microcosm Publishing), was published in January 2017.

Laz Carter is completing his PhD – entitled 'Going Global: Studio Ghibli, Global *Anime* and the Popularisation of a Medium-Genre' – at SOAS, University of London. His research interests include studies of stardom, authorship, *anime* and paratextual marketing materials. He also has a journal article forthcoming with the *East Asian Journal of Popular Culture*.

Tracey Daniels-Lerberg holds a PhD with a Women's and Gender Studies Certificate from the University of Texas at Arlington. Her dissertation, *Rethinking Resistance: Race, Gender, and Place in the Fictive and Real Geographies of the American West* draws on cultural and critical race studies, and environmental and feminist theory to examine representations of and writing by minorities and women. Her research and teaching interests include early and nineteenth-century American literatures and cultures of the United States.

Matthew Lerberg is an instructor at the University of Texas Arlington where he teaches courses in environmental humanities and animal studies. His primary area of study is environmental theory, animal studies, and critical theory in relation to Western literature, film, and art. His scholarly interests include how popular cultural representations of environments and non-human animals can help interrogate the ethics of human's relationships to both. His articles on popular culture, the environment, and animal studies have appeared in *Green Letters* and he has authored *Screening the Non-human* (Lexington Books, 2016).

Helen McCarthy is an independent scholar, writer and presenter. She began researching Japanese comics and animation in 1981, and written the first book in English on anime in 1993. She has since written more than a dozen books on anime and manga, and has contributed to a number of academic publications. Her works have been translated into seven languages. They include critical biographies of Osamu Tezuka and Hayao Miyazaki, and the shortest history of manga to date. She is the co-author of *The Anime Encyclopedia*, widely regarded as the key text in the field.

Jennifer E. Nicholson is a PhD candidate in English at the University of Sydney. Her doctoral research focuses on Shakespeare as a 'translator' of French sources in writing 'Hamlet'. She also hopes to consider francophone translations of the play, and to situate both doctoral and further research projects across both Shakespeare studies and world literature. The topic of her thesis stems from her wider interest in the unstable meanings generated in both interlingual and intralingual translation.

Eija Niskanen is the programming director for Helsinki Cine Asia and one of the founding members of Helsinki International Film Festival, and coordinates yearly Finland Film Festival event in Japan. She is doing Asian film and animation-related teaching and research at the University of Helsinki, currently working on the Moomins in Japan, for which project she has also been an exchange scholar at Meiji University in 2016. She has conducted industrial research on Finland–Japan co-production possibilities for Finnanimation in 2015 and for The Research Institute of the Finnish Economy (Etla) in 2010. Other publications include 'Ordinary Extraordinary: 3.11 in Japanese Fiction Film' in *Film on the Faultline*, ed. Alan Wrights, University of Chicago Press, 2015.

Emma Pett is a lecturer at the University of East Anglia specializing in audience and reception studies, with a particular interest in transcultural contexts of media reception and cultural policy. Her PhD was a collaborative doctoral award with the British Board of Film Classification (BBFC). Emma is honorary Research Associate on the 'Cultural Memories of British Cinema-going in the 1960s' project based at the University College London, and has previously worked at the Universities of Bristol and South Wales. Emma's current research projects are focused on the transcultural reception of East Asian media, audiences of immersive media and, with Karina Aveyard, community cinema cultures. Emma has articles published in *Participations*, *The Journal of British Film and Television* and the *New Review of Film and Television*.

Alice Vernon is a Creative Writing PhD student at Aberystwyth University. Her interests include women creators of comics and manga, particularly the work of CLAMP and Kaoru Mori. She is researching the Welsh landscapes in the comics of Carol Swain. Her article, 'Digital Sleep and the Performance of Lucidity in *Paprika*' was published in *Performance Research* in 2016.

Shiro Yoshioka is a lecturer in Japanese Studies at Newcastle University. His main research interests include Japanese popular culture, especially anime, fan culture, popular history, memory and nostalgia. He has written articles and book chapters on Ghibli and Miyazaki in English and Japanese, and is working on a monograph on Miyazaki, which overviews his life and career contextualizing it within a broader picture of history of Japan and the world as well as anime.

INDEX

CPSIA information can be obtained
at www.ICGtesting.com
Printed in the USA
LVHW081833041019
633221LV00013B/221/P

9 781501 354878